Praise for WEIGHT AND WISDOM

"Tigress and Nancy have done a great service by compiling this incredible anthology that is both political and deeply, deeply personal. *Weight and Wisdom* is an invaluable fat liberation history created by many of the very people who shaped the movement over the years. This is a must read for activists, advocates, and anyone who believes in creating a world where fat people can thrive."

AUBREY GORDON
Co-host of *Maintenance Phase* podcast
& creator of *Your Fat Friend* online essay series;
author of *What We Don't Talk About When We Talk About Fat*
& *"You Just Need to Lose Weight" and 19 Other Myths About Fat People*

"What a book! What a piece of art! This is what you get when you connect writers in the activist space to speak on the intersectional experiences that they have both lived and witnessed!

"This book is an essential read for those looking to understand the origins, present day, and future of fat liberation. Stories are masterfully crafted to draw readers in even if you are someone who has never experienced the harsh realities of weight stigma.

"*Weight and Wisdom: Reflections on Decades of Working for Body Liberation* provides a necessary foundation to have no nonsense conversations about the ways that modern society is complicit and more so, emboldened to declare that fat bodies do not deserve the same liberties, resources, and joy that smaller bodies readily partake of. It also (and rightfully so) reifies those with ample flesh to take up space unapologetically, offering a big middle finger to a world that is hell bent on seeing us suffer. Simply put, I love it here!"

JOY COX PHD
author of *Fat Girls in Black Bodies: Creating Communities of Our Own*

"*Weight and Wisdom* is expertly woven from insightful essays, eyewitness accounts, discussions, and oral histories about body liberation. The editors present an emotional tapestry that shows how local community efforts and social change efforts merge with personal need, political rage and creativity. *Weight and Wisdom* blesses us by teaching which people and what work has come before us."

KIMBERLY DARK
sociologist
author of *Fat, Pretty and Soon to be Old:*
A Makeover for Self and Society

"Storytelling is tremendously powerful. It helps us create a rich tapestry of human experiences and ideas, allowing us to understand the past and gain deeper context about where we are today. As someone who is still relatively new to this field, I am deeply grateful for the contributions in *Weight and Wisdom: Reflections on Decades of Working for Body Liberation.* The progress we've made in the fat liberation movement would not have been possible without the work shared in this book."

AARON FLORES, RDN
Certified Body Trust Specialist

"An important collection of short memoirs describing aspects
of the first several decades of contributions to eating disorders
and/or the weight-based oppression of fat people. While not exhaustive,
it is an excellent history documenting the beginning efforts to challenge
the cultural efforts to oppress and stigmatize bodies
based on an ideal shape and size."

CHEVESE TURNER
Founder, **Binge Eating Disorder Association**
Co-author of *Binge Eating Disorders: The Journey to Recovery & Beyond*
Co-founder of **Weight Stigma Awareness Week**
Lived Experience Recovery Coach

"This is a collection of very human stories from people who were
there at the time. Some are fond memories of a time of community
and hope. Others reflect on mistakes made and harms done.
Yet others speak of still-raw wounds. Yet we all continue to fight.
That is the one thing everybody agrees on—this is worth fighting for.
But the fight is still harder for some people than for others.
This book of personal recollections reminds us that we can, and should, build
on what has already been done—we don't need to start over
every generation—and we can learn from the mistakes that were made
and do better."

ANGELA MEADOWS, PhD
weight stigma researcher, University of Essex, UK
founder of the **Annual International Weight Stigma Conference**

WEIGHT AND WISDOM

REFLECTIONS ON **DECADES** OF WORKING FOR BODY LIBERATION

EDITED BY
NANCY ELLIS-ORDWAY
AND TIGRESS OSBORN
FOREWORD BY CALEB LUNA

PEARLSONG PRESS
Nashville, TN

Pearlsong Press
P.O. Box 58065
Nashville, TN 37205
www.pearlsong.com | www.pearlsongpress.com

Trade paperback ISBN: 9781597191036
Ebook ISBN: 9781597191043

LIBRARY OF CONGRESS CATALOGING-IN-PUBLICATION DATA

Names: Ellis-Ordway, Nancy, editor. | Osborn, Tigress, 1974– editor.
Title: Weight and wisdom: reflections on decades of working for body liberation/ edited by Nancy Ellis-Ordway and Tigress Osborn; foreword by Caleb Luna.
Description: Nashville, TN: Pearlsong Press, [2025] | Includes bibliographical references and index. | Summary: "Over the last 50 years in the United States, the medical establishment, the beauty industry, and the mainstream media have relentlessly forwarded the belief that fat is unattractive and unhealthy. While many believe that anti-fat ideas went unchallenged until the rise of body positivity, there have always been resistors. In the worlds of eating disorders treatment, Health at Every Size® advocacy, and fat activism, challengers to our cultural narratives have championed another way for decades. In this collection, 34 of those trailblazing rebels against body oppression voice the history of challenging the status quo and working to create a world where all bodies are valued. The result is a multifaceted compilation of stories from researchers, legal experts, clinicians, scholars, and activists who pushed back against weight bias and all its various harmful practices and outcomes. Through interviews and personal essays, Weight and Wisdom documents untold stories, reflects on shortcomings and successes, and invites readers to continue cross-generational dialogues to ensure body liberation"—Provided by publisher.
Identifiers: LCCN 2024044260 (print) | LCCN 2024044261 (ebook) | ISBN 9781597191036 (trade paperback) | ISBN 9781597191043 (ebook)
Subjects: LCSH: Body image. | Body weight. | Discrimination against overweight persons.
Classification: LCC BF697.5.B63 W425 2024 (print) | LCC BF697.5.B63 (ebook) | DDC 306.4/613—dc23/eng/20241125
LC record available at https://lccn.loc.gov/2024044260
LC ebook record available at https://lccn.loc.gov/2024044261

DEDICATION

I CONTEMPLATED THE IDEA FOR THIS COLLECTION for several years; it took the loss of Paul Ernsberger and all of his wisdom to motivate me to start. Far too many stories have been lost to us because they were not recorded anywhere. With that in mind, Tigress and I dedicate this volume to the trailblazers, benefactors, influencers, guides, and crusaders who are no longer with us to tell their stories. The contributors to the book were invited to add to this dedication; the names are listed in the order in which they were suggested to the editors.

Paul Ernsberger, Fall Ferguson, Linda Ramos, Claudia Clark, Joanne Ikeda, Miriam Berg, Caitlin "Cat" Pausé, Adrienne Bennett, Janet Conroy-Quirk, Mo Kalman, Elana Dykewoman, Pamela Vireday, Mara Nesbitt-Aldrich, Heather MacAllister aka Reva Lucian, Moe Lerner, Judy Freespirit, Crystal Kotow, Frances White, Amelia Mitchell, Lori Irving, Catherine O'Hara, Lew Louderback, Ann Louderback, Joyce Fabrey, Paula Dachis, Nancy Summer, Russell Williams, Louise Wolfe, Marvin Grosswirth, Ethel Weiss-Shedd, Sue Nyman, Susan Mason, Ruby Greenwald, Patricia Schwarz, Naomi Shadowitz, Neil Osbourne, Randi Hertz Suriano, Carla Joy DenHartog, Denise Washington, Butch Washington, Peggy Williams, Laura Hoesterey Baker, Jeri Carmichael, Roberta Stone, Darlene Cates, Elizabeth Fisher, Jerry Hoxworth, Mary Jo Hoxworth, Sandy Zitkus, Ronda Wood, Mary Frances Platt, Howard Clist, Natalie Clist, Sharon Russell Klose, Mary Ellen "Meg" Gwynne, Harvey Parker, Charles Van Dyke, Dot Nelson-Turnier, Wilma Kuns, Carl Neidershuh, Deb Albright, Margaret MacKenzie, June Bailey, Bunny Peckham, Donna Marie Ryan, Joyce Maloney, Carolyn "Carrie" Hemenway, Karen Wynn-Cohen, Kenneth Wachtel, Sherry Eckert, Michael Simpson

GENTEEL HELLRAISER
IN MEMORY OF LYNN MCAFEE (1949-2024)

LYNN MCAFEE IS A FAT ACTIVIST LEGEND. A founding member of the Fat Underground, Lynn also served on the NAAFA board of directors, and co-founded the Council on Size and Weight Discrimination. She was a radical rabble-rouser whose name is spoken reverently by other fat activists and feminists, a woman other fat lib icons consider an icon.

In early 2023 Lynn was hospitalized in southern California. I (Tigress) was about an hour away on business. Even though Lynn and I were strangers, she cheerfully agreed to a visit. We spent much of the next day together. Lynn was smart and sassy. We giggled over decades-old gossip. We discussed scholarship and strategy, socializing and socialization. We talked about destroying the system and working within the system. She told me her life in her later years, the people she treasured and the people she missed.

I was hesitant to turn our fun afternoon into a more formal interview, but after hours, she had shared so many important insights that I finally asked if I might record a bit of her talking about fat lib history and include it in this publication. She enthusiastically agreed, and we talked for at least another hour. Finally, I asked for just one more recording—her bio, so she wouldn't have to send me one later. That recording and the selfie we took would be all I'd make it home with. Sadly, the device I recorded on broke the next day. Returning home days later, I discovered that my "infallible" cloud backup had also failed. Only the bio recording remained.

I am heartbroken not to be able to share more of that day with our community. But I also treasure this gem that so encapsulates exactly who Lynn was. Here's what she said:

> Hi. I'm Lynn McAfee. Born in 1949. Grew up in the '50s and '60s as a wildly oppressed child. And then in the '70s, we BROKE OUT! And joined the women's movement. I was one of the founders of the Fat Underground. And I've just been a general hellraiser since then…in my own genteel way.

Y'all, the way she coyishly cooed "in my own genteel way"! So perfect! "How's that?" she asked. I told her I loved it, and asked if there was anything of professional note she wanted to add or if she wanted to just be a hellraiser. "Just be a hellraiser," she replied.

And so she was.

CONTENTS

CONTRIBUTORS

FRANCIE M. BERG, MS (she/her) is a teacher, historian, and author of 17 books, with homestead and ranching roots in the Old West. Born at home in the Missouri River Breaks, she grew up on a Montana cattle ranch and lives in Hettinger, North Dakota. She has worked as a county extension agent, and taught home economics in high school, college and adult education. A licensed nutritionist and graduate of Montana State University in Bozeman, she has a master's degree in family social studies and anthropology from the University of Minnesota. For 18 years Francie edited *Healthy Weight Journal*. Her nutrition books are: *Children and Teens Afraid to Eat: Helping Youth in Today's Weight-Obsessed World* (1997); *Women Afraid to Eat: Breaking Free in Today's Weight-Obsessed World* (2000); and *Underage and Overweight: Our Childhood Obesity Crisis—What Every Family Needs to Know* (2005). She has also written several western history books. In retirement, she writes a Buffalo blog: BuffaloTalesandTrails.com

GAYLE BROOKS, PHD (she/her) is vice president and chief clinical officer for The Renfrew Center. She received her doctorate in clinical psychology from Duke University. Dr. Brooks is a member of The Renfrew Center executive team and leads the Renfrew Clinical Excellence Board and the clinical training and research departments. She has administrative oversight responsibility for Renfrew's residential facility in Coconut Creek, Florida. For the past 30 years she has treated patients from diverse backgrounds who suffer from eating disorders. Dr. Brooks served as the eating disorders specialist in the HBO film *Thin*, has appeared on *Good Morning America,* and has been featured in the following publications: *The New York Times, People Magazine, Essence Magazine,* and *Perspectives*, the Renfrew Center Foundation's journal for professionals. A frequent presenter at conferences and workshops, Dr. Brooks speaks on topics such as the treatment of the complex patient, eating disorders and cultural diversity, the interplay between eating disorders and trauma, and eating disorders in mid-life women. Dr. Brooks is a former International Association of Eating Disorders Professionals (IAEDP) board member, serves on the IAEDP Senior Advisory Council, and is a former co-chair of the Academy for Eating Disorders (AED) Diversity special interest group.

HARRIET BROWN, MFA (she/her) is a professor of magazine, news, & digital journalism at the S. I. Newhouse School of Public Communications, and a sought-after speaker on college campuses around the country. She has written for the *New York Times* Science section, the *New York Times Magazine, O Magazine, Psychology Today, Scientific American,* and other publications. Her most recent book is *Shadow Daughter: A Memoir of Estrangement* (Da Capo, 2018). She has also written *Body of Truth: How Science, History, and Culture Drive Our Obsession with Weight—and What We Can Do About It* (Da Capo, 2015) and *Brave Girl Eating: A Family's Struggle with Anorexia* (William Morrow, 2010), which won a Books for a Better Life Award. In 2011 she won the University of Iowa's John F. Murray Prize in Strategic Communications for the Public Good for her work as an advocate for those with eating disorders.

BARBARA ALTMAN BRUNO, PhD, DCSW (she/her). Dr. Bruno's youth was colored by her parents' concern about her body size. She gave up dieting in 1974 and has spent much of her life since then seeking a better way for herself and others to live well in fatter bodies. She began teaching and counseling people to leave diets and use "weight problems" to lead them to better lives. She joined the National Association to Advance Fat Acceptance (NAAFA), became a local and national leader, and has been on NAAFA's International Advisory Board for a long time. Her book *Worth Your Weight: What You Can Do about a Weight Problem* came out in late 1996. She was a founding member of the Association for the Health Enrichment of Large People (AHELP), learned she was a grandmother of the Association for Size Diversity and Health (ASDAH), and became its education co-chair. She was on the editorial board of the *Fat Studies Journal,* wrote a brief history of the first century of Health at Every Size® (HAES), and brought HAES to her alma mater, Cornell University. Cornell's HAES work includes an ongoing program, Body Positive Cornell, publishing her HAES history, sponsoring a HAES symposium in 2019, and archiving not only her records but also those of Cheri Erdman and eventually Bill Fabrey, NAAFA's founder. She is now on the Council on Size and Weight Discrimination (CSWD). Overcoming size and weight discrimination and supporting living well at any size—especially fat—continue to be her passions.

DEB/DEBBY BURGARD, PhD, FAED, (she/her) is a psychologist and activist living in the San Francisco Bay area. She is a white cis lesbian disabled small fat, one of the founders of the care model known as Health at Every Size, and co-author of *Great Shape: The First Fitness Guide for Large Women* with Pat Lyons (1988). She created the BodyPositive.com website in 1997, the Show Me the Data listserv in 2001, the Poodle Science explainer video, and many other projects and publications. Her work aims to create community and spaciousness for fat people and reduce harm in healthcare systems, preferably while also having dance parties in the pool.

RAGEN CHASTAIN, BCPA, (she/her) is a speaker, writer, researcher, board-certified patient advocate, multi-certified health and fitness professional, and thought leader in the intersections of weight science, weight stigma, and healthcare. Utilizing her background in research methods and statistics, Ragen has brought her signature mix of humor and hard facts to health-care, corporate, conference, and college audiences from Kaiser Permanente and the Association of Diabetes Education Specialists national conference to Amazon and Google, Dartmouth University, the California Institute of Technology, and Canadian Fitness Professionals Inc. (canfitpro). Author of the Weight and Healthcare newsletter, the book *Fat: The Owner's Manual*, and the blog DancesWithFat, co-author of the HAES Health Sheets, and editor of the anthology *The Politics of Size*, Ragen is frequently featured as an expert in print, radio, television, and documentary film. In her free time Ragen is a national dance champion, triathlete, and marathoner who holds the Guinness World Record for Heaviest Woman to Complete a Marathon. She co-founded the Fit Fatties Facebook group, which has over 11,000 members, with Jeanette DePatie. Ragen lives in Oregon with her fiancée (and fellow fat activist) Julianne Wotasik and their adorable dog.

CARMEN COOL, MA, LPC, (she/her) is a politicized therapist, educator, speaker, consultant, and cupcake connoisseur. For the past 22 years her work has been to help people heal their relationships with food and their bodies, support the next generation of body liberation leaders, and shift the psychotherapy profession towards justice. She is the past board president of ASDAH, was named "Most Inspiring Individual" in Boulder, Colorado from the Boulder County REAL Awards, and was the recipient of the Excellence in Eating Disorder Advocacy Award from the Eating Disorders Coalition in Washington, DC.

CAROLYN COSTIN MA, MED, MFT, FAED, CEDS, (she/her) is a world renowned, sought-after eating disorders clinician, author, and inter-national speaker. Recovered herself, Carolyn recognized her calling after successfully treating her first eating disorders client in 1979. Carolyn was first to publicly say that people with eating disorders can become fully recovered. After 15 years in private practice and running hospital programs, Carolyn recognized a gap in the field and opened Monte Nido, the first residential facility in the U.S. combining standard treatment with meditation and yoga. Clients finally could practice daily skills necessary for full recovery such as grocery shopping, shopping for and preparing food. After selling Monte Nido Carolyn created The Carolyn Costin Institute, offering continuing education for clinicians and the certification of eating disorders coaches, filling another existing gap in the field. Carolyn continues to see a few clients, to offer consultations, and to speak at national and international conferences. She has written six books, the most popular being *8 Keys to Recovery from an Eating Disorder.*

REV. E-K DAUFIN, PHD, (she/her) is the award-winning author of the book *On Fat and Faith: Ending Weight Stigma in Yourself, Your Sanctuary and Society.* She is a fat-liberation intersectional multi-religious social change artist. She is a speaker, performer, coach, consultant, ceremony and workshop facilitator, educator, ordained feminist minister, and activist. She earned her doctorate in multimedia communication from Ohio State University. She is the founding adviser of the National Organization for Women's Campus Action Network at Alabama State University, an historically Black university in Montgomery, AL, where her company (E-K. Daufin *&* Associates) is headquartered. E-K. has performed and studied internationally, conducting ceremonies and workshops for myriad universities, libraries, and organizations such Canada's National Center for Eating Disorders and the Los Angeles Center for Alcoholism Prevention for Women. She has worked with many fat-positive organizations, including NAAFA (as cross-cultural liaison to the Black community, NAAFA50 fat fashion model, speaker, and workshop leader), ASDAH, the Fat Studies division of the international Popular Culture Association, the Binge Eating Disorders Association, the National Eating Disorders Information Center in Toronto, and others. Her multimedia work has been published in many forums, including in *The Los Angeles Times*, *ESSENCE*, the Associated Press, academic journals, monographs, and books. She has won many awards from organizations such as the Minorities and Communication Division and Commission on the Status of Women (Association for Education in Journalism & Mass Communication), the Academy of Television Arts & Sciences Foundation, and others.

AMY BAKER DENNIS, PHD, FAED, FACT, (she/her) is a researcher, educator, trainer, mentor, author, and clinical psychologist. Dr. Dennis has maintained a clinical practice for 45 years and has specialized in the treatment of eating disorders since 1977. She served on the faculties of Wayne State Medical School, the University of South Florida Medical School, and the Hamilton Holt Graduate School at Rollins College. She is a founding fellow of the Academy for Eating Disorders (AED), founding member of the Eating Disorders Research Society (EDRS), founding member of the National Eating Disorders Association (NEDA), founding fellow/diplomate of the Academy of Cognitive Therapy (ACT) and a certified cognitive therapist. She has received numerous awards, including Outstanding Contributions to the Field of Eating Disorders, presented by AED, and the Lifetime Achievement Award, presented by NEDA. She has lectured nationally and internationally and published extensively. Her most recent book is *Eating Disorders, Addictions and Substance Use Disorders: Clinical, Research and Treatment Perspectives.*

PEGGY ELAM, PHD, (she/her) is a clinical psychologist and publisher based in Nashville, TN. She has a master's and doctorate in psychology from Vanderbilt University and a bachelor's degree in journalism and English from Mississippi University for Women. She is the author of "Collateral Damage in the 'War on Obesity': Programming Kids for Eating Disorders," a chapter in Rebecca Weinstein's *Fat Kids: Truth and Consequences* (Beaufort Books, 2014), and (with Dawne Kimbrell, PhD) "Size, Lies, and Measuring Tape" (*Cognitive and Behavior Practice,*1995). She was the mental/emotional health expert and consultant for iVillage Inc. 1998–2000, edited the bimonthly newsletter of the International Society for the Study of Dissociation (*ISSD News*) 1999–2001, and was chair of ASDAH's media committee 2008–2010. She hosted the *Health At Every Size* weekly talk show on Radio Free Nashville 2005–2011. She founded Pearlsong Press in 2003, with the mission and vision of promoting liberation of body, mind and spirit, fat acceptance, and Health At Every Size. In recent years, as she cared for her elderly mother and now her disabled husband, she has scaled back her clinical work and has shifted the bulk of her practice to older people, providing counseling services in nursing/rehab centers and assisted living facilities, and via telehealth.

NANCY ELLIS-ORDWAY, PHD, LCSW, (she/her) is a psychotherapist with more than 35 years' experience, specializing in treating eating disorders, body image issues, stress, anxiety, depression, and relationship issues. She has a private practice in Jefferson City, MO. In addition to a master of social work degree from Washington University and a PhD in health education and promotion from the University of Missouri, she completed the Advanced Psychodynamic Psychotherapy training program at the St. Louis Psychoanalytic Institute. She has written chapters for five books and authored *Thrive At Any Weight: Eating To Nourish Body, Soul, and Self Esteem* (2019). She is the coeditor of *Weight Bias in Health Education: Critical Perspectives for Pedagogy and Practice* (2021) and the coauthor of "Weight Stigma as a Violation of the NASW Code of Ethics: A Call to Action" in *The Journal of Social Work Values and Ethics* (2022).

BILL FABREY, BSEE, (he/him) attended Cornell University and then obtained a BSEE degree (with highest honors) from the Rochester Institute of Technology in 1966. He was also very active in the student branch of the Institute of Electrical and Electronics Engineers (IEEE). While at RIT he was in the cooperative program with Eastman Kodak, receiving a patent, after which he taught electromagnetic field theory at RIT and then received a NASA fellowship at the Graduate School of Electrophysics at Polytechnic Institute of New York. He did engineering work after 1967, ultimately biomedical research, and founded the National Association to Advance Fat Acceptance (NAAFA), a human rights organization. He served as NAAFA's first president in 1969 and as a board member until 1991. In that year, he co-founded the Council on Size and Weight Discrimination (CSWD), eventually becoming its president. After his retirement in 2006 he became the proprietor of a mail-order company, Amplestuff, selling things like extra-large blood pressure cuffs and hospital gowns, extra-large clothing hangers, extra-wide socks, and many other items. He is also a member of ASDAH. As a biomedical engineer and a human rights volunteer, he tries to make a positive difference in the lives of others. At age 81, he advocates for disenfranchised peoples, Black Lives Matter, and the rights of native Americans and Indigenous peoples—while working to end the stigmatization of fat people. His posts can be seen on LinkedIn.

PEGGY A. HOWELL, RMT, CMT, (she/her) is a retired advertising and promotions manager, certified massage therapist, Reiki master/teacher and NAAFA board member. Peggy grew up in the Midwest, but has spent most of her adult life in California and Nevada. She served for 17 years as public relations director of NAAFA, a grassroots civil rights organization working to end discrimination based on body size whose programs include the Equality at Every Size campaign. Peggy has been a contributing patient-advice blogger for *U.S. News & World Report's For Better Blog.* As a representative of and media spokesperson for the size acceptance community she has appeared on many radio and television shows, including *Good Morning America, Anderson Cooper 360, Nat Geo's Taboo* and *The Dr. Phil Show.* At the age of 72 Peggy created an Instagram account with @fatacceptancewarrior as her handle. The objective is to show the world that fat people can live to be very old, just like anyone else. Her #oldfatty posts show old fat people living and enjoying life. Since her retirement from the NAAFA board in 2022 Peggy has spent most of her time reading, watching the Game Show Network, and brunching with her girls in Las Vegas.

DALIA KINSEY, RD, LD, (nonbinary/no pronouns) is a queer small fat Black registered dietitian, the creator of the *Body Liberation for All* podcast, and author of *Decolonizing Wellness: A QTBIPOC-Centered Guide to Escape the Diet Trap, Heal Your Self-Image, and Achieve Body Liberation.* Dalia rejects diet culture and teaches people to use nutrition as a self-care and personal empowerment tool to counter the damage of systemic oppression. Dalia's work can be found at https://www.daliakinsey.com/.

MICHAEL P. LEVINE, PhD, (he/him) is emeritus professor of psychology at Kenyon College in Gambier, Ohio, where he taught from 1979 through 2012. In the field of eating disorders his commitment to research, writing, and advocacy focuses on the intersection between sociocultural risk factors, prevention, and community psychology. He has authored three books and three prevention curriculum guides and has co-edited three books on prevention. In 2015, as co-editor with his long-time collaborator and colleague Linda Smolak, PhD, he published a two-volume *Handbook of Eating Disorders* (Wiley & Sons Publishing). In 2021 he and Dr. Smolak published a new, extensively revised, and expanded edition of their 2006 book *The Prevention of Eating Problems and Eating Disorders* (Routledge/Taylor & Francis). In addition, Dr. Levine has authored or co-authored approximately 115 articles, book chapters, and book reviews, and has presented his work throughout the United States, as well as in Canada, England, Spain, Austria, and Australia. Dr. Levine is a fellow of the Academy for Eating Disorders (AED), which has awarded him their Meehan-Hartley Award for Leadership in Public Awareness and Advocacy (2006), and their Research-Practice Partnership Award (2008).

CALEB LUNA, PHD, (they/them) is an artist, public scholar, and theorist of the body. They are an award-winning educator and scholar, the bestselling author of *Revenge Body* (Nomadic Press, 2022; Black Lawrence Press, 2023), and co-host of the podcast *Unsolicited: Fatties Talk Back.* Publishing, performing, and curating across genre and medium, their cultural work examines race, size, sexuality, and disability in media and culture. Ultimately, they are interested in engaging embodied difference as a generative resource toward fatter understandings of collective freedom. Dr. Luna holds a PhD in performance studies with a designated emphasis in gender and women's studies from the University of California, Berkeley. They are currently an assistant professor of feminist studies at the University of California, Santa Barbara.

PAT LYONS, RN, MA, (she /her) has been a registered nurse for over 50 years (primarily in community-based health programs for low income BIPOC people), a fat activist since 1986, and co-author of *Great Shape: The First Fitness Guide for Large Women* (1988), which became part of the foundational development of Health at Every Size (HAES). She has contributed chapters to several other books on weight bias issues. She co-authored research studies at UC Berkeley on negative effects of dieting, and co-authored the first published study on weight bias barriers to ovarian cancer screening identified by large women. As a consultant in the regional office of health education at Kaiser Permanente in Oakland from 1989–2007, she led efforts to educate physicians and staff to reduce bias in health care and develop the HAES model. She has been a speaker at numerous national and international conferences for health professionals and women's health programs. She collaborated with fat activist and size acceptance leaders to establish the Association for the Health Enrichment of Large People (AHELP) in 1990, which eventually led to the formation of the Association for Size Diversity and Health (ASDAH).

MARGO MAINE, PHD, FAED, CEDS, (she/her) is a clinical psychologist who has specialized in eating disorders for over 35 years. A founder and former advisor of the National Eating Disorders Association and founder and fellow of the Academy for Eating Disorders, her most recent book, *Hair Tells a Story: Hers, Yours, & Ours* (Toplight, 2023), explores women's relationship with their hair, a neglected aspect of body image. Dr. Maine is also author of *Pursuing Perfection: Eating Disorders, Body Myths, and Women* at Midlife and Beyond; *Treatment of Eating Disorders: Bridging the Research-Practice Gap; Effective Clinical Practice in the Treatment of Eating Disorders; The Body Myth; Father Hunger;* and *Body Wars;* and senior editor emeritus of *Eating Disorders: The Journal of Treatment and Prevention.* She is the 2007 recipient of the Lori Irving Award for Excellence in Eating Disorders Awareness and Prevention, the 2014 recipient of the Don and Melissa Nielsen Lifetime Achievement Award, and the 2015 NEDA Lifetime Achievement Award, and a 2016 honoree of the Connecticut Women's Hall of Fame. She maintains a private practice, Maine & Weinstein Specialty Group, in West Hartford, CT. She loves the Earth and gets up early every day to celebrate it.

JUDITH MATZ, LCSW, ACSW, (she/her) is a therapist, nationally recognized speaker, and consultant on the topics of diet culture, binge eating, emotional eating, body image, and weight stigma. She is co-author of *The Diet Survivor's Handbook, Beyond a Shadow of a Diet, The Making Peace with Food Card Deck,* and *The Body Positivity Card Deck,* and author of *Amanda's Big Dream.* Her new workbook on chronic dieting, binge eating, and body shame will be published in 2024 (PESI Publishing). Judith's work has been featured in media including *NPR, The New York Times, Good Housekeeping,* and *Psychotherapy Networker.* She has a private practice via telehealth in Illinois. Find her at www.judithmatz.com and on Instagram @judmatz.

ALLEGRA O'HARA, BA, (she/her) lives and works on unceded Yuggera and Turrbal land in Meanjin (Brisbane), Australia. She has researched and written about systems of oppression and the people that they oppress. A passion for systemic change has led to pursuit of a master of gender studies degree with a plan to write a thesis on non-normative understandings and articulations of love. She brings to this book very little of what neo-liberal imperialist institutions would define as "formal" experience in the world of weight-based oppression and fatphobia, instead bringing a wealth of "informal" knowledge gained from living as a fat person. One goal in writing her chapter was to contest positivist hierarchies of knowledge and show that valid and valuable knowledge doesn't always need a scientific seal of approval. It is important to her to note that her experiences as a fat person are inherently informed by other subjectivities. She is a white small-fat cisgender woman physically located in the English-speaking global North, and acknowledges the power and privilege these subjectivities afford her.

LILY O'HARA, PHD, MPH, (she/her) is a mid-sized fat woman who has experienced external and internalized weight-based oppression throughout most of her life. The first crack in the once-impenetrable wall of internalized scientific and cultural beliefs about body weight that held her prisoner for so long appeared in the mid 1990s, and she has spent the years since working personally and professionally to dismantle the wall brick by brick. She is currently associate professor of public health at Qatar University. She is a public health and health promotion educator and practitioner with experience in Australia, United Arab Emirates, and Qatar, and a longstanding member of ASDAH and NAAFA. Her fat studies research focuses on analyzing oppressive public health approaches to body weight and their inequitable impact on people with larger bodies, and developing ethical, evidence-based, salutogenic public health initiatives for body liberation using a social justice-oriented approach to the Health at Every Size framework. Her research and practice also focuses on developing critical health promotion competencies of the community, workforce, and institutions. She is the co-developer of the Red Lotus Critical Health Promotion Model, and most recently the Quality Assessment Tool for Critical Health Promotion Practice (QATCHEPP).

TIGRESS OSBORN, MFA, (she/her) is the executive director of the National Association to Advance Fat Acceptance (NAAFA). Founded in 1969 in the United States, NAAFA is the world's oldest documented fat rights advocacy organization. As leader of the most diverse board in NAAFA's 54-year history, Tigress has championed an intersectional approach to fighting anti-fatness through education, advocacy, and support. Her work with NAAFA has been featured in *USA Today, Huffington Post,* and *Newsweek,* and heard on *BBC AntiSocial* and *ABC News.* Tigress also hosts and produces the NAAFA Webinar Series, which features a wide variety of activists, scholars, and artists from fat community. Tigress founded Full Figure Entertainment in 2008 in Oakland, CA, and co-founded the PHX Fat Force in Arizona in 2019. Tigress is a justice, equity, diversity, and inclusion (JEDI) consultant and educator whose clients have ranged from major tech companies to small nonprofits. She is a two-time women's college graduate with a BA in Black studies from Smith College and an MFA in creative writing from Mills College. Learn more about NAAFA at naafa.org. Follow Tigress @iofthetigress on your favorite social media.

ELYSE RESCH, MS, RDN, CEDS-S, FIAEDP, FADA, FAND, (she/her) is a nutrition therapist in private practice with 40 years of experience, specializing in eating disorders, intuitive eating, and Health at Every Size. She is the co-author of *Intuitive Eating* (now in its fourth edition), *the Intuitive Eating Workbook,* and *The Intuitive Eating Card Deck—50 Bite-Sized Ways to Make Peace with Food.* She is also author of *The Intuitive Eating Workbook for Teens* and *The Intuitive Eating Journal—Your Guided Journey for Nourishing a Healthy Relationship with Food,* and a chapter contributor to *The Handbook of Positive Body Image and Embodiment.* She has published journal articles, print articles, and blog posts and does regular speaking engagements, podcasts, and extensive media interviews. She is nationally known for her work in helping patients break free from diet culture. Her philosophy embraces the goal of reconnecting with one's internal wisdom about eating and developing body liberation, with the belief that all bodies deserve dignity and respect. She is a social justice advocate and a member of the Healer's Circle of Project HEAL: Help to Eat, Accept, and Live. She supervises and trains health professionals and is a certified eating disorders specialist and supervisor and fellow of the International Association of Eating Disorder Professionals and the Academy of Nutrition and Dietetics.

JON ROBISON, PHD, MS, MA, CERTIFIED INTRINSIC COACH®, (he/him) holds a doctorate in health education/exercise physiology and a master of science in human nutrition from Michigan State University, where he served as assistant professor for a quarter of a century. He has spent his career working to shift health promotion away from its traditional, biomedical, control-oriented focus, with a particular interest in why people do what they do and don't do what they don't do. He has authored numerous articles and book chapters on a variety of health-related topics, and is a frequent presenter at conferences throughout North America. He is co-author of the book *The Spirit and Science of Holistic Health: More than Broccoli, Jogging, and Bottled Water, More than Yoga, Herbs, and Meditation,* a college textbook and guidebook for practitioners who wish to incorporate holistic principles and practices into their work. This book provided the foundation for Kailo, one of the first truly holistic employee wellness programs. Kailo won prestigious awards in both Canada and the United States, and the creators lovingly claim him as its father. He has been a national leader in the Health At Every Size movement for almost three decades. He has implemented Health for Every Body®, a unique alternative to weight loss programs at the worksite, in over 20 cities across the United States in the past 15 years. He is also one of the featured health professionals in the powerful documentary *America the Beautiful II: The Thin Commandments*, and has been helping people struggling with weight- and eating-related concerns for more than 25 years. As a Certified Intrinsic Coach he understands that behavior is the outward manifestation of thinking and feeling, and that behavior modification approaches that focus on extrinsic motivation rarely result in sustained change and, in fact, often inhibit intrinsic motivation. Aside from his work, his passions include his wife Jerilyn, their son Joshua, music, humor, and a 14-lb living teddy bear named Ginger.

ESTHER D. ROTHBLUM, PhD, (she/her) is professor emerita of women's studies at San Diego State University and editor of *Fat Studies: An Interdisciplinary Journal of Body Weight and Society*. Her research and writing have focused on the stigma of weight, weight and employment discrimination, and weight across cultures. She has edited over 20 books, including *Overcoming Fear of Fat* (with Laura Brown, 1989). Her most recent book, *The Fat Studies Reader* (with Sondra Solovay, 2009), was reviewed in *The New Yorker*, the *New York Times, MS Magazine,* and the *Chronicle of Higher Education*, among others, and received the Susan Koppelman Award for Best Anthology by the Popular Culture/American Culture Association and a Distinguished Publication Award from the Association for Women in Psychology. Esther Rothblum is a member of the NAAFA advisory board and a founding co-chair of the Size Acceptance Caucus of the Association for Women in Psychology.

DANA SCHUSTER, MS, (she/her) is a mostly retired health & fitness instructor and fully retired vocational evaluator who has a master's in rehabilitation counseling. She co-taught the Kaiser Permanente Great Shape exercise class for 13 years, co-founded Women of Substance Health Spa (open 1997–2001), taught exercise classes at Every Woman Health Club in Redwood City, CA, and currently teaches a conditioning class via Zoom. Since 2005 Dana has been involved in school wellness policy development and implementation as an avid promoter of the Health At Every Size model, and has been described as a "freelance agitator & advocate for integrity." Family (husband, two adult sons, one daughter-in-law, and one adorable grandson) and close friends are central to her happiness.

BRANDIE SOLOVAY, BA, JD, (she/her) is a fat legally blind lesbian attorney who practices discrimination, disability, immigration, and criminal defense law. She is director of the Fat Legal Advocacy, Rights and Education Project

(FLARE!), which she runs out of her law office, and is also the supervising attorney and legal director at two San Francisco nonprofits. She received her BA from the University of California, Santa Cruz with a major in legal studies and a minor in film. Her JD is from John F. Kennedy University School of Law, where she completed over 1,500 hours of public interest legal work. She has been practicing law in California since 2009, and is passionate about advocating for underserved and marginalized individuals and educating people about their rights. Through the FLARE! Project she is excited to improve access to imaging for higher weight individuals, assist fat people in getting needed accommodations in healthcare, employment, education and at places of public accommodation, and help create federal, state, and local laws that protect people from height and weight discrimination. She understands that racism, white supremacy, and weight discrimination frequently intersect in ways that disproportionately burden certain communities, and she is dedicated to closing the legal loopholes that allow that injustice to continue.

SONDRA SOLOVAY, JD, (they/them) is a lifelong vegetarian/vegan fat and disability justice activist committed to understanding anti-fatness in the context of white supremacy, ableism, and other systems of oppression. They used the law (or their vision of what the law should be) to fight weight-related discrimination through their law office's Fat Legal Advocacy, Rights and Education Project (FLARE!). Sondra helped pass size discrimination laws and regulations, including helping write the San Francisco law's enforcement guidelines. They taught law with a social justice perspective. Their first book, *Tipping the Scales of Justice: Fighting Weight-Based Discrimination,* was the first to look at weight as a U.S. civil rights topic. Along with Esther Rothblum, Sondra was co-editor of the award-winning *Fat Studies Reader,* which helped establish the field of fat studies, and co-creator of the play *Fat F*ck,* which was produced in San Francisco and New York. They contributed to *FaTGiRL* and *FAT!SO?* zines, danced with Big Burlesque, and was a fat cheerleader with the Bod Squad. Being fat and disabled, they were personally impacted by the discrimination they fought in education, healthcare, employment, and public/social settings. They live with their human and furry loves in California; they are grateful to them and their wonderful brother for their support.

CAROL SQUIRES, BS, (she/her) is a Midwest-born baby boomer. She has a bachelor of science degree in photography and anthropology from Southern

Illinois University, Carbondale. After graduation she worked as a portrait photographer for a few years in her hometown. In 1981 her life took an exciting turn when she fell in love and moved to the San Francisco Bay Area. Quickly she found herself drawn to the Bay Area fat community and was introduced to the radical concept of loving her fat body. The once-shy fat girl soon found herself posing nude for the book *Women En Large: Images of Fat Nudes* by Laurie Toby Edison, with text by Debbie Notkin, performing on stage with FAT LIP Readers Theatre, and dancing with Big Moves, a size-diverse dance organization. She lives joyfully with her partner of 40 years and their two dogs.

LISA TEALER, BS, (she/her) is a Black woman, Bay Area native, longtime size diversity and community health advocate. She is a former board member of NAAFA, where she developed a size diversity toolkit to assist individuals and organizations in creating a size inclusive mindset and environment. For many years she was a size inclusive fitness instructor and taught classes for women of all sizes based on the book *Great Shape: The First Fitness Guide for Large Women*, which was written by her mentors, Pat Lyons and Deb Burgard. She also co-owned a health club focused on women of ALL sizes and fitness levels. Lisa worked for close to 40 years in both the biotech industry and in community health. She continues her diversity, equity, and inclusion work as a consultant and leads a grassroots community health organization dedicated to eliminating health disparities in underserved communities across generations. She has given presentations and participated on several panels focused on diversity, inclusion, and health equity. Lisa serves on several Bay Area community advisory boards, including Sequoia Hospital, Stanford Cancer Institute, and the University of California San Francisco Cancer Center. Lisa has an undergraduate degree in biology from Mills College and a diversity management certificate from the Bauer College of Business, University of Houston.

PATTIE THOMAS, PhD, (she/her) is a medical sociologist and sociology professor at the College of Southern Nevada. She is unapologetically fat and has lived with chronic illness and disability for most of her adult life. She has written, produced, and presented many endeavors to support fat liberation, fight fatphobia, and confront medical profiling and ableism for over 25 years. She is co-author of *Taking Up Space: How Eating Well and Exercising Regularly Changed My Life* (Pearlsong Press, 2005), with her husband Carl Wilkerson, MBA. Dr. Thomas and Mr. Wilkerson co-produce the channel *PDA Nation* on YouTube, often addressing ableism and fatphobia with humor and satire. Dr. Thomas also produces sociology videos on the channel *Living Sociology* on YouTube.

MARILYN WANN, MA, (she/her) is a longtime fat activist. In the mid-'90s she created the print zine *FAT!SO?* and in 1998 put together the *FAT!SO?* book, using her writing and other people's contributions from the zine.

ROSIE YOUNG, MSW, (she/her) is a social worker and fat activist in the Baltimore metropolitan area. Her work in the fat liberation space focuses on promoting inclusion and access to eating disorders treatment for all bodies, as well as connecting parents to resources for raising children who are critical of diet culture.

FOREWORD

CALEB LUNA

WHEN I READ *THE FAT LIBERATION MANIFESTO,* originally published in November 1973 by Fat Underground[1] members Judy Freespirit and Aldebaran, for the first time, I remember being struck by how little had changed in the decades since the document was published. Reading in the 2010s, I was taken aback that we had seemingly been having the same conversations for so long. Much like discovering other famous and infamous historic events, such as the Minnesota Starvation Experiment[2], along the journey for fat liberation, it occurred to me that our histories had been so successfully strategically suppressed in order to keep us on a hamster wheel of sorts—the same conversations about weight loss, fashion and self-esteem as distractions from the central demands of our movement.

Reading *Weight and Wisdom* troubled that picture. Rather than the same conversations, this collection details all the small benchmarks that made these conversations possible. It is more than a breath of fresh air. It feels like a soft, fleshy, warm hug from the living ancestors who have been on the front lines of this movement for decades. Each chapter sketches out more and more of the histories that have been invisibilized by colonial capitalist white supremacist diet cultures that are intent on having fat people hate our bodies. These stories fill in the gaps of how this movement was founded, the shapes it has taken, the stumbling blocks, the outright failures, and the successes. It brings insight into how we have gotten to where we are at this time of writing, as 2023 comes to a close.

This collection comes to be such a comprehensive look at the history of the movement of fat liberation from nearly every angle. It brings together activists, practitioners, and everyday people as they detail how the movement and its demands have shifted over time. We hear from lifelong fat people and fat advocates, as well as non-fat parents and lovers of people, and practitioners and professionals who have had fat clients and patients. We trace the shifts in cultural and medical landscapes as they begin to dictate and diagnose body size. The stories in this collection situate the history of fat oppression and disordered eating within larger historical contexts of the Vietnam war, *Diagnostic and Statistical Manual of Mental Disorders (DSM)* editions and diagnoses, social media, and more. We witness more clearly and intently the relationship between civil rights movements, women's liberation, and gay rights, as fat liberation models itself after each movement and has been influenced and supported by each movement's members as well.

Along the way, the reader will encounter familiar organizational names such as The Fat Underground, NAAFA, ASDAH, NEDA and HAES; individuals like Marilyn Wann, Sondra Solovay, Charlotte Cooper, Paul Ernsberger, and Bill Fabrey. They will also encounter many more names of individuals, publications, and organizations that have been, until now, largely lost to history. Barbara Bruno sketches the connections between civil rights movements of the 1960s and early fat activists. Jon Robison points to the consistency with which poor faith science around fatness and body size has been perpetuated. Carmen Cool reflects on the powerful impact of being treated for eating disorder recovery by a fat practitioner. Gayle Brooks points to how issues of disordered eating predate the formal movement for fat liberation and the field of eating disorders recovery.

I feel immense gratitude to those whose invaluable labor is captured within these pages: the labor of doing, of remembering, and of writing. And to those whose labor this book can't hold. And to you, dear reader.

This is not a book one reads to learn to love their body. Nor is it one to read to discover the magical cure to self-esteem, or to disordered eating. These are the conversations that have been allowed to float to the surface of mainstream discourse: conversations that individualize systems and histories into personal failures. This is the book that bears witness to the ancestors and elders who have been pushing the needle from the beginning. People who saw injustice in how they themselves and their loved ones were treated and decided to challenge that. It does not hide or shy away from the accompanying challenges, stumbling blocks, missteps, and outright failures incurred over the decades.

This is the book to read to situate oneself within a powerful fat lineage, to understand our history, and to move forward doing better. We must learn where we have been in order to understand where we have to go. This collection does the important labor of illuminating our past in order to shine a light on our future paths.

FOOTNOTES

1. Largely credited as the first Fat Liberation group, comprised of a group of women in LA in the 1970s. We learn in this book that they were originally a chapter of NAAFA.

2. A 1944 experiment that studied the effects of starvation (i.e., dieting) on the body.

CONTENT WARNING
LANGUAGE AND TOPICS SOME READERS MAY FIND CHALLENGING

TIGRESS OSBORN

FAT LIBERATIONISTS AND OTHERS who work toward social justice and body liberation use the word "fat" both neutrally and positively. We believe that normalizing "fat" as a descriptor deflates the power of the word as an insult. Using the word "fat" as just one of many ways to describe a body, and accepting that being fat is just one of the many ways to have a body, helps free people of all sizes from the burdens of body oppression. Still, we must acknowledge that for many people, especially those new to fat liberation frameworks, trauma related to being fat or being called fat can make it difficult to be exposed to this word. If you are one of those people, please be aware that this collection will expose you to the F-word. Often.

This collection will also expose you to the O-words. Many body liberation activists and/or professionals working toward body liberation avoid using the terms "overweight," "obese," or any variations thereof. These terms, as well as the entire framework labeling fat bodies as inherently diseased, are recognized as pathologizing and as contributing to weight stigma. Many of us object to the medicalization of fat, and some choose to indicate this objection visually by replacing letters with punctuation, as is done with vulgarity or slurs ("ob*sity"). In this book, we have allowed each contributor to handle O-word terminology as they do in their own work. Thus, readers should be aware that they will encounter these words in this text.

Pieces in this collection include discussion of disordered eating, body dysmorphia, depression, and other mental health issues.

Pieces in this collection refer to weight loss, both intentional and unintentional. In some cases, this includes mention of specific numbers.

Pieces in this collection frankly discuss white supremacy and colonialism.

Many of the contributors to this collection hold privilege in one way or another, particularly racial privilege, socio-economic privilege, and privilege related to gender or sexual orientation. Some discuss this privilege, including reflections on the ways in which lack of awareness of their own and their colleagues' privilege harmed marginalized people in eating disorders treatment, HAES, and fat liberation. We recognize that it may be difficult for some readers to encounter explicit discussion of and examples of white supremacy, colonialism, and oppression.

We know that it may be challenging for some readers to learn that people whom they consider heroes or role models have been considered otherwise. We urge you to remember that the impacts of problematic behaviors on those who were harmed outweigh the discomfort of being asked to understand and learn from reflections on problematic behavior. We invite you to examine fragility—your own and the collective fragility of privileged groups within our liberation work—in order to contribute to building inclusive communities for body liberation and other anti-oppression work.

This is a 2023 collection looking back at the '60s, '70s, '80s and '90s. As such, it is demographically representative of what our movement and professional circles looked like during those decades, not what they should have looked like then or what they do look like in the more intersectional landscape we are building today. This book should not be considered comprehensive or definitive. It is a sampling of important voices, not a documentation of the only essential voices. There always were, and always will be, more stories to collect.

Health at Every Size, also known as HAES (pronounced "haze"), is a registered trademark of the Association for Size Diversity and Health. ASDAH was founded in 2003, and has held the trademark for Health at Every Size since 2011. ASDAH's founding and other aspects of the organizations' history are discussed in several chapters of this collection.

HAES was trademarked to ensure that commercial interests such as diet companies, pharmaceutical corporations, and bariatric surgeons could not co-opt the terminology and use it in ways that are counter to the intentions of HAES frameworks. ASDAH become the "guardians and keepers" of the phrase for legal purposes. This move was widely supported by fat activists, but the decision was not unanimously supported. Some activists believed then and still believe that "ownership" of the language, even by a community-responsive and collaborative group, ultimately limits its use by the community and is its own kind of gatekeeping.

In 2024, ASDAH introduced updated HAES principles and a new supporting framework after two years of deep and broad engagement with various segments of fat and HAES community to ensure that the principles reflect ASDAH's values (abundance mindset, accountability, collaboration, curiosity, trailblazing, transformation, and joy) as well as other values of the fat liberation movement (including, but not limited to, intersectionality, inclusion, and bodily autonomy). According to ASDAH, "The Health At Every Size® Principles and Framework of Care are continuously evolving alternatives to the weight-centered approach to treating clients and patients of all sizes."

Today's HAES Principles are as follows:

- Healthcare is a human right for people of all sizes, including those at the highest end of the size spectrum.
- Wellbeing, care, and healing are resources that are both collective and deeply personal.
- Care is fully provided only when free from anti-fat bias and offered with people of all sizes in mind.
- Health is a sociopolitical construct that reflects the values of society.

In addition, ASDAH has created the HAES Framework of Care to help healthcare practitioners and others ensure that they are truly HAES-aligned in their work. Further information about the Principles and the Framework are available at asdah.org/haes.

Health at Every Size and HAES are used in this publication with ASDAH's permission.

LOOKING BACK

NANCY ELLIS-ORDWAY

"If there's a book that you want to read,
but it hasn't been written yet,
then you must write it."
TONI MORRISON

SEVERAL YEARS AGO while attending a conference, I spent the evening with several young people, new graduates, who were eager to learn more about eating disorders, fat activism, and weight stigma. When they realized how long I had been in the field, they peppered me with questions about history, influencers, attitudes, programs, ideas, theories, treatment approaches, controversies, challenges, changes, and on and on. Their curiosity was boundless. I could draw on my own limited memory, but I wanted to be able to refer them to print resources. I realized I needed to write a book, and I needed to draw on the memories of many others to help me. I also realized that many of the people who have been in the field for a long time are aging and their stories will not be available forever. I started calling and emailing; luckily, many folks responded.

I knew this task was larger than I could manage alone. While I knew many folks in the clinical world, I needed someone with more background and contacts with the activists. I also needed someone with a younger, more current experience in the field. I was delighted when Tigress Osborn agreed to be my co-editor. While we agree in many ways, she has brought a perspective to this project that is very different from my own and has introduced me to people I would not have met otherwise. She has kept me focused and on track while challenging me to think in ways new to me. Thanks to Tigress, this book is far better than what I originally imagined. I am grateful for the opportunity to work with her and for this volume we have produced together. Plus, I discovered that she loves collecting stories as much as I do!

The book you hold in your hands is an attempt to gather some of those stories, told from first person points of view. It is by no means a complete history; the number of participants was limited by publishing restraints, time, and availability. While I set out to gather memories, I feel very fortunate that the authors also have included the wisdom that comes from experience and have expressed compassion for our younger selves who didn't know as much as we do now. For all of us, it has been a journey of growth, evolution. and progress.

It is hard to remember that there was a time in our culture when thinness was not so idealized, when adiposity was not so villainized, and when diet companies did not dominate the conversation. For those of us who can remember the 1950s or earlier, society was different in many, many ways, including different attitudes about body size. While some individuals might have been scrutinized for being larger, for the most part variations in body size were much more likely to be accepted as a normal part of human diversity. Even in the medical field, concern about malnutrition, which had been endemic for most of human history, only gradually gave way to concern about ob*sity.

This began to change as various entrepreneurs discovered that there was money to be made selling products and programs that promised weight loss. Profitability then became linked to finding new ways to disparage the condition of living in a larger body. Adiposity became medicalized and linked to a growing list of illnesses. Fatness took on a moral quality. Bias became discrimination and oppression, not only in the medical field but also in employment, education, housing, media, and financial opportunity. This resulted in a cultural shift in which it became acceptable, even expected, to be mean and hateful to people of size. Eventually we had a term for this: weight stigma, which refers to anything that devalues larger bodies and overvalues thinness.

There is a correlation between the increase in weight stigma and the increase in eating disorders and body dissatisfaction. If people are treated badly in society for being larger, it only makes sense that individuals would try to make themselves smaller, by any means necessary. Even those who were already small were terrified of gaining weight and being treated badly.

Different groups of folks began to push back against these beliefs and assumptions in different ways. This is the thread that runs through the chapters in this book. Weight stigma resulted in eating disorders, and clinicians responded by developing and studying treatment approaches. Weight stigma resulted in the medicalization of adiposity, and scientists and scholars pushed back through research and data gathering. Weight stigma resulted in discrimination and oppression of larger people, and activists fought back by disrupting that narrative whenever possible. Weight stigma resulted in widespread shame and body dissatisfaction, and advocates developed ways to intervene and promote body acceptance and positivity.

All these ideas were once new and untested. Over time they have been developed and refined and are still works in progress. We have made both progress and mistakes. We build on what has been done before; we learn from what did and didn't work.

In every social justice movement there comes a time to pass the torch to a younger generation. It fills me with joy to see the growing group of scholars, researchers, clinicians, and activists who are ready to carry this work forward. There is still much to be done, and knowing our history can help us continue the work.

ICE CREAM FOR BREAKFAST
FAT LIBERATION STARTS AT HOME

ALLEGRA O'HARA *and* LILY O'HARA

INTRODUCTION

PATTI LATHER ENCOURAGES US to sit in the ruins that result from the deconstruction of the white-supremacist-neoliberal-capitalist patriarchy.[1] She urges us to embrace the mess, the chaos, and the unknown, and to refuse to tidy up for the sake of others. Whilst reading this chapter, we encourage you to do the same. Sit with any feelings of confusion, doubt, or uncertainty, and find solace in the unresolved.

We do not aim to give you the definitive guide to the histories of weight-based oppression or fat liberation. Instead, the narratives we offer are simply meant to enrich your own thoughts and understandings. We aim for this chapter to reassure you that knowledge is exponential and incredibly subjective. In other words, it's OK not to know everything.

We are daughter (Allegra) and mother (Lily), and our views and experiences are both individual and inextricably intertwined. Throughout this chapter, wherever we share the same perspectives, we use the term "we." Wherever the perspective is individual, we identify the specific person. In this chapter, we discuss fat liberation and anti-weight-based oppression upbringing and parenting, critique the language used in the fat liberation movement, and describe our approaches to weight-based oppression and fat liberation.

We try to embody an ethic of fat liberation and anti-weight-based oppression in all facets of our lives. But we also cannot deny the extent of weight-based oppression in society. This creates a complex space that so many of us occupy: the borderlands between the revolution required for fat liberation and the abject pressures of a weight oppressive society. Feelings of doubt, frustration, and even betrayal are inevitable. These complexities make up so much of the fat experience and yet so often don't feel adequately represented. In giving you an honest reflection on our experiences with fat liberation and weight-based oppression, we aim to change this.

FAT LIBERATION AND ANTI-WEIGHT-BASED OPPRESSION UPBRINGING AND PARENTING

I (ALLEGRA) COME TO THIS BOOK less so with academic and career experience, but with a lifetime of lived experience. I am a mid-sized fat person in her 20s, and while negative feelings about my fatness are not at the forefront of my mind, being fat is a significant factor in my identity. I was very fortunately raised by a mother (Lily) whose approach to life and parenthood has been underpinned by fat liberation and a fight against weight-based oppression. I was taught that every day of my life as a fat person is an act of rebellion. Being the naturally contrarian person I am, any chance to be rebellious was music to my ears.

Although it is over 25 years ago, I (Lily) have a clear and distinct memory of the two red lines that seemed to illuminate the white plastic test kit. I was pregnant with my second child and co-author of this chapter (Allegra). It was very much a planned and wanted pregnancy. Sometime later an ultrasound revealed that the baby would be assigned female at birth, and I felt a rush of delight—a second daughter to raise as a strong fat liberationary feminist. I had grand plans! As a parent of three daughters, I have proactively and painstakingly worked to cultivate a fat friendly family environment imbued with a deep appreciation for the natural diversity of human bodies (and all other life forms). I was zealous in enacting the principles of the Health at Every Size® approach.[2] When reading Harry Potter books to my kids, I would censor any negative descriptions of fat people. I am a mid-sized fat person, and always referred to myself as fat. We discussed the use of the term and how it is just a neutral descriptor, though not everyone feels this way because it has been used as a pejorative term for so long. When Allegra asked to have ice cream for breakfast one day, I said yes. And the next day, and the day after. And although part of me wondered if it was the "right" thing to do (it's impossible to escape those insidious messages about "healthy" food), I was determined to stick with it, and on the fifth day she decided she was sick of ice cream and asked for dippy eggs with toast soldiers instead. Phew, HAES® principles vindicated.

As my daughters got older, we had more sophisticated discussions about why some bodies were idealized and others vilified. With Allegra in particular, we talked about the role of capitalism, neoliberalism, sexism, the patriarchy, and cis-heteronormativity. I not only wanted to protect my daughters from the toxicity of systemic weight-based oppression, but also to raise daughters who would feel capable of contributing to the liberation of people from this tyranny. Raising children, and indeed living and working in a society that prizes a thin body over all others and (erroneously) equates thinness with "health" is tough.

Although Mum (Lily) describes her approach to creating a fat friendly household as proactive and painstaking, our home environment never felt that. To me (Allegra), our family was just like every other family. I now know that this was not the case. Going to friends' houses, I began to see that other families had very different relationships to food, physical activity, and their bodies than what we practiced at home. As Mum touched on, food was simply just that in our house. For our family there were two meal options: home-cook or takeaway. Refusing to give in to insidious messages about "healthy" food, Mum never referred to takeaway food as "fast" food or "junk" food. This was a conscious decision on Mum's part that has stuck with me to this day; I can't actually remember a time when I've used the phrase "fast food." As kids, we came to understand that food isn't something to covet or to fear. Takeaway food was never used as a treat or reward but was just another meal option. Comments were never made on how much or what we ate, and my memories of mealtimes center more on family bonding and antics than the food itself.

Mum (Lily) mentioned that her aim was to raise her daughters to be strong, capable, and unapologetic in the face of adversity. I like to think that my actions over the years speak to how much Mum and her approach to parenthood have empowered me to fight weight-based oppression. In grade six, at 11 years of age, I decided to talk to my teacher about her diets, which she very unprofessionally had told her students about, being problematic. In a grade 10 physical education lesson, I, albeit quite anxiously, stood up for myself and refused to participate in the measurement of my body mass index. More recently, I told my doctor that I would not simply "try exercising" as they suggested when I asked to be medicated for depression. While none of these acts were a walk in the park, I could always count on the support of my mum.

Reflecting back on my childhood, it actually took me quite a while to pinpoint moments that felt particularly fat liberationist. I realize now that this is exactly what Mum (Lily) worked so hard for. Fat liberation was simply the norm in our house. I know that this cannot have been an easy task, but I will forever be grateful for Mum's dedication to instilling in me knowledge and practices of fat liberation and anti-weight-based oppression. Her commitment to fat liberation created a beautiful, supportive household in which I've always felt confident and comfortable to be myself.

LANGUAGE CRITIQUE

We now turn to an exploration and critique of the language and terminology used in the fat liberation movement. While planning this chapter we were both often unsure of what phrases or terms we thought were most appropriate. We threw around a few different terms, but none of them felt true to what we're trying to capture: the fight against oppression based on body weight. Although we decided on using "fat liberation" and "weight-based oppression," the decision-making process also revealed interesting insights into how fatness is talked about.

Among both the general population and in academic circles, popular terms related to fat liberation and weight-based oppression include "body positivity," "diet culture," "fat phobia," "weight stigma," and "weight bias." We take issue with these terms based on their tendency to minimize the full extent of the issues, and their emphasis on the individual. The overly simplistic nature and narrow focus of these terms means that they fail to account for the very real oppression fat people are subjected to.

In popular media, an increase in the use of the terms "body positivity" and "diet culture" has contributed to the downplaying of the fat experience. An emphasis on the "positive" in body positivity forces an idealistic understanding of marginalization based on weight, negating the trauma that also ensues. The phrasing of "diet culture," on the other hand, is pointedly placid. To describe something as a culture does not necessarily insinuate that it's a bad thing; think "sneakerhead culture" or "coffee culture." The use of "culture" neutralizes the trauma of being oppressed. With thin celebrities and influencers using the terms "body positivity" and "diet culture" more frequently, they have subverted the oppression of fat people and created a neutral cultural understanding that continues to center thin people.

While "weight stigma" and "weight bias" are terms more commonly found in academic literature, they, too, have the same minimizing effect. The use of "stigma" and "bias" to describe what is in actual fact oppression completely undermines the severity of the situation. Like the term "culture," both weight stigma and weight bias imbue a sense of neutrality. They are phrases used to make weight-based oppression more digestible and less confrontational or political. Weight-based oppression is sanitized and made clinical by terms like "weight stigma" and "weight bias." No better evidence of this is the fact that such terms have been co-opted by the "ob*sity" medical-industrial complex to call for *more* efforts to eliminate fat people. Weight stigma is regarded as undesirable purely because it prevents people from getting treated for their fatness, which is classified as "diseased." To come back to Patti Lather, the vast mess of weight-based oppression is minimized, cleaned up and sanitized by framing it as weight bias or stigma. This is to the detriment of fat people.

"Fat phobia" is another term we take issue with. A true phobia is a psychological condition characterized by an uncontrollable, irrational, and lasting fear of a certain object, situation, or activity.[3] Anti-fatness is not an anxiety disorder. Rather, it is the hatred of fatness that results in weight-based oppression. The term "fat phobia" is therefore both ableist and seriously inaccurate.

In addition to minimizing the severity of weight-based oppression, all of these terms work to divert attention away from the broader systemic and structural changes that are required to bring about equity for people with fat bodies. This diversion is achieved by emphasizing the individual. Heavily informed by neoliberal individualism, the body positivity movement overlooks institutional change as it suggests that the solution is for individuals to simply choose to be positive about their bodies. Weight stigma and weight bias also reiterate this emphasis on the individual through their focus on capturing individual people's experiences of weight-based oppression as opposed to the systems driving it. Fat phobia focuses on the internal attitudes, beliefs, and behaviors of individual fat haters. None of these terms capture the ideological and institutional systems that create and perpetuate the oppression of people based purely on their adiposity. While all of these terms have been seen as progressive and contributing to fat liberation in some way, we believe it is time to consciously choose language that captures the full scope of the problem (weight-based oppression) and the desired outcome (fat liberation).

OUR APPROACH TO WEIGHT-BASED OPPRESSION AND FAT LIBERATION

WE BOTH NAVIGATE WEIGHT-BASED oppression and fat liberation in a similar manner. We agree that our responses hinge on choosing our battles and knowing what approach will appeal best to our audience. We think it's important here to recognize that being able to choose our participation is a privilege and understand that not everyone is afforded this luxury. Not having a wealth of academic knowledge, I (Allegra) don't always feel confident taking a more fact-based, "scientific" approach to discussing weight-based oppression. Instead, I find using emotional reasoning far more beneficial. Speaking to my experiences as a fat person in a fat-hating society, the hardships I face, and the trauma that has been inflicted upon me has been a useful tool to educate less knowledgeable people about weight-based oppression. I've found that when talking with people in the medical industrial complex in particular, an emotional appeal is the only way to get through to them. Positivist, neoliberal, fat-hating ideologies are so heavily ingrained that information countering these views is often inconceivable to others. An appeal to others to see my humanity has been a far more effective approach.

Interestingly, I (Lily) have come to the same conclusion. I trained as a scientist and have worked in public health for over 30 years. For my PhD I analyzed public health approaches to body weight. I have published articles meticulously detailing the scientific inaccuracies underpinning the "war on ob*sity"[4] and the scientific evidence supporting the HAES approach.[5] I work in an academic public health department. I have conducted scientific studies on weight-based oppression[6-8] and the impact of HAES-informed health promotion programs. [9-12] I am deeply committed to science. And yet I have stopped using scientific arguments for fat liberation and against weight-based oppression. I have come to the same conclusion as Allegra. Our stories of lived experiences are far more powerful. I won't give up on the science, but it is our stories, the stories of our lives and of our children's lives, that I believe are far more impactful.

Both of us have also learned to take on an ethic of compassion when being faced with weight-based oppression. Now you may be thinking, what place does compassion have in an effort against oppression? We have found that trying to be more compassionate in recognizing the institutional ideologies that inform people's beliefs about fatness is a helpful tool. Mum (Lily) has taught me (Allegra) to remind myself that most people haven't had the same exposure to fat liberation and don't have the same knowledge of weight-based oppression as I do. For us, this brings a sense of ease. Compassionately recognizing the biases or gaps in someone's knowledge allows you to focus on the institutional issues as opposed to focusing on the person you're interacting with. Doing so also has the potential to ease some of the frustrations towards particular individuals that both of us often feel. Extending some form of compassion can help suspend the distracting emphasis on *why* people think certain things, and instead highlight opportunities for education and change. Often I (Allegra) complain to Mum (Lily) that someone said something fat hating, and she'll be like, "well yeah, because of x, y, z ideologies," and I'll be like, "ah, OK, yeah, that makes sense."

Of course, this compassionate approach doesn't help to redress systemic and structural oppression, nor is it easy to adopt in the face of overt fat hatred from family, friends, or work colleagues. In these situations, we can both find ourselves emotionally reactive. I (Lily) have lived and breathed fat liberation for over 30 years and I still find my heart racing, tears forming, and throat constricting when I am met with aggressive pushback after speaking up against weight-based oppression. Recently I had a work colleague literally shout at me in both online and in-person meetings that I had to stop arguing against the use of the O words, and that my stance was "ridiculous" because "everyone knows that 'ob*sity' is a public health crisis." The colleague then proceeded to try and rally support from other colleagues to assist in their efforts to stop me from making such "outrageous" requests. Was I cool, calm and collected? Absolutely not. I may have seemed it from the outside, but on the inside I was both furious and fragile, incapable of speaking to them directly about the matter. After 30 years of fat liberation work, I am still emotionally reactive. I still feel this viscerally. Whenever I hear anyone use the term "ob*sity," it still feels like I've been kicked in the guts, literally, not metaphorically. So yes, this work is difficult, but it has to be done. The stakes are too high to disengage. The real issue is not whether we choose to address weight-based oppression, but how best to do so.

Just like Mum (Lily), I (Allegra) am often faced with acts of weight-based oppression in the workplace. I recently worked in a women's clothing store and, while I loved my job, it was a constant minefield of oppressive comments about weight and bodies. At least once a day I heard someone say, "This would look better if I lost weight." Comments like, "Yeah, but it highlights my stomach" or "I'd prefer if it covered my flabby arms" were also frequently thrown around. These weren't things I overhear in conversations between other people; they were said to me directly. So I found myself caught in this awkward position between being the professional salesperson and feeling the need to assert my fat liberation beliefs. I was not going to affirm their hatred for their body, but I also really wanted to sell that dress. Deep breaths, Allegra; remember that this person is a product of their oppressive and hateful environment. No, compassion is out the window; I'm annoyed. I'm literally standing in front of this person; how could they think this was ok to say? Internal eyeroll over, I would rattle off some vague comment of resistance: "That's not necessary," or "You don't work for the clothes, the clothes work for you," and try to move on with my day. When I tried to talk about these experiences with friends or family, the comments would often get dismissed with retorts like "That person was just talking about themselves, it's not about you." But this *is* about me. Customers were actively expressing disdain for a body or parts of a body that look like mine. The oppression is endless. Despite having a plethora of fat liberation tools in my tool belt, I still find myself frustrated and disappointed at both the initial situation and my friends' and family's lack of understanding about the impact it has on me. Although my feelings of anger and dejection are taxing, they also fuel me to keep pushing for fat liberation and never settle for a society ruled by weight-based oppression.

One of the strategies that has supported me (Lily) to sustain this essential work, especially in the face of fierce opposition, has been connecting with other fat liberationists and creating fat liberation community. Deb Burgard started the Show Me The Data listserv in 2001, and it was the first opportunity for me to interact with other people from all over the world who were interested in deconstructing the science around weight-based oppression. In 2003 I ventured on a fat liberation road trip across the USA that included meeting many of my fat heroes for the first time in person. In 2004 Marilyn Wann's Fat Studies listserv broadened the scope of connections to include people interested in the scholarship of fat. In 2006 I attended the first ASDAH conference in Ohio, and throughout the 2000s I attended more ASDAH conferences and National Association to Advance Fat Acceptance (NAAFA) conventions. More recently I have attended International Weight Stigma Conferences in person and Fat Studies New Zealand conferences online. Through these listservs, my road trips, conventions, and conferences, I have built communities in which I feel "normal," accepted, valued, communal, and most importantly, energized to continue the work of fat liberation.

For me (Allegra), I often feel like I'm not making "real" change by just speaking to my experiences. I frequently question if I'm doing enough and often feel that I should be more aggressive and unrelenting when faced with weight-based oppression for it to be considered valid activism. Being vulnerable is also incredibly taxing, but then being understanding about people's lack of knowledge can feel like you're giving them a pass. However, the reality is that an all-guns-blazing-at-all-times approach isn't sustainable for the self.

We've found that self-preservation is essential to being able to navigate weight-based oppression. It's important to put yourself first and recognize when you have the energy to engage with these difficult issues. Sometimes not engaging is a necessary choice that has to be made to keep yourself going. Our activism, no matter the form, can't occur if we're run down or burned out.

In this chapter we discussed fat liberation and anti-weight based oppression upbringing and parenting, critiqued the language used in the fat liberation movement, and described our approaches to weight-based oppression and fat liberation. We hope that others starting on the fat liberation path, through personal and/or professional interest, will develop the strategies they need to dismantle weight-based oppression and build fat liberation. For no one is free from weight-based oppression until all fat people are liberated.

FOOTNOTES

1. Health At Every Size® and HAES® are registered trademarks of the Association for Size Diversity and Health and used with permission.
2. We present the term "ob*sity" in a censored form to minimize harm, and disrupt and contest the pathologization of higher weight, in accordance with fat liberation researchers, health professionals, and social justice advocates.

REFERENCES

1. Lather P. *Engaging science policy: from the side of the messy.* New York, NY, USA: Peter Lang Publishers; 2010.

2. Association for Size Diversity and Health. HAES Approach n.d. [Available from: https://asdah.org/health-at-every-size-haes-approach/.

3. Johns Hopkins Medicine. Phobias n.d. [Available from: https://www. hopkinsmedicine.org/health/conditions-and-diseases/phobias.

4. O'Hara L, Taylor J. What's wrong with the "war on obesity?" A narrative review of the weight-centered health paradigm and development of the 3C framework to build critical competency for a paradigm shift. *SAGE Open.* 2018;8(2):1–28.

5. O'Hara L, Taylor J. Health at Every Size: A weight-neutral approach for empowerment, resilience and peace. *International Journal of Social Work and Human Services Practice.* 2014; 2(6): 273–82.

6. O'Hara L, Tahboub-Schulte S, Thomas J. Weight-related teasing and internalized weight stigma predict abnormal eating attitudes and behaviours in Emirati female university students. *Appetite.* 2016; 102: 44–50.

7. Thomas J, Quadflieg S, O'Hara L. Implicit out-group preference is associated with eating disorders symptoms amongst Emirati females. *Eating Behaviors.* 2016; 21: 48–53.

8. O'Hara L, Alajaimi B, Alshowaikh B, editors. Experiences of weight-based oppression in Qatar. Qatar University Annual Research Forum and Exhibition (QUARFE 2020); October 28, 2020; Doha, Qatar.

9. O'Hara L, Ahmed H, Sana E, editors. Impact of a brief Health at Every Size-based activity on body positivity and internal weight-based oppression.

Qatar University Annual Research Forum and Exhibition (QUARFE 2020); 2020, October 28, 2020; Doha, Qatar.

10. Ritchie B, O'Hara L, Taylor J. Kids in the Kitchen Impact Evaluation: engaging primary school students in preparing fruit and vegetables for their own consumption. *Health Promotion Journal of Australia.* 2015; 26: 146–9.

11. Vogler J, O'Hara L, Gregg J, Burnell F. The impact of a short-term Iyengar yoga program on the health and well-being of physically inactive older adults. *International Journal of Yoga Therapy.* 2011; 21(1): 61–72.

12. Shelley K, O'Hara L, Gregg J. The impact on teachers of designing and implementing a Health at Every Size curriculum unit. *Asia-Pacific Journal of Health, Sport & Physical Education.* 2010; 1(3/4): 21–8.

Foxes in the Henhouse
Size Acceptance through 18 years of *Healthy Weight Journal*

Francie M. Berg

EALTHY WEIGHT JOURNAL BEGAN in April 1986 as a free service that evolved into a pilot program. Initially titled the *Obesity Newsletter*, I typed a four-page review of research briefs and short items and mailed it to doctors with weight treatment programs. Most of them belonged to the American Society of Bariatric Physicians.

The *Journal* grew out of a healthy lifestyle column I was writing for some 50 newspapers. Research in the new field of obesity was breaking fast, often taking surprising turns. In investigating weight issues for the column, I was continually surprised to find new research that had not yet filtered through to clinicians or the general public. It was an important knowledge gap that needed bridging.

As a licensed nutritionist, granted by our state dietetics association, I had a master's degree from the University of Minnesota in family social science and archaeology and a BS from Montana State College at Bozeman in family consumer science. I'd worked as a home economics teacher and home extension agent in Montana and North Dakota. At the time, as a stay-at-home mom of two preschoolers I was on the volunteer list of various organizations, so the writing opportunity came as a welcome challenge.

Our free pilot program lasted 11 months, and then we offered the *International Obesity Newsletter* for subscription with an immediate base of 300 subscribers. In a few years it was mailing to over 2,000 subscribers in 37 countries.

The journal evolved through the years—broadening to encompass an international audience with not just obesity but related topics of weight, dieting, eating disorders, and health. A series of name changes reflect these milestones:

1986—*Obesity Newsletter*
1987—*International Obesity Newsletter*
1989—*Obesity & Health*
1994—*Healthy Weight Journal* (At this point I asked my advisory board

if this title seemed judgmental. Their reply: "You are in the process of redefining healthy weight. It's what you've been doing all along.")

Throughout, the journal had 3 goals:

1. To provide readers with current obesity research and information in a concise and easy-to-read style.
2. To expose deception and fraud in the field.
3. To reduce size prejudice, promote respect for persons of size, and support a reshaping of inappropriate attitudes toward weight.

And yes, there was one more goal at the start:

4. To promote the prevention of obesity. Prevention programs were active in other advanced countries, but had not yet been addressed in the U.S.

Note that at the time I really thought—as did others—that we'd solve the problems of weight with all that science going on. After all, there were already a number of so-called "medically sound" ways of losing weight at the great medical universities, led by noted physicians and surgeons who claimed long-term success.

Weight loss treatments seemed effective. People obviously lost weight—with some methods they lost a lot of weight. Few asked what happened next.

But in September of that first year I had reviewed a Swedish medical study that shocked me. It reported four-year "success" with an initial quick weight loss followed by weekly sessions. Half the patients began with six weeks of only 600 calories a day; the other half had their jaws wired shut up to 19 months. Drop-out rate was 31%. Two men died—in the second and fourth year—and a third man who shifted from jaw wiring to surgery died after surgery. I was horrified. But questioning the experts seemed radical, even rude.

The Federal Drug Administration, our investigative arm, backed them up. (Little did I know then that the foxes were already in the henhouse.)

That those physicians were claiming one-year weight loss—or even less—as permanent, long-term success escaped my notice at first.

My goal in writing was always to push the envelope—write what no one else had written—new information that would make a difference.

In January I suggested cautiously that clinical studies "showed little success."

By October 1987, in what now seems an understatement, I wrote, "It has to be said, long term results are disappointingly low."

Ours was one of the first publications to question the efficacy and ethics of weight loss treatment. Through it all I tried to find the truth and report it objectively.

THE SIZE ACCEPTANCE MOVEMENT

BY 1988 BILL FABREY of New York, the inspiration behind the size acceptance movement, began calling me every few months telling of the group he had started, NAAFA, and their developments—books, *BBW (Big Beautiful Woman)* magazine, *Radiance: The Magazine for Large Women*, and the people involved.

It was impossible not to be impressed by Bill and his cohort.

These were large people who had had enough. Enough of trying to lose weight and instead gaining more; enough of being discounted as "unworthy" and blamed for their size. Many were large women who became even larger through their efforts to lose.

I quoted Bill's sources, probed the new size acceptance viewpoint, and reviewed their books. Sometimes we reprinted a guest feature from their newsletter.

Oddly, they were fighting an uphill battle against what was happening to them, trying to get on with their lives. But other people—in particular, health professionals and often their own families—were making it extremely difficult.

I was intrigued. Certainly, they had valid points.

Then suddenly one day it dawned on me—I needed to give these very articulate people the opportunity to tell it in their own words. Their voices needed to be heard—every word.

My readers were the perfect audience. This was a legitimate group with plenty of anger about how they were being treated by health providers as well as others, and of course, this included me.

But my message soon changed. The size acceptance people absolutely won me over.

We began including a size acceptance article in every issue—and I attended and participated wholeheartedly in size acceptance conferences.

Our first regular size acceptance feature led off the July/August 1991 issue: "Fighting for Acceptance in the Fitness World," by Pat Lyons, RN, MA and Deb Burgard, PhD.

Wow! Pat and Deb let us have it in the first paragraph:

> There are few things more insulting than having a relative, friend or a total stranger hand you a diet book or article about

weight loss, professing concern for your health as justification for rudeness. Sometimes they slip in the phrase, 'You have such a pretty face...' allowing our imagination to infer how ugly they think our body is.

They proceeded to quote numerous humiliating examples! In detail!

> There are ways of preparing for these incidents, dealing with them on the spot and surviving afterwards. One thing you must not do is accept abuse silently and give a home to the feelings of anger, sadness and shame that fester within and immobilize you. You can be witty. You can terrify someone by hurling abuse in return. You can be dignified and aloof and ignore the creep. Or you can tell him or her to go to hell. It's up to you. Be sure to get the incident off your chest. Don't brood over it.

> Call a friend and share every last detail, even what shamed or embarrassed you the most. You have every right to anger, sadness or any other feeling. If you can't reach a friend, write it. Get it out of your system.

> We have a right to take up space, live fully in our bodies and fully in our lives. By dealing with our feelings honestly and supporting one another in this right we make it easier for ourselves and those who follow in our footsteps.

Dietitians responded in surprising ways. They invited me to speak at their state and national conventions. I found that about one-third agreed with me totally (usually with some experience they knew their patients gained back all the weight they lost); one third were interested and listening; and one third rejected my message—these were the bright young dietitians just out of school with all the answers.

One came up to me after I spoke at a conference and said, "I heard you speak several years ago—and I disagreed with everything you said!" She laughed, "Then I found you were right, and now I teach just what you do."

We included wonderful writers who told their personal stories. Lynn McAfee of the Council on Size and Weight Discrimination; Alice Ansfield, editor and publisher of *Radiance: The Magazine for Large Women;* Miriam Berg, president of the Council on Size and Weight Discrimination; Carol Johnson on "Raising Largely Positive Kids," Laura S. Brown, PhD, and more. I came to admire them all.

The feature was a great success—and an important learning experience for the professionals who treated them! Most of them really wanted to help.

Especially the nutritionists in my own field.

Letters to the editor were generally supportive:

> "Thank you for the article on discrimination in the medical community toward overweight people. When I presented this to my Dietless groups, it brought up a lot of feelings and horrible memories. I value your journal and read it cover to cover. Thank you for adding to the education and acknowledgment of issues confronting people who struggle every day with their food and weight."
> —Caron Asada, PhD, clinical psychologist, La Mesa, CA

> "Your *Healthy Weight Journal* has been EXTREMELY helpful to me since its inception many years ago. My work in truly helping large people become healthier has been greatly influenced! Many, many thanks!"
> —Janet Sundberg, MS, RD, Murphysboro, IL.

One letter was signed by 10 health leaders:

> "The recommendations for treating obesity developed by C. Everett Koop's Shape Up America! and the American Obesity Assoc. that you presented in the May/June 1997 issue would be truly comical if they were not so potentially damaging. There is considerable evidence these actions will result in violation of the Hippocratic principle 'First, do no harm!'"

Obesity research was breaking fast—but was scattered among many disciplines, and not readily available to educators and health care providers.

I knew some of those surgeons did real damage to the women who submitted their healthy innocent bodies to the knives and ill-fated experimental surgeries, powerful drugs, VLCDs (very low calorie diets) that went on too long and caused permanent damage, and other gimmicks that were little more than quackery itself.

But there was no proof. It was impossible to attack them directly—they could demolish me, and probably would if they had half a chance.

I described their techniques and consequences as plainly as I could. Plenty of dietitians, health providers, and eating disorders specialists agreed with me. They invited me to speak at their conferences, and what they told me afterwards was often revealing and quite shocking.

There were reports of serious investigations, which we quoted. Researchers at the University of Rochester, NY reviewed a number of five-year-old studies—almost everyone had regained to initial weight or higher. In fact, the typical person had gone on at least two additional weight-loss programs lasting two weeks or more. Still, those dieters were optimistic about losing weight in the future. They blamed themselves (as did their doctors!) and vowed to do better next time.

Researchers in psychiatry and behavioral sciences at Stanford University School of Medicine rechecked their weight-loss five-year results. They were chagrined to find theirs was just another episode in a long series of weight loss efforts for their patients. Most had tried many other weight-loss plans during the intervening time.

A nutrition specialist wrote an article for us on summer weight-loss camps for kids.

> The typically severe dietary restrictions at camps stimulate binge eating after camp is over and may foster weight gain through biological changes. Such camps are most likely to attract families that are desperate about their adolescent's weight and want to have their child 'fixed.' The obese adolescent becomes the victim as parents first delight in initial weight loss, then despair and blame him or her as weight is regained.

QUACKERY, FRAUD AND FANTASY

ON THE QUACKERY FRONT was an amazing array of products, one after another: Cal-Ban 3000, Berry Trim, Metabo-Slim Formula 22, the Magnetic Belt, Figure-Tron body shaper, Vision-Dieter glasses, Relaxacizor and Nemectron.

Slimnonics Electro Body Toner ("Attach the pads, turn up the pulse, adjust the controls for rhythm and intensity—then read, sleep, visit or watch TV"); Cell-U-Loss Body Toner ("Hundreds of vibrating fingers dissolve cellulite and flabby muscle on tummy, thighs, rear and hips"); and the Fat Magnet ("Breaks into thousands of particles, each acting like a tiny magnet, attracting and trapping many times its size in undigested fat particles...all the trapped fat and calories are naturally flushed out because they can't be absorbed").

Fibre Trim, Phoenix Fiber Cookie, Chinese Slimming Tea, Metabo-Slim Formula 22, Quicktrim II, Healthy Greens, Great Earth Formula-PM, Starch Blockers, Grapefruit Super Pill II, Rotation Diet, Absorbital 2000, Fat-off 75, Guar Gum, Cho Low Tea, Herbalife's Diet Disc, Nutri-Calc HD, HCG Shots, Electronic muscle stimulator, toning tables, Fat Blocker, Spirulina Tablets, Co-enzyme Q10, Bee Sweet Grapefruit Diet, Slender-Mist Appetite Spray and Primary Plan Tablets.

In all I reported on over 200 questionable and fraudulent weight loss products.

By 1989 we started publicizing the Slim Chance Awards, the worst quackery of the year, telling our readers "It's a Slim Chance you'll lose weight with any of these."

That year we dared to challenge diet professionals with their deception:

> Diet programs are becoming entrenched in hospitals and clinics for the financial rewards they offer. Medical personnel and scientists who otherwise would champion balanced health programs are caught in a moral dilemma that pits the need to strengthen their institutions against the scientific integrity of total disclosure.

We hailed the success of the National Association to Advance Fat Acceptance (NAAFA) that same year, when they reported that Hallmark Cards gave in to their letter-writing campaign on threat of boycott. Earlier Hallmark had chided their criticism of "fat joke" cards by saying humor is "Good for the spirit! And we intend to continue this tradition of good humor in a way we hope all our customers will find appealing." NAAFA stuck to their guns and won. Good for them! Hallmark backed down and promised to "avoid any subject matter that might be considered insensitive to fat people."

Many of the highly touted quack products cost only $39.95. They were vulnerable to ridicule—and we probably took advantage of that. They were breaking FDA rules, so I felt sure they wouldn't sue.

Still, they could be deadly.

I well remember a very nice man—a lawyer—who called many times over the years, telling me of one quack product or another he'd discovered. He was a heartbroken man, and at the same time horrified, and hoped to do what he could to stop the flow of quackery.

His terrible experience: One evening his beloved wife consumed a double dose of her "Slimming Tea." They went to bed and in the morning when he awoke, she lay dead beside him.

ABUNDANT RESEARCH

THERE WAS PLENTY of research to cover.

All kinds of weight-loss programs—drugs, gastric surgery, very-low-calorie—effects of weight cycling, exercise programs, smoking issues, diabetes, behavior modification, breastfeeding issues, genetics, overeating children, Prader-Willi syndrome, weight and fat distribution, hypertension, metabolism, energy intake, anxiety and depression links to binge eating, holiday weight gain and how to avoid it, social eating, artificial sweeteners, and much more.

Not all studies, I began to discover, were as transparent as that early Swedish study had been. Experienced "diet doctors" were learning which aspects of their research were best published, which to omit, and how to highlight success by "cherry picking" their best subsets.

Studies of eating disorders were in their infancy—anorexia nervosa, bulimia, binge eating disorder, dysfunctional eating, the starvation syndrome, purging, excessive exercise; there was a lot to learn. Eating disorders groups held tearful conventions as bewildered parents bared their souls and begged for help for damaged or dying children. I attended some of them.

I can't forget one father—a truck driver. A truck driver! He sat in an empty chair next to me at refreshment time and told me about his two daughters. The older had starved herself to death. "Then I heard my younger girl in the bathroom—gagging!" Tears filled his eyes, and his voice dropped to a whisper.

In 1989 we reported on the *U.S. Weight Loss & Diet Control Market Report* released by Marketdata Enterprises. It listed nine major segments from health spas and weight loss clinics to diet books and appetite suppressants.

The report said half of U.S. women were currently dieting and that "(w)omen who want to lose weight average five weight-loss regimens per year." In other words, women finished one diet, lost the weight, regained and started another, regained—and started another and another. Were they blaming themselves for each failure and expecting to do better next time?

The most expensive programs listed were: Residential Spa for two weeks ($2,200), Hospital Weight Loss for four months ($1,200), one year of Nutrisystem clinic at $45 per week ($2,250), Weight Watchers meals at $3 per day for one year ($1,095).

At that time my subscribers were mostly professionals—physicians in the weight loss industry, dietitians, nutritionists, and health specialists. The reigning royalty were the "thin white male obesity doctors" who made a lot of money telling women what to do—including their dietitians, who did the dirty work of cleaning up after their invariably "successful weight loss" ventures ended and the victims gained it all back.

I was there for the entire "Garren-Edwards Gastric Bubble melodrama," from beginning to end. Dr. Garren flew over from Britain to report at the first obesity conference I attended after his bubble was approved by the FDA. He explained his method and his studies, showing 35 kg losses at 10 months. Afterward, scientists and physicians crowded around with a multitude of questions.

"Yes," he told them, "The bubble reduces appetite and provides more stomach satisfaction with less food." The FDA had agreed that the bubble might trigger sensory receptors in the stomach to signal the brain, or perhaps stimulate hormone production to make the person feel full, or maybe it affected emptying of the stomach. (I reported in the November 1987 issue on the surprising weakness of the FDA.)

In less than a year 20,000 gastric bubbles were sold and 2,000 physicians trained in the insertion technique. Somehow, they couldn't duplicate the Garren studies.

The FDA then limited the bubble to "those morbidly obese or whose weight is a major factor in other life-threatening medical conditions, in whom expected benefits outweigh the risks." By February 1987, widespread use of the gastric bubble was being discouraged by the American Medical Association.

Physicians quietly withdrew their bubbles.

Already, enthusiasm had moved on to Very Low Calorie Liquid Diets (VLCDs) of 800 calories or less, with their "amazing, miracle" results. Large patients lost one-third of their size in months. These were based, it was claimed, on safer formulas than the liquid diets that had caused deaths in the 1970s.

I knew Peter G. Lindner, MD quite well. He was one of the famed "diet doctors" of the 1980s, and co-author with George Blackburn, MD of Harvard an early study that "proved" VLCD success. But Lindner grew increasingly despondent, and then he died. His good friend told me he was discouraged because he made a five-year check of all his former patients and not one of them—not one!—had kept off for five years any of the weight they had lost so successfully for him.

But by then the Lindner-Blackburn study had taken on a life of its own. So popular was the VLCD in the late 1980s and early 1990s that it is hardly an exaggeration to say medical and scientific journals published hundreds of nearly identical short-term studies, all lauding its success. None suggested there would be rapid regain and sometimes terrible side effects.

No one talked about the deaths.

Much later it was revealed that VLCD companies wrote the studies, and well known "obesity experts" were paid to attach their names to the studies, which were inserted into medical journals.

Then came SlimFast and its imitators in huge stacks blocking grocery aisles for a couple of years. Next, thigh cream. And after that the fen-phen/Redux tragedy.

One cult after another, as one scientist complained. And these were just the legal, medically sanctioned cures.

In 1993 we put out a special report: *Health Risks of Weight Loss,* a devastating 194-page report that included risks of weight cycling and the great toll of semi-starvation.

We explored the mortality increase from weight loss and weight cycling that was showing up in the large population studies and appeared to be a determining factor in whether there were health risks for large people after all. It was summed up as "The public needs to know."

This marked a turning point in how health professionals viewed the diet industry, and consumer groups took up the mantra "Diets don't work!"

At the same time, we dissected starvation studies—real starvation in what we then called third world countries, as well as the classic World War II Minnesota Starvation study by Ancel Keys, and VLCDs—all of which produced similar effects in physical deterioration, antisocial personality changes, isolation, and food preoccupation.

In the Keys study, 32 formerly idealistic, good-humored young men became loners, sarcastic, self-centered, argumentative, and intolerant of each other when their daily food intake dropped to half and they lost one-fourth of their weight.

These same personality changes are well known to professionals who work with anorexia and bulimia nervosa patients. Starvation is not pretty.

Another long-time concern of ours was whether obesity treatment was causing eating disorders. Some leaders dared to say it outright: "Eating disorders always start with a diet!" Likely it was true, along with the rest of their accusations.

But not until the December 18, 1996 issue of the *Journal of American Medical Association* did the nine members of the federally funded National Task Force on the Prevention and Treatment of Obesity, which set our national health policy, disclose their financial affiliations. Eight of them had financial ties with at least two and up to eight commercial weight loss firms each. They served as consultants on company advisory boards, conducted industry research, and reaped honorariums and grants from diet-drug and weight-loss companies.

All along, as it turned out, the foxes were in charge of the hen house!

SIZE ACCEPTANCE IN THE NUTRITION FIELD

BY 1994 we were able to say, editorially,

> We are proud that many of today's leaders in the new healthier treatment programs have been our readers for years and say they have gleaned inspiration from these pages in developing innovative concepts.

We are further delighted, and somewhat surprised, to be a rallying point for size acceptance groups from all over the world who thank us for our allegiance to truth, justice, and better living for people of all sizes. It is gratifying to know we are making a difference. We appreciate and value your support in this adventure.

We invited Pat Lyons and other strong voices in the size acceptance field to speak at our own organization, the Society for Nutrition Education and Behavior (SNEB). With a few others we worked to shape our focus into being size accepting. Many of our members were college professors and extension staff, so we were educating educators who taught thousands of teachers and had long-term influence on the next generation of nutrition professionals. In general, they were very accepting of our size acceptance message.

In founding our Weight Realities division of SNEB we included these tenets:

- Human beings come in a variety of sizes and shapes. We celebrate this diversity as a positive characteristic of the human race.
- There is no ideal body size, shape, or weight.
- Self-esteem and body image are strongly linked. Helping people feel good about their bodies and who they are can help maintain healthy behaviors.
- Good health is not defined by body size; it is a state of physical, mental, and social well-being.
- People of all sizes and shapes can reduce their risk of poor health with a healthy lifestyle.
- Health promotion programs should be accepting of size diversity.

One special group I worked with were the WIN Wyoming group of nutritionists, who adopted similar goals as our size acceptance tenets and the Canadian Vitality principle for their entire state. We worked together both in Wyoming and at our national meetings.

I began writing a book to help professionals who work with young people fight their way through the maze of weight issues. I remembered a catchy phrase Pat Lyons had dropped on us way back when we first met: "Health at Any Size." It really rang a bell, and even worked just fine with the acronym HAAS.

My Canadian friend Linda Omichinski said, "It's catchy, easy to remember, tested, and addresses the non-diet continuum. We focus on health and self-acceptance rather than dieting and weight loss. And the media will love it as well!"

NEW CHALLENGES—DO NO HARM

THEN—18 YEARS was long enough. In 1997 I sold the journal to BC Decker, a Canadian publisher in Hamilton, Ontario, while continuing to edit it till 2004, when my good friends, professors Wayne C. Miller, PhD and Jon Robison, PhD, stepped in as editors. They even changed the title—to *Health at Every Size*. YES!

The dread war against obesity was rapidly heating up, and for the first time it directly zeroed in on children. In an early editorial the new editors asked, "Who is protecting our children, the ones most vulnerable?" And they were forced to conclude, "Increasingly, our children are becoming the casualties of this war!"

As for me, I had a book or two or three to write. All those years with a serious deadline and much to learn had served me well. I felt well-armed, knowledgeable, and ready for what lay ahead.

What I needed to tell health and nutrition professionals working with youth was a simple, profound message. "Focus on Health at Any Size: Eat well, live actively, and feel good about yourself and others. Do no harm."

Freelance Agitator

Dana Schuster
as told to Rosie Young

THE CONCEPTS OF NON-DIETING, size acceptance, and advocating for weight-neutral medical care were totally new to me in the early 1990s. As a privileged white, cisgendered, straight, fat, married mother of two young sons, this paradigm felt revolutionary and freeing after two decades of dieting and body disparagement. Once I learned about it, I embraced it with gusto, and my personal and professional lives were radically altered from that point onward.

Growing up, my family was very health conscious. My dad was a surgeon, and my mother had been a nurse. Health was the crux of everything. Food was wrapped up in that, and our privilege allowed us to enjoy home-cooked nutritious family meals together. I also grew up in a safe neighborhood that allowed for outdoor play and I swam competitively from the time I was six years old. While I don't remember eating being directly associated with judgement about how my body looked, this idea still became embedded in my mind and would lead to years of chronic dieting.

When I was twelve my father died suddenly, and my mother had to get a job after not working outside of our home for 14 years. I took over domestic tasks, as my older sister was a teenager and making some separations. My mother didn't do emotions, so there was no help for her or us to process the trauma of our father's death. We were expected to just carry on. I oversaw the family meals, so while my mom wasn't always present, food was there. It was very self-soothing, and became my go-to comfort.

Dieting became a focus in my mid-teens. I had this notion that I had some responsibility for my father's death, and I witnessed my mother's distress at losing her husband. She and my sister would argue and yell and I got so scared it would push my mother over the edge and we'd be without her too. I felt I was the one who must fix this, by calming the waters and keeping everything under control. I believe trying to keep my body in check was part of that effort.

It wasn't until my early 30s that I learned there was a way off the weight-cycling carousel. I had heard that psychological trauma caused people to be fat, so I asked my doctor to refer me to a psychologist. I thought the therapist was going to fix me—heal my trauma so I would lose weight. Instead, I learned about this wild notion of weight neutrality and the Health At Every Size approach to wellness.

At that point Pat Lyons's and Deb Burgard's book *Great Shape: The First Fitness Guide for Large Women* was pivotal for me and led to my participation in a Great Shape class taught by Beverly Steckel at Kaiser in Redwood City. A few years later Pat Lyons offered a training to become a Great Shape instructor, which fat activist Lisa Tealer and I (among others) took. Lisa and I subsequently talked each other into taking up the mantle of leading the local Great Shape classes when Beverly Steckel stepped back from teaching.

The Association for the Health Enrichment of Large People (AHELP) was started in 1991 by Joe McVoy, PhD, a psychologist on the East Coast, to bring together professionals trying to better serve individuals who were in larger bodies. AHELP held a conference in San Francisco in the early '90s, and although I wasn't a member I was able to attend parts of the conference open to the public. The conference brought together people in the Bay Area who were promoting a non-diet paradigm, who then decided to start a local group for ongoing networking and support. I became involved in that group early on. Pat Lyons organized the first meeting at the Kaiser in Oakland where she worked. Subsequently, Deb Burgard started the email listserv for this "Think Tank," as well as the Show Me the Data listserv for those particularly interested in research discussions.

All proponents of the new paradigm were welcome to participate in what eventually came to be known as the SF Bay Area HAES Think Tank, although in the beginning the group was mostly health professionals. That began to change as more activists joined. It was a time when Marilyn Wann and others were ramping up local guerrilla activism and acts of civil disobedience against weight-focused events and organizations. The participating activists wanted Think Tank members to get involved with direct action, which led to some conflict for those who felt they couldn't take on additional commitments.

In 1996, while teaching the Great Shape class, Lisa and I found out about a women's health club in Redwood City that closed suddenly with no warning to its members. We both independently had the thought, "Wouldn't it be amazing to have a whole facility that was totally about the joy of moving your body, finding what you liked, and taking care of yourself from a weight neutral, body positive perspective?" I brought up the idea in class the next week, and Lisa confirmed she'd been thinking the same thing, and then the class totally bulldozed us with enthusiasm. They said, "You guys have just got to do this. We'll help." So we went for it, with class members' assistance with funding and set-up, and the encouragement and support of Pat Lyons. Women of Substance Health Spa opened in January 1997.

Our members were varied in terms of body size, age, race, ethnicity, and sexual orientation, although many were in their 50s and 60s and most were in larger bodies. We'd have fat women who'd come in the first time and say, "Seriously? You're not going to talk about weight loss?" or "I couldn't possibly get in a bathing suit. I haven't been in a bathing suit in years, and you want me to get in a pool?" These same women, within months, would be driving to the pool in just their bathing suits with the attitude "So what if a cop stops me? Big deal!" The transformation people underwent was profound and amazing to be part of. We had parties and educational events and often had potlucks—it was all part of our philosophy. Exercise, delicious food, social gathering: these are all wonderful parts of life, all to be enjoyed, and they all benefit wellbeing.

In 1999, Marilyn organized a huge protest against a fatphobic billboard that 24Hour Fitness had erected on a prominent freeway-visible intersection in San Francisco. The billboard had a picture of space aliens and read, "When they come, they'll eat the fat ones first." On President's Day a group of us gathered in front of the 24Hour Fitness on Van Ness Avenue. We were protesting fat bias with signs and enjoying exercising in our fat bodies on the sidewalk and on the center median! News cameras were everywhere, and the protest received both local and national news coverage. Partially because of that day, work began towards passing an ordinance in San Francisco to prohibit discrimination based on size. The ordinance passed unanimously in May 2000.

Shortly after those events, Jennifer Portnick, another fat positive fitness instructor, became involved with the Think Tank. She shared with us that she had been turned down by Jazzercise to be a certified instructor due to her body size. She hooked up with attorney Sondra Solovay, and they were able to use the San Francisco ordinance to negotiate on Jennifer's behalf. In 2002 they made a mediated decision to settle, and Jazzercise agreed to drop their "fit appearance" standard for franchise owners. The 24Hour Protest, the San Francisco ordinance, and Jennifer's settlement were pivotal flashpoints in the fat activism movement, and were great examples of people coming together to make real change.

When the dot-com bubble hit Redwood City in early 2000, Women of Substance Health Spa couldn't hire anyone to come work for us. Many of our members were older adults who sold their homes amidst a suddenly hot housing market and moved away. Renters were getting hit with huge rent increases and could no longer afford a gym membership. Meanwhile, I was working around the clock, Lisa had cut back her time at her other job to be there for the gym, and it was doing us both in.

Women of Substance was open for about five years, closing in the spring of 2001. Looking back, it probably wasn't sustainable from the get-go, because we refused to do the things that gyms survive on. We refused to sell any product focused on changing size or appearance. We refused to work with companies peddling weight loss. We didn't sign people up and then hope they never came, which was the standard modern gym model. Instead, we created a community of women who fundamentally changed how they viewed and cared for themselves. When we closed, our members, who were used to being treated as completely valuable and worthwhile as they were, went to new fitness environments and started getting the traditional messages. They wouldn't stand for it, and they began to spread the philosophy of size acceptance in these facilities, advocating for exercise access for all bodies.

After Women of Substance closed in 2001, my focus shifted to bringing size-positive education—which I called MYOB (Mind Your Own Body)—into San Mateo County schools. As someone who had often done volunteer work in my children's classrooms, l was able to leverage those relationships to bring HAES workshops to student, staff, and parent groups. There were many wonderful size acceptance resources available by this time—Marilyn Wann's transformative YAY Scales, teen-focused card decks with body positive affirmations, and The Body Positive work of Connie Sobczak and Elizabeth Scott, to name a few. Then in 2005 the federal government issued requirements that every school receiving funding for food programs had to develop a school wellness policy to be in place by the start of the 2006 school year.

Not surprisingly, the language in the bill was very weight focused. Fortunately community collaboration was mandated, despite that not being the way schools traditionally developed policies. I was horrified by some of the things our local districts had first come up with, so I started sharing people's stories and scientific documentation of the harms of using a weight-focused lens. As a "freelance agitator," not employed by any educational or business entity, I could be relentless, whereas the folks who worked for the school system might be at risk of getting fired if they pushed back against accepted doctrine. Volunteering to do tasks no one else wanted to do—like taking notes or writing the first draft of documents—was an excellent technique for making sure the Health At Every Size perspective was embedded from the start.

At the same time, San Mateo County formed a task force they initially called the Childhood Obesity Task Force, comprising about 250 people including doctors, nutritionists, and community organizations and individuals who worked with youth. It took two years of constantly challenging the status quo and talking about the damage caused by a weight-centered approach before the name and focus of the group finally shifted away from this bias.

AHELP dissolved in 1996, which left a void for non-diet health professionals interested in national organizing. In 2003 Claudia Clark, a psychologist at Bowling Green State University in Ohio, got some funding and support to start the Association for Size Diversity And Health (ASDAH) under the umbrella of the university. She issued invitations to folks she'd known through AHELP to come for a one-day meeting at the university to plan this new organization. There were about 30 or 40 people in attendance, including many early voices in the size acceptance movement such as Paul Ernsberger, Barbara Bruno, and Miriam Berg. The morning consisted of presentations about the science and why there was a need for this type of organization. About a dozen people met as a steering committee in the afternoon to discuss the nitty gritty of how to get ASDAH off the ground. Several individuals volunteered to take on roles such as membership chair, treasurer, etc., and there were impassioned discussions about what the mission, goals, and principles of the organization should be.

Colleagues Joanne Ikeda, Karin Kratina and others had previously authored lists of tenets outlining the principles of Health At Every/Any Size, and these were used in ASDAH's discussions. The Bay Area Think Tank had adapted those tenets to use as screening criteria for people interested in joining, and had added activities and beliefs that would preclude one from participation as well. There were several folks (including myself) advocating to incorporate those preclusions in ASDAH's guidelines. There were others, especially Miriam Berg, who felt strongly that the focus should be on what HAES was rather than what it wasn't, feeling the latter would be too exclusionary. Both sides were adamant, so Claudia assigned Miriam and me to jointly complete a first draft of the mission, goals, and tenets over the next several weeks. At the time it seemed to me to be a recipe for failure, but it turned out to be an incredible process and valuable lesson on the art and skill of advocacy, listening, and compromise.

Sadly, ASDAH's original mission and goal statements were mired in a narrow vision where social justice beyond body size was not addressed. The goals were mostly reactionary—they focused on pushing back against the weight-centered health field that endorsed dieting and exercise for weight loss. Most of the attendees at that first organizational meeting were cis white women, including both lay advocates/activists and those who were employed in educational/health related professions. As I recall, Veronica Cook-Euell was the one Black participant. What we produced was reflective of our limited diversity and lack of consideration of intersectionality and racial disparity issues.

The first few years of ASDAH were focused on offering members support, increasing membership, and building infrastructure. It wasn't until our first conference in 2006 that we had the chance to gather in person as a community. Held at Case Western Reserve University, where Paul Ernsberger was a professor, in a lovely rural facility known as The Sheep Barn, there were about 40 participants in attendance for the weekend event. It was very successful in many ways, and yet there was a huge controversy that erupted with the first keynote speaker, Richard Koletsky, MD, who was a close colleague of Paul's. The expectation of participants was that all presenters would be HAES proponents and weight neutral in their work. Dr. Koletsky started talking about how losing 5% of one's body weight could make a big difference to health. It caught most everyone off guard, and the reaction in the room was visceral. Within a few minutes Lindo Bacon stood up, stopped him, and said, "This is not Health At Every Size."

Paul was furious and very hurt, as this was his valued colleague whom he'd invited to come. Others were angry that the speaker had been challenged and interrupted, as this was not the correct protocol at a professional conference. At the same time there was a passionate contingent who felt that those who were not completely pro-HAES were the enemy, and we felt betrayed. It was immediately clear that the group could not proceed with the conference as planned without addressing this incident. Deb Burgard facilitated a circle discussion to allow everyone an opportunity to share their feelings, and helped the group get to a point where most of the planned elements of the conference could proceed.

Not long after that first conference ASDAH took steps for the organization to operate outside of the university umbrella, due to Claudia's anticipated disability retirement. Claudia dealt with the IRS, which directed ASDAH to become a 501c6 nonprofit organization. Deb Lemire and Veronica Cook-Euell researched and developed organizational bylaws. An election was held to select a board of directors. Fortunately several people who had been part of the initial steering committee stepped up to run for office, and I volunteered to run for president. The Redwood City PO box address and banking location were chosen because they were close to where I lived.

NAAFA had been around for quite some time already, having been founded in 1969. Many of the attendees at ASDAH's first conference were also NAAFA members. ASDAH felt it was important to be a separate organization from NAAFA, since our membership was mainly therapists, dietitians, and eating disorders professionals. NAAFA leadership initially suggested ASDAH might be a professional arm of their organization rather than a totally separate entity. Looking back honestly now, I believe ASDAH had embraced an elitist attitude that we were doing professional work and NAAFA was not.

ASDAH partnered with NAAFA to hold concurrent conferences for about four years. Combining the conferences was initially a benefit to all members, as everyone who was planning to attend the NAAFA convention could take what they wanted of the ASDAH offerings, and vice versa. As president of ASDAH at the time, I was responsible for overseeing the planning and coordination of workshops, presentations, and breakouts to mesh with NAAFA's offerings. While most of the leaders of NAAFA were respectfully collaborative, when a new president came in who seemed to have a different view of ASDAH, things became contentious. ASDAH was not allowed to make any independent decisions about conference structure or content without approval from NAAFA. The finances were all run through NAAFA, and we weren't always in agreement about budgeting choices. Eventually ASDAH decided to go back to hosting independent conferences every couple of years. However, NAAFA and ASDAH determined that they did not want to be competitors, but rather wanted to actively support each other. Over the years, having different but complementary priorities and skills has been mutually beneficial.

In the early days it was a very steep learning curve for ASDAH, and many mistakes were made. Most of us had little awareness of the structural racism embedded in the language and concepts surrounding health in general, nor in the hierarchical structure of the organization. Many of us ignorantly referred to fat discrimination as the last acceptable societal/legal prejudice. By focusing exclusively on promoting acceptance of fat bodies and preventing discrimination based on body size within healthcare, we perpetuated the embedded white supremacy we hadn't yet acknowledged.

As the leadership of ASDAH changed, new skill sets helped the organization to move forward to be more visible and effective in promoting Health At Every Size. When Deb Lemire came in as president, her social media savvy and incredible creative energy become infused in the work. Then Fall Ferguson became president and brought awareness of social justice issues and intersectionality. Under Fall's guidance ASDAH began to move to undo the harm of white supremacist structures and pay attention to the experiences of marginalized folks through an intersectional lens.

Each ASDAH conference has had at least one significant controversy that, in retrospect, highlights both organizational and individual leaders' limitations in listening to marginalized voices. One of the most significant occurred in 2009 when Susie Orbach was invited to be the conference keynote speaker. There were strong objections from fat activists who felt pathologized by Susie's early writings in *Fat is a Feminist Issue* and said that inviting her was a betrayal of the fat community. ASDAH leadership felt strongly that bringing her in to talk about her new book *Bodies* might create an opportunity to cultivate her as an ally. ASDAH tried to mitigate the concerns raised by removing Susie's keynote designation and shifting to an interview format wherein Fall Ferguson would directly address the harm to fat people in Susie's writings. The questions to be asked were shared ahead of time with those who'd been against inviting her. Fall was brilliant, calm, and very direct during the interview. This event came to be referred to as the "Orbacle," which activists such as Charlotte Cooper have written about. The truth is that *Fat is a Feminist Issue* was both hugely impactful and freeing for many people while at the same time hugely problematic. Just like ASDAH.

For each of the major moments of controversy in ASDAH's history, there are lessons to be learned. Each conflict was a puzzle piece falling into place that contributed to a growing awareness of how the organization needed to be more inclusive. Barriers had been erected that people are still struggling to get past. The need to acknowledge our mistakes, genuinely apologize, and work hard to do better is absolutely essential. We didn't see how ASDAH was not a safe place for marginalized voices, beyond body size. We spent many years naively believing that just inviting people to join was enough, but of course it didn't address our underlying white supremacy and potential to do harm.

A turning point occurred for me when Jessica Wilson, a Black dietitian, joined the Think Tank. At the time, Fall and several other ASDAH leaders were part of the group. At one meeting Jessica bravely spoke up about the harm of the white supremacy, racism, and discrimination baked into HAES and the structures of both the Think Tank and ASDAH. Several of us white folks with unexamined privilege immediately became very defensive and said things like, "There are other Black people in the organization who don't feel the way you do. This must be your personal issue." I went further in my inexcusable cluelessness by asking her to educate us about what we'd specifically done or said to make her feel harmed. I'm pretty sure we checked off all the boxes of white fragility in our initial responses.

ASDAH owes a lot to people like Jessica who forced us to confront our structural racism problem. This led ASDAH to hire Lisa Marie Alatorre to educate the board and general membership about oppression, intersectionality, and white privilege. The Advisory Board was formed, facilitated by Lisa Marie and composed of folks with multiple marginalized identities. Individually many of us also began to do our own work to understand our internalized racism. ASDAH tried to help the broader HAES community understand why this shift was crucial and why we needed to start centering the voices that we should have been listening to all along. ASDAH lost some members because of this shift, as not everyone saw that you cannot isolate fat bias from other types of oppression.

At the 2013 ASDAH conference Lisa Marie was hired to be present to help deal directly with racist issues when they arose. Barbara Bruno had been doing some great work at Cornell with intersectional social justice and HAES oriented folks, and they attended that conference. One of the young women of color from that Cornell group bravely stood up during a plenary session and interrupted the guest panel stating, "This is colonialism. What you're saying is racist." The organizing committee stopped the session and brought Lisa Marie in to help everyone understand and process what was happening. Some people left and didn't come back. We offered to provide them with support, but I don't know that it was accepted. There were others who indicated this was the most important health related conference they had ever attended.

Carmen Cool became president of ASDAH after Fall Ferguson. She had a different style of leadership with different strengths, and she was also very committed to continuing and expanding the work of the Advisory Board. Unfortunately the subsequent president and leadership team seemed to be in a different place around these issues, and the Advisory Board got left by the wayside. This became public knowledge at ASDAH's extremely well-attended conference in Portland, OR in 2018, and was hugely discouraging to many. However, that may have been exactly what the organization needed to go through to then throw out most everything from the past and truly start from a new place.

The new ASDAH and more inclusive HAES approach is still emerging, and that process will take time. The pandemic has thrown additional hurdles into the mix. On a personal level, I stepped back from what had for many years been the primary focus of my life and work since first being introduced to the HAES concept. I was fearful at one point in time that ASDAH was going to collapse, but no longer have that fear. It now seems abundantly clear that the goal of dismantling weight-based structures and bias towards marginalized individuals is truly guiding our organizations and the individuals committed to them.

"WEIGHT PROBLEMS" SHAPED MY LIFE

BARBARA BRUNO

I REALIZED THAT AFTER 20 YEARS OF DIETING and failing to keep my weight down, diets didn't work for me. More and more nasty things were being broadcast and written about people who were not "acceptably thin." I didn't buy into them: I was happily married and had always had many friends and lovers, was athletic and active in fitness, was intelligent, Ivy-League educated, and independent in spirit.

My first oasis was provided by Bob Schwartz, a fitness professional who wrote *Diets Don't Work* and led group sessions encouraging people to (re) discover their natural hunger and satiety cues. I lost a noticeable amount of weight while enrolled in his program, and he wanted to hire me, but I wanted to do some things differently.

My weight loss got many people's attention, and my MSW degree and social work license allowed me to run groups and classes I first called "Thinside Out." I had decided that diets made people fat, and my work encouraged people to discover their hunger and satiety, as well as taking care of what else in their lives they had tried to remedy through weight loss.

Having run several of these groups and classes, I decided to go for my doctorate. Trying to find a doctoral program that allowed me to focus on non-dieting, weight, the contextual therapy of Bob Shaw, MD of the Family Institute of Berkeley, and the solution-oriented therapy of Bill O'Hanlon, MS was nearly impossible. None of the more traditional doctoral psychology programs offered me support. I finally found a non-traditional external degree program through Columbia Pacific University that allowed me to work with a mentor, whom I educated about non-diet weight loss.

Two years after I got my PhD I saw on a TV program a very fat and smart woman named Lynn McAfee. She had been very fat even as an infant and had been subjected to diet pills and diets as a very young child. I realized that she must have been naturally fat and had not just become a fat child via diets, and then I got angry at how badly fat people were treated by society and medicine. Their size was not their fault! They had not done anything wrong!

Probably via McAfee, I discovered the National Association to Advance Fat Acceptance (NAAFA), a civil- and human-rights group for fat people. I had been involved in the racial civil rights movement through both my parents' influence and my best friend's father, Whitney Young, Jr., head of the National Urban League. Young had always asked me what I was doing to help the Negro (what Black people were called at that time), but it wasn't until Lynn McAfee's appearance that I realized fat people were the group I would spend my life helping.

I discovered that there had formerly been a local chapter of NAAFA that had been discontinued. I managed to resurrect it with the guidance of Pat Coles, its last leader in my Hudson Valley area. A couple of other former members and I rebuilt the chapter and began programs building on civil rights—including contacting legislators and doing other activism—and human rights—including fitness and health-oriented programming, trying to find healthcare professionals who did not insist that every symptom be treated via weight-loss diets, literature, fashion shows, and social events. We published a monthly newsletter, *The RoundUp*.

I attended my first national NAAFA convention in the late 1980s, in California. There I saw more fat people together than I'd ever seen—many more than at our local meetings—and many were beautifully dressed and groomed. They had dances and parties, speakers and workshops. On a macro level compared to our local monthly meetings, the week-long NAAFA convention provided an oasis for people whose daily life consisted of harassment, insult, degradation in pay and nearly no opportunities whatsoever that thinner people were afforded.

The field of eating disorders was not very prominent at that time, although there was a lot of attention and profit around "compulsive eating," the notion that people were fat because—their fault—they could not keep from eating too much, and most must be lazy. Oprah Winfrey decided that people were fat because they had been molested.

One day I got a mailing, "Treating Obesity in the '90s." This first program, to be held at a hotel in Virginia, included most of those people whose names I recognized from the few anti-diet books I had found. I signed up immediately. The founder of the program was Joe McVoy, a psychologist who specialized in treating people with eating disorders.

I was on a small plane headed for a Virginia airport near Mountain Lake. On the plane was someone whose name I already knew via the very few books available that did not agree with the pro-diet, anti-obesity stance that swamped the market, reading lists, and treatment programs at the time. Deb Burgard had co-authored *Great Shape: The First Fitness Guide for Large Women* with Pat Lyons. Among that sparse group of books were Laura Brown and Esther Rothblum's *Overcoming Fear of Fat; Shadow on a Tightrope*, an anthology on fat oppression edited by Lisa Schoenfielder and Barb Wieser; and *You Count, Calories Don't* by Linda Omichinski.

At Mountain Lake I found my spiritual and professional home. Those of us who attended that conference named our group AHELP, the Association for the Health Enrichment of Large People.

Between NAAFA and AHELP, I was no longer alone in the anti-diet desert.

Since I was at that time thinner than most NAAFA members, lived in the New York City suburbs, and had a doctorate, I appeared on a number of television and radio programs and in print media, speaking on behalf of fat people's rights and against dieting as the solution to their problems. A "sixties child," I was accustomed to marching and picketing for civil rights and against the Vietnam War. Activism was part of my nature and my practice.

I attended all the AHELP meetings, including some more local ones, and got on the NAAFA board of directors and then on its international advisory board. In late 1996 my book *Worth Your Weight: What You CAN Do About a Weight Problem* was published.

Near the millennium, we AHELP folks and our associates sought a name for the work we had been doing. We debated "health at every size" vs. "health at any size." I no longer recall why "every" was chosen over "any." We deliberately pushed back against the profit- and prejudice-driven notion that health equaled lower weight.

A few years after AHELP stopped meeting, planes crashed into the twin towers of the World Trade Center, as well as the Pentagon and in Pennsylvania. The world as I knew it ended. I left my anti-diet, pro-health work and played a lot of solitaire on the computer. What did weight matter when people were trying to kill all of us—not just fat people?

After a lot of inner work and spiritual counseling, I realized that there could not be peace in the world if people could not even be at peace within themselves. There could not be peace if people were struggling against weight mandates, or as long as there were weight-loss programs and so-called "obesity experts" and medications profiting from people's weight insecurity.

I returned to what was now the HAES movement and found that ASDAH, the Association for Size Diversity and Health, had formed during my absence. I was thrilled to learn that its founder, Claudia Clark, a psychologist at Bowling

Green State University, had been inspired by one of my activism workshops at AHELP and had then hosted ASDAH's introductory meeting at her university in 2003. Despite my absence, I felt like ASDAH's grandmother!

I remained active in NAAFA and ASDAH for a few more years, and then decided I would step into the background of the HAES and fat acceptance movements. There were many, many more young and active people who were ready, willing, and able to take the reins.

However, I wanted to reach more people. Our world had been in worse and worse shape. Conflict and eating disorders were increasingly widespread. I approached my alma mater, Cornell University, with a proposal to spread HAES to its tremendously capable, smart, and younger population. I wanted their intelligence, hard work, and energy to go out to help our world—which sorely needs it—rather than be wasted by struggling with food and their bodies.

I sponsored several members of Cornell Health and its extraordinarily open-minded director, Kent Bullis, MD, to attend ASDAH's 2015 conference in Boston. Bullis was one of the very few physicians who were aware of the failure of the diet and weight = health paradigm. So many students with eating disorders were arriving at Cornell, struggling with ubiquitous anti-fat messages—now mostly through social media rather than other traditional media—that Cornell was open to a HAES approach. With encouragement by a national wrestling champion and Cornell nutrition graduate, Clint Wattenberg, Body Positive Cornell began, using programming developed by Connie Sobczak and Elizabeth Scott. Happily, the program has been running for undergraduate and graduate students, faculty, and staff, with peer-led support groups meeting via Cornell athletics, mental and physical health, the Greek (fraternity/sorority) system, BIPOC and LGBTQ groups, as well as a Body Positive Club and speakers. Groups of faculty and staff have met. Peer leaders can receive credit for their work. In 2019 Cornell sponsored a HAES symposium that featured Cornell-related, HAES-related speakers including NAAFA's founder, Bill Fabrey, and Paul Ernsberger, PhD, a biomedical researcher and educator at Case Western Reserve Medical School.

I wrote a history of what I considered the first century of the Health at Every Size movement, which was printed by Cornell University in 2018.

I am delighted that Cornell has archived much of my work and will also archive Bill Fabrey's NAAFA-related work.

I am thrilled that our work is continuing and being spread out into the world by increasing numbers of smart, capable people, who can use their energies and abilities to make a very big difference for us all.

THE OPTIFAST® DEBACLE
ON MESSING UP, LEARNING, AND DOING BETTER.

JON ROBISON, *as told to* RAGEN CHASTAIN

AFTER I GRADUATED FROM THE UNIVERSITY of Michigan in 1973 with a degree in music literature, I did what I wanted to do originally, which was not go to college, but instead play music professionally. I went on the road for about 15 years. That's not a very healthy life, being in a bar five or six hours a night with all the smoking and drinking. So I decided to try running, which is very odd because in junior high and high school I was a skinny uncoordinated kid. I was the last kid to be picked on the team—any team. I could never climb the ropes in the gym or do the pushups. It's not the same as what fat people experience, but I think it helps me understand conversations about body image a bit better, because I always felt that I was way too skinny and simply not enough. Combined with a pretty serious case of ADHD (in the principal's office a lot), it made those school years difficult. Playing and singing in bands was my joy and probably my savior.

I really got into running while I was on the road, and perhaps surprisingly was pretty good at it. And as I was getting a little bit tired of being on the road 12 months a year I had the thought, "Well, maybe I'll go back to college and get a degree in exercise physiology." I went to Michigan State University (MSU) and started to work on a master's degree in that field. During that time I also got really interested in nutrition and started thinking that it might be fun to teach college. I knew that big universities often frown on "just" master's degrees if you want to be a professor, so I thought, "Well, what the hell? I'll get a PhD in exercise physiology." But I also had this keen interest in nutrition. So I collaborated with the nutrition department and worked concurrently on a master's degree in nutrition and a PhD in exercise physiology. I graduated with all three degrees in 1992.

In the mid-1990s I got involved with an internal medicine physician, who ran—here we go—wait for it—an Optifast® program! In case you're not familiar with Optifast, it's referred to as a protein-sparing modified fast, which is a way-too-kind "scientific" way of saying you starve people until they lose a shitload of weight. And you do that by not letting them eat any food. You heard that correctly. Feeding them just basically "milkshakes" of around 800–1,000 calories a day! You may remember the picture of Oprah from way back then trotting across the stage with a wagon full of what looked like human fat cells—that was the Optifast program.

We had exercise physiologists and social workers and psychologists, and we did group counseling as well as intensive medical monitoring. And lo and behold, people lost lots and lots of weight, which you would expect given that they were starving. Sometimes they lost a hundred or more pounds, over the course of six months, eight months. But six months after that, I would see many of these same people walking down the street and I noticed that they would cross over to the other side of the street from where I was walking, because most of them had gained all their weight back and more.

I was doing what I was taught in my exercise physiology classes and in my nutrition classes (by the way, as far as I know, they're still teaching basically the same nonsense right now, this many years later), but it felt horrible. A psychologist joined the practice and, right from the beginning, she was horrified at what we were doing. In fact, I learned later that she actually joined the practice hoping that she could convince the doctor to stop doing what we were doing. Eventually she did convince all of us that we needed to stop this nonsense. Frighteningly, the Optifast program is still available and widely promoted today. On the brighter side of things, this woman later became my wife.

During this time, I also met a professor at MSU named David Garner, whom people in the eating disorders world will know because he's quite famous in the field. He used to say to me, in this very quiet voice, "Jon, what are you doing?" And I would say, "Well, we're trying to help people with health issues and weight and diabetes, and blah, blah, blah." He'd say, "Have you read the literature? You really should read the literature." And I'd say, "But hypertension and diabetes, and all that other stuff." And he'd say, "Jon, read the literature." And he just kept repeating that suggestion over and over again.

And so, the combination of being frustrated and feeling terrible with what was going on with the Optifast program clients and the shame that they were feeling (though I'm the one who should have been feeling the shame), plus interactions with my future wife and Garner's gentle prodding, prompted me to start reading the literature. Lo and behold, of course I discovered that this remarkably ubiquitous cycle of dieting followed by weight regain had been known about for years! We should have known better. All of us should have known better.

During the course of reading the literature, I came in contact with people who ended up being my mentors. People like Pat Lyons, Cheri Erdman, and Marilyn Wann. I read their books and spoke to them and learned from them. And then I got involved with AHELP—the Association for the Health Enrichment of Large People. I went to a couple of their conferences, and they were just eye opening; they were mind-blowing in every way because they showed me quite clearly what I had been doing to people. I care about people and that's why I went into the fields of study that I did in the first place. I was so, so upset with myself because of the harm I had done that I decided that I was going to devote considerable time and effort going forward to doing things differently and changing people's minds about the status quo.

I started to learn and then teach about this new paradigm. I taught college for 25 years at Michigan State and Western Michigan universities. I only taught classes that I designed, and they were all from a Health at Every Size perspective. "Dying to be Thin" was a class I developed with Esther Park, who is an eating disorders specialist completely grounded in Health at Every Size. It became one of the highest student-rated courses in the MSU nutrition department. But it made many in the faculty and administration uncomfortable, and eventually they made us change the name to "Prevention and Treatment of Eating Disorders" because they thought "Dying to Be Thin" was too "radical." (P.S.: We changed nothing except for the name—exactly the same content).

There have been many changes in the size acceptance/HAES community culture since I got involved. One thing I notice is that when I got involved back then with AHELP and so forth, it was very white. Now I'm learning more about the relationship between weight stigma, racism, and Black bodies from people like Sabrina Strings and Da'Shaun Harrison. I think the movement is doing a better job of including more marginalized voices, though of course there's still a lot of work to be done. I think in American culture overall there have also been some improvements, although it feels like we're in a period of dangerous backsliding in many areas in the present moment. I remember that when I was traveling and introducing these ideas to people and organizations years ago and people would ask for referrals to individual practitioners, it wasn't easy to find them and there weren't many to be found. Now if somebody emails me or texts me from whatever town it might be, I'm usually able to find somebody whom I feel comfortable recommending. We have not hundreds, but thousands of practitioners now around the country who are doing the right thing. Nutrition professionals, psychologists, social workers, and more. Of course, I understand that in terms of weight stigma, structural oppression, and access there is a long, long way to go, but I do see positive changes.

Thinking about some of the more memorable events from the past, I want to start by saying that my memory is sketchy at best. I've had multiple sclerosis for 30 years, and one of the things that it has affected is my memory. I do remember this one time, I think at an AHELP Conference, when Glenn Gaesser, PhD was speaking. Glenn is a brilliant scientist who I think has done a lot of good for the weight-neutral health and size acceptance movements. He spoke at the conference, and he wasn't quite all the way there yet in terms of Health at Every Size. I won't go into specifics about it, but there was a lot of firm criticism. He took it well. I loved the way that my mentors helped him to understand how his privilege (thin, white male like me) continued to show up in the equation. Pat Lyons and Deb Burgard had just written a book about exercise called *Great Shape: The First Fitness Guide for Large Women*. Glenn gave a keynote lecture, and then he got lectured to a bit because he just wasn't quite there. He was learning, but he was still somewhat rooted in the whole healthism thing.

More recently I got into a discussion with a nutrition professional on LinkedIn who was talking about connecting intuitive eating or mindful eating and weight loss. Honestly, I wasn't as kind as I could have been about it because I figured she ought to know better. I responded on LinkedIn saying, "Please don't do this. *Please* don't do this. You can do great harm with this." I think I referred her to my friend and colleague Michelle May, MD, and they got connected. Eventually the nutrition professional came around and is now aware of the mutual exclusivity of the two concepts.

After my personal experiences with weight loss programs and my study of the literature, I have become so passionate about the damage that we do to people. I have bumped heads and made some enemies over the years, for sure.

When I think about what I might have done differently, I'll be honest that I'm not sure that Health at Every Size was the best term to use because it does lend itself some to healthism. I was part of what is called the "health promotion community," and I've written lots of white papers and blogs and a couple of books discussing the issues with that community, including the complete lack of understanding of social justice issues. The National Wellness Conference and the American Journal of Health Promotion Conference are both places I spoke at for decades, and there was little to no understanding around social justice. It was all white, upper class, mostly thin people, and mostly women. And it was all about what you ate and how much you exercised and that was pretty much it. If you did those things "right" then you were "healthy." And if you didn't, you weren't "healthy." It was a narrow and misleading conceptualization of what health is really all about.

Today there are so many different overlapping intersectional issues going on that can be complex and confusing. But at the same time it's important because it's not just about thin upper middle-class people jogging and eating broccoli. That's why the first book I wrote was called *The Spirit and Science of Holistic Health: More Than Broccoli, Jogging, and Bottled Water; More Than Yoga, Herbs, and Meditation*. The word "health" has gotten so bastardized, which is why we moved from "health promotion" to "wellness" and now to "wellbeing." The truth of the matter is that if you go back and look at original definitions of the word "health" from decades and hundreds of years ago (Indigenous cultures, for example), they were very holistic—mind, body, spirit, and even ecological. It got "un-holisticized"—driven by a patriarchal, mechanistic, privileged, white conceptualization of the world.

Being mostly retired now, I think about the fact that, considering 25 years of teaching and all the conferences and publications, I've had the opportunity and honor to speak to thousands of people about these issues. I still hear from people who say, "I took your course in 1991, and now I'm an eating disorders specialist," and "I do HAES work and I never would've done that if I hadn't heard you speak at that conference…" Though I know I have a lot of privilege that others doing this work don't have, it still hasn't been an easy road, but those realities make it all worthwhile. I know there are many other people that I positively impacted that way as well, that I just don't hear from. And that makes me feel really good. And it balances out the sometimes hurtful responses that I have gotten from people still stuck in outdated, scientifically bereft paradigms. I just have to remind myself of that.

So, I guess if I've helped people better accept themselves, and trained other health professionals to do the same by having more care and less judgment for people, I'd be really happy with that as a legacy.

NAAFA's Early Years

Bill Fabrey

A LOT OF PEOPLE ASK HOW I GOT INTERESTED in the problems of fat people, especially since I was thin myself when I was growing up. Well, without knowing it, I was an admirer of the large figure from the age of five years old. I always liked girls, from kindergarten on, and somehow or other they were always chubby. When I was nine I developed a crush on a girl who lived across the street who was eight years old. It lasted five years! She was the kind of girl who caused mothers on the street, including mine, to say things like, "Diana has such a pretty face—it's such a shame she has that weight problem." I always thought to myself, "What weight problem? She looks great to me!"

Around the age of 14 I admitted publicly that I admired fat girls when I went to my mother and pointed out a picture in a magazine of a woman who was perhaps what today would be a size 18. I told my mom that I thought the woman had a perfect figure by my standards. After she regained her composure, she explained to me that the woman was pretty but "very overweight," and that if I thought that was attractive, I must be going through a phase. (The phase has so far lasted over 60 years, and I'm still counting.)

After that, I came to face a total lack of acceptance on the question of my taste in women—from family, from friends, and from society. In fact, there was virtually no recognition in the media of the existence of others like myself, and I felt pretty isolated. I noted that there were plenty of books and articles written about gay men and women, but almost nothing about those whose sexuality involves attraction to a larger partner. I began to read anything I could find on the subject, and came to the opinion that there was a huge gap in the world's understanding of fat people and their admirers.

When I dated in high school and college, my dates were always plus-sized girls and women. The one exception was when a thin female friend and I both

76

wanted to go to a certain prom, and neither of us had dates, so we asked each other to the prom. But it never would have occurred to me to think of her as anything other than a friend.

In 1964 I married Joyce, a very plus-sized woman. In living with her and getting to know and understand her issues, I became very angry at the way that she was treated every day of her life. For example, when we were engaged and applied for a marriage license, blood tests were required under New York state law. She went to a new doctor in her community to receive a blood test and was shown into his office. When he asked why she was there, Joyce replied that she was engaged to be married soon and needed to obtain a blood test. The astonished doctor replied, "Who would want to marry you?" When Joyce, between her tears, told me the story on the phone, I was furious.

Events like these set the stage for an anger that built up inside me, anger that was later to be used productively.

One day in 1967, three years after Joyce and I were married, I read an article in the *Saturday Evening Post* magazine called "More People Should be Fat" by a man named Lew Louderback. In the piece he suggested that a large number of people at any given time are temporarily thin, at a low point during their dieting, and are making the rest of us miserable by their "born-again-thin" attitude and making themselves unhealthier than if they had stayed fat. And that fat people are terribly mistreated by our society.

I leapt out of my chair, galvanized by the thought that I had discovered a kindred spirit, and the truth had finally come out. I thought it would be a great idea to order some reprints of the article from the *Post* and give them to those friends and relatives who had been unsupportive throughout the years, and perhaps anyone else I bumped into who needed convincing. But I was told by Curtis Publishing that reprints were available only in quantity, with a minimum of 500, for around $80, which was big money in those days. So, I thought, maybe I could get together a few other people, including Louderback himself, to place a single order for the reprints.

The moment I thought of "getting people together" I realized that ordering reprints was just a start, and I was onto something big. I remembered that in the U.S., most everything that gets anything accomplished is done through an organization, and I realized that it was up to me to start one, since nobody else had. My next thought was to fear that I could find nobody who would take the idea seriously, and the thought after that was to realize that for me to be driven by that fear would be counterproductive. I decided that once I had the thought to start an organization that might have the potential to help so many people, it would be morally dishonest to walk away from it.

In February 1968 I wrote to Mr. Louderback with my ideas for the NAAFA[1] organization, and he responded that he liked the idea and that I should flesh it out a bit more. He and his wife agreed to meet with me and my wife, and at that meeting, we all agreed that if I could find a sympathetic attorney, come up with a constitution, and round up some friends to serve on a board, we could start an organization.

Soon thereafter Louderback was awarded a small advance to write the book *Fat Power,* and I put plans to start the organization that would eventually become NAAFA on hold for a year while I helped him with some of the research for the book. My thought at the time was that people would take us more seriously if we had a well-researched book that espoused our positions on the role of fat people in society and how fat people could be healthier and happier. The book was published, and did not make much of a splash, but I consider it to be the "Bible" of the size acceptance movement. Most of what Louderback said more than 30 years ago has withstood the test of time, and is still valid. But the book has been out of print for many years, and it's hard to find copies of it today.

In the early spring of 1969 I sought out an attorney referral from the county bar association in Long Island, NY, and prayed that I would be taken seriously. I was, and got an appointment with a lawyer named John Trapani. The moment I walked into his office I knew I had come to the right place. His secretary (Eileen Lefebure), who ended up becoming one of our co-founders, was fat. With his help, and with hers, I drafted a constitution and bylaws, going through three drafts in the process. Then I rounded up the few friends I had left who didn't think that this was a harebrained scheme, and we all met on June 13, 1969 to sign and ratify the constitution. NAAFA was born that day!

Well, I can tell you that I was pretty naive. Louderback, being more mature, said he thought that our task was harder than demolishing a brick wall, but I believed that all we had to do was to put the truth in front of rational people and in a few short years size oppression would be a thing of the past. I soon realized that we faced major problems convincing most people to even listen to the message. And our main opposition was not intellectual truth, but the emotional reactions of people who had invested a lifetime in believing themselves or others inferior because of weight.

We faced serious opposition from our friends and our parents, and even my own wife was doubtful that it was worth trying. She went along with it for the same reason that some women take up golf—because they won't spend much time with their husbands if they don't. My parents were openly hostile to my efforts, feeling that I was wasting my time and energy on a fruitless project. It wasn't until the 1980s that they began to see and even respect what we were trying to do, after I got quoted in the *New York Times* and the *Wall Street Journal* several times.

Getting NAAFA going caused me to make some tough career choices, have new experiences, and develop new friends. In 1969 I had to leave most of my old friends behind who did not understand why in the world I would do what I did. My career choices were dictated by the fact that in the 9-to-5 workaday world an engineer cannot ask his boss for an hour off to line up some people for a Phil Donahue show. I was forced to work as an engineer for small companies who respected my technical skills, and who were willing to put up with frequent disruptions in my schedule. Eventually I became a consultant, paid by the hour.

The first few years of NAAFA, until perhaps 1980, were partly administrative—answering phone messages and the mail, mailing literature, processing $6 memberships, revising literature, meeting monthly with a democratically elected board of directors, being interviewed by the media, and so forth. We had so few members (less than 100 in 1970, and less than 1,000 in 1980) that at no time was our survival as an organization assured. The media were interested, but mostly viewed us as a curiosity. Gradually reporters doing their homework began to ask more intelligent questions, and interviews were less sensationalistic—although this trend was later reversed in the category of TV talk shows, which became more sensationalistic in the 1990s and later, and with which we decreasingly cooperated.

In those years the media did not include the internet. People didn't even have home computers. The publication of a more-or-less-regular newsletter for members began in October 1970. The newsletter commenced after membership applications and media interest took an upturn after the *New York Times* ran a large article with photos on August 18 of that year. In the years to follow a regular annual convention was held, starting with a single-day event in New York City. By the end of the 1970s conventions were three-to-five-day affairs held in various locations, and included workshops, some meals, pool parties, dances, hospitality suites, and a dating and a pen-pal program. There were local chapters around the U.S. and one in Canada. By the end of the 1980s conventions had been held in Chicago and Los Angeles (each twice). Sometimes NAAFA held special fundraising events in cooperation with a local chapter, to raise money and encourage membership.

The goals of the organization were set in the original constitution in its preamble and were fairly broad. In plain English, it was proposed to help fat people in as many ways possible to live better lives in a society that was clearly hostile to them. The people that NAAFA was dedicated to helping were treated as an existing group of people, not as slender people who were temporarily fat. This is an important distinction, as there have always been efforts to "help" fat people by devising ways of making them less fat. These are almost always futile in the long run, even counterproductive, but extremely profitable to those offering such "help," at the expense of the health and sanity of their customers.

However, because the goals were stated so broadly, it was quickly obvious that the work of NAAFA had to be more than political. If we talked about offering a weekend conference of planning ways in which we could fight size discrimination in hiring and promotion, for example, five people might show interest; but if we offered a weekend of dances and workshops, a few of which dealt with size discrimination and many of which also offered support, then 100 to 300 people might show up.

Many people found partners within the movement, or, armed with their newly found self-esteem and set of behaviors, were able to find partners outside the movement. At NAAFA we found out that the need for social interaction with others who don't disapprove of your body was so powerful that we could not attract members without offering such social activities, so NAAFA-Date was born, and we started holding dances and mixers in several cities. Some in NAAFA, including Lew Louderback, respectfully withdrew from leadership when that happened, because their vision was primarily one of activism and education.

Eventually, because of publicity, the social component of NAAFA activities was the only side that some members and outsiders saw, cared about, or were aware of. There was even an editor of a plus-size fashion magazine whom we invited to be a guest speaker but declined, and later told us that she had heard we were a "sex club." It was never one of our goals to be a "sex club," but we were dealing with human beings with human needs, and they often came to NAAFA with the primary goal of finding a partner. Some succeeded, and some failed.

For the record, all but one of the original co-founders who helped me get NAAFA off the ground were happily married, and none were seeking an improved social life for fat people or for themselves. We were all political animals, and initially believed that the solutions to size discrimination were political in nature. None of us, I believe, were that wise about human nature; wisdom came later, with experience.

We had many successes and many failures, and every year NAAFA and the size acceptance movement both add to each of those lists to this day. Successes, in my view, were often related to the "ripple effect"—things that a few people do can affect how many people think or behave.

NAAFA set an example for the plus-size fashion industry, which initially sneered and held its nose when we began holding plus-sized and super-sized fashion shows at our conventions. After they found out that the market for plus-sizes was the only one that was expanding, while other markets were shrinking, they reluctantly started churning out more clothes in larger sizes, and even held fashion shows for them. Today, few people deeply immersed in the plus-size industry remember or understand the role that size acceptance groups have played in their industry.

NAAFA helped to convince some healthcare professionals that inhumane treatment of fat patients was not only wrong but counterproductive, and could result in fatter or less healthy patients in the long run. We also enlisted a few allies in those professions to help back up our claims. (Some healthcare professionals realized this on their own, without our help, when certain truths presented themselves within their practice or research, as eventually they always do.)

NAAFA built some of the tools that later generations of fat people could use, if they wanted to, to reconstruct their self-esteem and improve their health and well-being. However, many or even most fat people did not and still do not reach out and grasp the tools to help themselves. It is extremely hard for people who have lived with oppression all their lives to break away from that mindset—especially when so much of the media and society itself are telling them they are correct to think badly of themselves.

NAAFA inspired writers of books and magazine articles, as well as occasional media coverage in TV, radio, and even film, to take another look at the issues of health and aesthetics; to recognize that beauty and attractiveness were not necessarily functions of pounds and inches; and to understand that bad health and a higher weight do not necessarily have to go hand in hand.

NAAFA helped build awareness in some people who never joined the organization, but may have made a choice of careers in graduate school, for example, that later helped work against size oppression. I have spoken with several of these people over the years, and I have to assume that there are many more.

NAAFA was the source of a number of "spin-off" organizations that felt that they could tackle some aspect of size oppression better than NAAFA was doing. This began around 1971 with the Fat Underground of Los Angeles, which had started as a NAAFA chapter but quickly realized that NAAFA was too "mainstream" for what they had in mind. It has never ended—new organizations spun off and continue to do so.

Although not all new size-related groups are NAAFA spinoffs, most have been influenced or motivated in part by what NAAFA did, whether they realize it or not. I have always spoken in favor of such groups, having come to believe long ago that it is not possible to address all the issues of size discrimination effectively within one organization. For example, it is hard to convince Jane to respect the work of Susie and vice-versa when Jane believes that the answer to the problem is to hold a plus-size beauty pageant, but Susie believes that the answer to the problem is to picket any company who fires an employee for weighing over some limit, or wants to smash scales every year on No-Diet Day.

I've hinted above at some of the things that we could have done better. It is possible that if NAAFA had concentrated on a fewer number of issues affecting fat people, it might have gone farther with those issues. Other problems include things over which the organization had no control. Today, for example, we supposedly have an "obesity epidemic," but the terminology, which is completely bogus, was coined by an unscientific surgeon general and has been promulgated ever since by the media and those who stand to gain from widespread fear of the "epidemic," especially in children. I call it the "Chicken Little" effect. It is hard to see how size acceptance could have prevented that. There are more fat people and there are more very fat people these days, but there is no epidemic.

Another failure, if that is the right word, was organizational. Partly because of the "big tent" philosophy, there were at many points in NAAFA's history a disconnect between NAAFA leadership and its members, and a great deal of members over the years "voted with their feet," not renewing their memberships and withdrawing their support. In part this was a leadership failure to recognize what people expected to receive as members, kind of a "customer service" problem. And in part it has been the all-too-human failures of leaders failing to see the long-term big picture and getting bogged down in squabbles, personality issues, and who-is-sleeping-with-whom-type power struggles. These kinds of things are endemic in most human organizations, but in 1990, during a period of disputes with the officers, board members, and some regular members, a group of trained intervention counselors was hired by NAAFA to make recommendations. They stated that NAAFA's leadership dynamics were unusually messy and were built into the system. One of their recommendations was a friendly divorce (my words) between warring factions, which is ultimately what took place during that era.

Because of such matters, it sometimes seemed that since the very beginning, for every two steps forward taken by the organization there have been one or one-and-a-half steps back. Historically, groups of oppressed minorities that try to better themselves by forming organizations tend to expend nearly as much energy fighting internal battles as they do in fighting the outside enemy, and NAAFA was no exception. Through the years this has happened time and again, and yet a lot of good was accomplished. Many people's lives were powerfully affected by the endeavor. And today the size acceptance movement still includes NAAFA and several other groups that focus on various aspects of the problems of fat people.

Since this is a report of successes and failures of the first 20 years, I would have to count some of my personal failures, to the extent that they have impacted the organization.

My being the founder and the principal activist for such a group in the beginning was very stressful on my marriage to Joyce Fabrey, who was one of the co-founders, and we counted that stress as one of the five reasons we decided to separate and then divorce. The effect on NAAFA itself was primarily to reduce my productivity at the time. My subsequent marriage to activist Nancy Summer in 1981, which lasted 23 years, was also stressful, sometimes for similar reasons, but also a very productive period for NAAFA because we learned from each other, and she became president of NAAFA for a time and put out a very successful run of newsletters as the editor for several years. Many of the concepts devised by Nancy are still in use today, and we remained good friends after our divorce.

The disputes of 1990 were particularly rancorous in part due to resentment of a few leaders about Nancy's strong leadership and personal qualities. Members and leaders who were homophobic objected to her strong support of the lesbian and gay communities within size acceptance. Those communities, especially the groups of lesbian and bisexual women within the movement, were extraordinarily creative and inspired by the goals of size acceptance, but were often regarded with mistrust and even hostility by some NAAFA members, despite my best efforts, even from the very beginning of the organization.

The combatants in the 1990 disputes agreed to go their separate ways and remained cordial or even friendly in their relations when it was called for within the movement, and that has worked. But some of the late '90s disputes in NAAFA were not settled so amicably, and left some wounds that have never completely healed. I have not been personally involved in any of these disputes since 1990; I have chosen to remain a friend and ally with all sides. I hope I am considered an "elder statesman."

When I look back at the early history of NAAFA, and the first 42 years, I am struck by a shift in my own thinking about the goals of size acceptance, and where our energies should be allocated.

In the early years, just the notion that one's weight was a poor indicator of one's health, longevity, worthiness, and beauty was pretty radical for its time. (In mainstream Western society, today, it still is a radical position!) In the beginning I was inspired by other movements—gay rights, Black civil rights, empowerment for women, for minority religions, the elderly, and so forth. The earliest NAAFA literature that I drafted omitted any assumption about the readers' sexual preferences, for example.

Yet the term "inclusivity" did not yet exist, and I strongly felt at the time that we had so much on our plate with weight issues that we would be diluting our energies if we tried to fight those battles at the same time as fat rights. In fact, when I spoke to the president of a disabled veterans' rights organization, he told me frankly that his group would not want to be tied in with a group espousing fat rights.

Time and again I could see racism, ageism, looksism, and homophobia play out at the NAAFA chapter level, all the way up to our own board of directors. If chapters couldn't hold meetings because nobody could agree on what side of town to hold the meetings, which included conflicts of transportation, race, parking problems, personal safety, and expense, how could we pursue fatphobia when we allowed other phobias to weaken us? If the board couldn't give a "distinguished achievement" award to a newsmagazine for its excellent fat coverage because of the lesbian focus of that publication, and half of the board feared that NAAFA would be judged badly by any perception of giving support to lesbians, then how could NAAFA hope to encourage inclusivity? After that battle, as chair I broke a tie vote, only made possible when the award was downgraded to an "achievement" award. I guess the lesbians weren't distinguished enough!

There was even what I called a "size pecking order." At conventions, we noticed that supersize members took an unsupportive view of what today are sometimes called "small fats" (those who are much smaller, yet still considered fat by society). Our largest board members were known to walk up to a smaller attendee and say something like "Why are you here—you can't have any problems at your size!" One of our board members actually said that to a guest speaker in an elevator. Yet at the same time, the smaller attendees were known to sometimes say, about those who were much, much larger than they were, something like "You poor thing, how do you even get through the day at that size? Have you even tried to lose weight?" Or to remark, "OMG, these people have let themselves go!" Noting that many of the men present seemed to be most attracted to the largest members, some smaller fats were resentful of that fact, and took their resentment out on the women who were getting the attention.

Neither I nor the early board of directors were prepared for any of these problems of human interactions, and I avoided trying to dive into trying to steer the organization to the high road of inclusivity. Yet when I joined the board of directors ("leadership team") of the Association for Size Diversity and Health (ASDAH) in 2008, I began to see some of these issues discussed in earnest, at a higher, more professional level. Around 2011, perhaps (maybe when the late Fall Ferguson was chair), the ASDAH board voted to hire experts on inclusivity to present a weekend-long training session by phone, and I abstained, due to my long-held reservations about our size acceptance and HAES goals risking being diluted by all the other possible battles that could occur. (I was alone on the board with these concerns, but didn't want to be a nay-sayer to block progress, if the group wanted to learn more about inclusivity.)

However, in the process, I gradually changed my mind about the whole matter of inclusivity. After 42 years of feeling one way, I became convinced that all the social ills—racism, homophobia, xenophobia, oppressive treatment of Indigenous peoples, age discrimination, size discrimination, poverty, and so forth, were inextricably linked, and all have to be fought.

In addition to the training I received on the ASDAH board level, I have to credit three individuals for having the largest effect in my transition on this topic: Dana Schuster, the Rev. Dr. E-K Daufin, and Deb Burgard. I am sorry I didn't do it sooner, as various disenfranchised persons might have helped lead NAAFA and all of size acceptance in a more inclusive direction.

This is not to denigrate the many years of hard work and dedication of many NAAFA leaders whose goals were not focused on inclusivity. I just believe that all of us might have been more morally and ethically productive had we done so sooner. Yes, a different direction might have alienated some members, but might have brought in more, different members whose perspectives would have lent more depth to the work that we did.

My explanation of the history of the internal problems in NAAFA is, of course, not a detailed one, but it is my own. If you asked any of the participants in any of the disputes for their versions, you would undoubtedly get as many different explanations as the number of people that you asked, and probably a lot more detail than you wanted.

In the years I've written about here, NAAFA influenced many thousands of lives, perhaps even hundreds of thousands, sometimes without even knowing who they are. Mostly, their lives are better because of what size acceptance has done and is doing. That is why we must continue.

FOOTNOTE

1. NAAFA originally stood for "National Association to Aid Fat Americans" and was later changed to "National Association to Advance Fat Acceptance."

Thoughts on Surviving Misogynoir in Size Acceptance and Fat Lib

Rev. Dr. E-K Daufin, *as told to* Tigress Osborn

WITH NAAFA AND WITH ASDAH, I have a before and after story. Neither story has been free of racism, sexism, misogyny, misogynoir, classism, because—it's planet Earth. But thanks to a lot of work by some brave people, it has become better recently—better than it was in my earlier experiences, at least. So much of my early life was dealing with family, doctors and school—it was just a beat-down about being too fat. "You should diet and exercise and starve yourself" and all the rest that doesn't make you thin, or not for long.

I think we intersectional fat libbers should explain (and others should receive or get to steppin'!) the wisdom of focusing on what happens to the biggest of us and the Blackest of us, and the most kinkiest-haired of us and those with the most Africanized features. I'm talking about colorism. As I work for intersectional social justice, I try to acknowledge the ways in which I *am* privileged. I try to make it clear that I know that people who are even bigger and darker skinned than me get *even more* of the problem and *even more* literal pain.

When I first came to NAAFA I was the super young one at most events, and I was also the only, or one of the very few, Black people. One thing that I thought *was* handled really well in early NAAFA was the fashion show. I was a small fat then, a size 18 (22/24 now). Being in theater, I thought I would love being in fashion shows, but I was always too fat for "straight" shows. And that was before the time they even had the *one* size 10 or 12 in shows with white models. There was Ebony Fashion Fair, a Black-themed fashion show—they would go to different cities and pick one person from the local area to give it that local flavor. In LA they already had their one plus-size, who was a size 10! And in the white fashion shows, the plus-size model would be a size six or eight. At NAAFA I had to do a little audition. I started improvising, you know, and I was dancing around on the runway and stuff. They LOVED it, and so did I. But they would only let me model one outfit. They explained to me—they said, "Look, we think you're great! But because of fat oppression, we can't have the thinnest of the fat models doing more than one outfit or seeming preferred." And even though I was sorry that I wouldn't get to strut my stuff more than once, I understood that. One of my core beliefs is that let's help the group or person who is most profoundly and directly hurt.

But—intersectionality, you know—I *do* wonder now, if I had been a small-fat *white* woman, especially if I had had long blonde hair, and maybe blue eyes, if they would have still given me only one runway shot. I was the *only* Black person in the fashion show.

I don't remember which came first, the chicken or the egg; whether I first learned about the NAAFA convention from a newspaper ad in the *Los Angeles Times*, or whether I was already on their mailing list and learned about the LA NAAFA convention that way. It was all snail mail back then, United States Postal Service. People were happy to have a NAAFA member who was Black-identified and a writer. They just didn't want to accommodate my Blackness or support me or defend me or enforce their own rules, but we'll get to that story in a minute.

There *were* other related blessings to going to NAAFA conventions. I *did* meet a white woman who was involved with one of the largest Goddess worshiper or feminist witch circles in the country. She got me into that circle because we met at LA NAAFA. She's like, "Aren't you—? You seem like you're—?" She saw the Goddess in me. So I got that entrée there.

In my early days in NAAFA I was writing for the welcome packet. I was also getting and placing some fat positive things in the Sunday *Los Angeles Times,* which had about a two-million circulation. On my day job as a tenure-track university assistant professor, those were seen as nothing because they weren't in a juried journal. But I was very involved in NAAFA, and doing all this free labor for them. And I was named the Black Community Fat Liaison.

This was long before social media, but I was promoting fat acceptance socially. The trouble was that at the social dances there would be one or two Black or Latino men who were basically "the studs." At least one of them, I later found out, was kind of an amateur gigolo. At the conference men were called fat admirers, but I don't even call those "stud" Black and Brown men fat admirers because it's not the *fat* that they admire so much as the *whiteness* that they want. Seemed to me that the couple of Black guys were after only the white women. It was all about the Western colonial gaze, white aspirational beauty standards minus the skinny. I love to dance, but the white men there who were fat admirers, none of them asked me to dance. None of them. And then the Black guys, they just wanted to dance with the white women and did stuff that was indicating they wanted to have intercourse with them right on the dance floor! And I'm looking for love, you know. I'm looking for respect. I'm looking for passion—sexual, emotional, intellectual. And the male attention was for *white* fat women.

It was really making me literally sick to my stomach. I watched these men sometimes leaving with women, perhaps to have sex, and coming back later to get another one to leave with. That's what those women wanted, or what some of them would settle for. And those white women, and legions since, seemed to be thinking, "Well, this is the way all Black men are." That's not true! That's so untrue! And I hated seeing things go down that way.

I finally was so fed up on the third night of the LA convention that I just left. As I left, this one Black guy finally came after me. Maybe he had gotten all his white pigeons by the third night. He would've gone to my room with me, but no friggin' way would I have done that. *And* I still lived in LA and I was commuting from home to save money. He said he lived in LA too, so I did give him my phone number. I thought outside of the convention setting he might be different. I found out later that he didn't have his own place. He was full-time couch surfing, and the women he'd met at NAAFA dances around the country would send him money. And he would work them. And they would let him, until they got tired of that. Then I found out that NAAFA had paid his way to the conference! And I thought, *I'm working for them. I'm the liaison, and I'm paying my own way from the little money I have, but they're giving him a free ride?*

When I found out all this stuff I stopped seeing him and stopped talking to him, because he just became disgusting to me. But then I'm at the next NAAFA conference in Chicago, and he's there! I wanted nothing to do with him, and he kept getting right up under me. He tried to grab my breasts and my butt at the pool party. Then when I left, he tried to get in the elevator with me. He wouldn't let me get in the elevator without him. He held the door open. He got in and I got out, and I got back in and he got back in. I waited for another; he waited, too. I tried to walk away. He followed. I didn't want to get caught in a stairwell with him. So I called hotel security and they came and got him, and let me get on the elevator by myself. They were two Black men security guards who came and helped me. Instead of saying, "Oh, he's just being a guy," they came and helped me. And they said, "If he bothers you at all, you let us know."

If they hadn't been there, I thought maybe he would have raped me. It was a horrible feeling. It was frightening.

NAAFA had a clear, very strict conference code of honor about what you do and do not do. NAAFA was way ahead of the curve on asking for good sexual consent, each step of the way. When I got back to LA, I reported what he did to me. The board had a complaint process, and the person was supposed to be banned from conferences, and the organization, if they'd violated the code of conduct. I had proof—many witnesses. This was before email, so it was a longer and more difficult process—typing up a letter, making copies, sending the letter, making sure someone signs for it, and so forth. And I had to keep reminding them that I was waiting for an answer. I kept urging them. And finally they sent me a letter that said, "We find that you have no grounds." Basically, you know, your complaint is nothing. This was horrible! Later, a sweet but powerless insider told me this: "The board decided that they valued a Black fat admirer much more than a fat Black woman member. They know their audience." That cut me to the core. I left NAAFA after that, for a long time. I didn't come back to it until the last few years, and only then because you (Tigress Osborn), as a then-lead board member, now executive director, were so kind and encouraging.

Around that time there were a couple of fat women magazines run by fat white women. One of those owner/editors had a Horatio Alger story. I think that with only a high school education she started and even ran the magazine from her kitchen table. That was back when you couldn't produce a glossy, professional print magazine on your home computer, or send it to Kinko's, or anything like that. She learned about what I was doing in NAAFA. She found me in Los Angeles, at my home number. She also found out that I was a PhD, an assistant professor at that point, also writing about fatphobia for the *Los Angeles Times*, *Los Angeles Herald*, and other places. I was also working, leading art and spiritual, ceremonial, fat-positive circles and workshops for the Alcoholism Center for Women. They used to have this incredible prevention program. And any woman who had had major trauma in their life, the ACW considered at risk for alcoholism.

The magazine publisher had learned about all that, and she said, "I want you to write a series for me." I asked, "How long?" She said, "Oh, as long as you want! I don't care how long it is. I'll cut them up and we'll pace them out over a year." I wrote them that way. She wasn't gonna pay me anything. But I volunteered because it would get out in this slick-covered magazine that had big women in it. So I did all this work. I sent her the first three articles in the series she had invited me to write. In fact, that she had insisted I write! And I did all this work when I was supposed to be focusing my energy and efforts on juried journal research to get tenure, so I wouldn't get fired from the universi-ty—"publish or perish."

When she got the articles, she called me and said, "These are terrible. This is not what Black fat women experience." This white woman told *me* that this is not what Black women experience. She said, "They're happy to be fat and the Black men love them fat!" What I had written had a lot of data and research, as well as personal experience, in the article. I said, "Well, where are these happy, fat Black women that you've seen? They're not at NAAFA. Where are they?" And she said she had seen fat women going to church, on their way to church with the big hats, wearing bright-colored clothing—that was it. That was her "proof" that my own lived experience as a fat Black woman, and my research with other women, was wrong.

Later, that magazine would print articles where they would advise white women to go into Black and brown communities to get those men because those men "love fat women." That was the magazine's advice to their readers, and that was their wrong and predatory take on Blackness. She said that my story was worthless because it wasn't accurate, because she *knew* how easy it was for Black women who were fat. That's all she wanted to hear.

Years later, I was a member of the Association for Size Diversity and Health, the old ASDAH, which is different from the ASDAH of today. As it had been with NAAFA, everyone was so happy at first to have a fat Black woman par-ticipating, because it made them feel better—made them feel that they weren't racist. I was able, through a lot of hard work and sacrifice, to be there, able to meet with them and do things for them and spend time with them.

ASDAH had a very active listserv group on Yahoo at that time, so that'll tell you the era. We had trouble with racism and misogynoir. For instance, when one person had put up Meghan Trainor's "All About That Bass" video, saying that this was a wonderful fat lib, fabulous HAES example—when I saw it, I said, very gently and respectfully at first, "This is problematic." I talked about the misogynoir, the colorism, that all the women were all smaller fats, *if that*. I said this, and then the thin white person who had posted it basically responded, "You're wrong. I still like it. I don't care about any of that." And then others started piling on me.

As this hostility continued, I gave the example that I described here, about the magazine publisher who decided that because she saw some Black women dressed up going to church on Sunday, all fat Black women face no fatphobia, or discrimination, or harassment. One of the men on the listserv, who had been an encouraging fat ally in NAAFA and who does so much good work in the movement, told me that he knew the editor of this magazine, that she wasn't racist, and instead, I must have written a crappy article. These white HAES experts on the listserv—none of whom had been a professional multimedia journalist, who had not earned PhDs as a Black woman, etc.—just started beating down on me about what a bad writer I must have been for the magazine editor to have rejected my work. And I was like, *wait, wait, wait—I've been doing academic and popular writing, getting fat lib stuff out there, national awards, university teaching, social action. Why you gonna go there?* Back then, no one intervened on my behalf. In today's ASDAH, I think I would have way more support on that issue.

I'd also like to talk about PCA, the Pop Culture Association, because I talked about ASDAH and I talked about NAAFA. PCA is an academic organization. In the fat studies area ethics, nothing that is accepted for conference papers can talk about intentional weight loss, or use the O-word. A Black man at the academic institution where I was teaching told me about PCA's fat studies area and gave me the gift of *The Fat Studies Reader.* And I was like, *Wow, I'm not alone.* When I got to the PCA fat studies part of the conference, it was so wonderful to be around my fat people. However, the racism was way worse when I first got there.

And the *Black* studies area at PCA—at least the people I met and the people I proposed my papers to—thought I was crazy. They weren't seeing any intersection; in fact, they were only acting like it's a shame. It's a shame to be Black and fat, and they didn't want to deal with me.

In fat studies I was also a Black woman fighting the whole misperception that Black women don't have to deal with sexism because we're Black. I was shouted out, shouted at, and shouted down so many times, because I would speak up when they would make these blanket statements that were not true for fat Black women, not statistically and certainly not in my very broad and long experience.

Yet unlike Black studies, *fat* studies accepted my papers. One year Crystal Newman, a fat Black University of Louisville counseling psychology MEd student, founder of Fat Positive Louisville, presented on racism in that organization and resourcing groups such as Standing Up for Racial Justice to address anti-Blackness in fat lib spaces. I intervened in support of Crystal when a white woman audience member kept insisting that racism in fat studies is a non-issue and didn't matter. Suddenly not only were a couple people turning around in their seats screaming at me, but one woman got up and called me a Black bitch as she walked out! And nobody, nobody, did anything. People stood there. People acted like it never happened. They just went on to the next panel.

One woman, only one woman, came to me later and said, "Are you okay?" I was not, and I told her so. She wrote about it later and sent me what she wrote because she thought it was so supportive of me. But her attempted support was also very hurtful. She was trying to be helpful, but she had experienced me through her own stereotype of the "strong Black woman" who can endure anything, pain-free. She talked about how it didn't faze me a bit and how I "took it in stride." And I said, "You know, I was messed up *for days* afterward."

I was going to leave PCA. Whenever I was hurt in these spaces no one wanted to say anything, because administration wasn't saying anything, and they didn't want to get in bad with administration. Or they would come to me afterward and whisper something when no one saw them with me, because God(dess) help them if they should be seen as an ally to me. A turning point for me was when Laura Jennings, PhD, of the University of Illinois Urbana-Champaign, presented a beautiful paper about why fat studies needed diversity. It's not published anywhere, but I wanted her to publish it. She said she just had her notes and an outline, and I said, "Send *that* to me! I need it—I need to sleep with it under my pillow. I need to send it to everyone! I need to bring copies to any conference I go to!" She's not in academia anymore. She's writing novels. But she told people, "E-K has done all this work. She's a great researcher; she's a great human being. If we don't shape up, not only is she going to leave, but we won't be able to bring others next year." I decided to try again. I've tried again with many fat community spaces.

People have asked why I have given these organizations, these fat community spaces, another try. "Why don't you just do your own thing, start your own organization?" I felt like I wanted to, but I was often tapped out emotionally, energy-wise, and even financially. It's difficult. My whole life has been do-it-yourself. I don't want to have to do *this* all by myself, too. I want fat lib and HAES spaces to do better. I want social-justice-oriented folks everywhere to do fat positive intersectionality better.

That's the purpose of my book, *On Fat and Faith: Ending Weight Stigma in Yourself, Your Sanctuary and Society.* I believe in taking a rest when you have to. And so I've taken breaks from these organizations and other social justice spaces at times because I needed to. People denigrate the term "licking your wounds," but you gotta do something for your wounds! Because it *is* wounding.

Being a Black woman in these orgs has been wounding. But I have given these fat lib organizations another chance because they're fighting upstream just to say that fat folks are not crap, that we deserve some kind of decent healthcare, that we are worthy of help and intervention and rest at *any* weight. Talking about racism in these spaces has been difficult but necessary. It has cost me. I didn't get the political boost and the gigs and the acceptance I could have had, even in size acceptance and fat lib, because I have been so frank about racism. Others have appeased white folks, but I have not. But I *have* always provided a path through, a way for white folks and for all folks to unlearn some of the poison they know and learn some of the antidote they need to know. It's a path that requires work. I'm not going to just bless them, like, "OK, now you have no racism! You're wonderful. Not a racist bone in your body, not a twitch of misogynoir in your top!" I won't do that. It requires work.

THE CASE FOR FAT STUDIES

ESTHER ROTHBLUM

Transcribed from the webinar
"Critical Fat Studies: From the Academy to the Community,"
March 4, 2022, moderated by Harriet Brown, Syracuse University,
Newhouse School of Public Communications.
Sponsored by a 2022 CUSE Grant,
Newhouse School of Public Communications,
Department of Nutrition and Food Studies,
and the Fat Studies Working Group.
(Edited for clarity and length.)

I WANT TO BEGIN WITH SOME TERMINOLOGY, which I think many of you may be familiar with. In English, many medical terms are based on Greek and Latin. If you think of any illness, disease, medical procedure, the name is usually a Greek or Latin word. When groups organize, they often take the original word like "homosexual" and replace it with something shorter and more informal, like "gay." Sometimes they even recreate or use a word that has been used against them, like "queer." Similarly, the word "obesity" is based on Greek, and as groups organized, they began to reclaim the word "fat." In the *Fat Studies Journal*, we always put the terms "obese" or "obesity" into quotation marks, and we prefer "fat." I also want to point out that the words "overweight," "underweight," and "normal weight" assume that there is this normal weight that everybody would be if they ate the same and exercised the same. That is just not true. If you took 100 babies, gave them all the same amount of food and same amount of exercise, they would grow up to have very different body sizes. So I'm going to be using the term "fat."

Fat studies: In our introduction to the *Fat Studies Reader*, we defined it as "in the tradition of critical race studies, queer studies and women's studies, fat studies is an interdisciplinary field of scholarship marked by an aggressive, consistent, rigorous critique of the negative assumptions, stereotypes, and stigma placed on fat and the fat body." In this field, it advocates respectful treatment of people, regardless of size. It asks why we oppress people who are fat, and who benefits from that oppression, which I think is very interesting, and argues that weight, like height, is a human characteristic that varies across any population. In that regard, fat studies resembles other academic disciplines that question discriminatory practices based on race, ethnicity, gender, age, and so on.

What I'm going to be talking about today is the academic part of fat studies, the history of fat, and the intersection of fat with gender, race, income, and sexuality. And I'm going to try to focus on the questions I always get asked: "But aren't they unhealthy?" and "Why can't they just lose weight?" And then I'll end with talking about publishing in the field of fat studies. I'll talk a little bit about my own research on weight and stigma, the anthology *The Fat Studies Reader*, and other work by fat studies scholars.

What got me interested in fat studies was back in 1983, I was at a conference and the performance group called Fat Lip Readers Theatre was performing. I had been told by well-meaning colleagues not to study what was then called "weight stigma." People said, "You'll never get a job" and "but aren't they unhealthy," that kind of thing. So when I heard this group perform, I knew this was going to be a big part of my life. Much later, they put out a VHS tape called "Nothing to Lose."

I want to point out that this is not a new field of study, so I'm going to review what was around in the 1980s in what is now called fat studies. There were books called *Shadow on a Tightrope: Writings by Women on Fat Oppression*, *The Fat Black Woman's Poems*, *Transforming Body Image: Learning to Love the Body You Have*, and *The Dieter's Dilemma: Eating Less and Weighing More: The Scientific Case Against Dieting as a Means of Weight Control*. These were some of the early books that I remember reading. I was also very influenced by the work of Susan and Wayne Wooley, who were at the University of Cincinnati Medical School. I point this out because some of the earliest research on fat studies came out of health and medicine, which might seem counterintuitive, but often it was medical professionals who understood that people were not losing weight; they could lose weight, but they would put it back on, and there were a lot of problems with the so-called health risks related to weight.

I also want to put this in a larger context, that fat studies is very much a field that affects women, although of course, it also affects men and children. In 1986 Susan Brownmiller wrote a book called *Femininity*. In this book she argues that across historical time, and across the world, there have always been ways that women are supposed to look and act. If you look at old drawings, and more recently, old photographs, women look very different across cultures but there's some similarities. She says that women are expected to look and dress in ways that immobilize them. These constricting norms are thought to be the invention of women themselves, whether this is wearing high heels or corsets. Without conformity to these norms, women cannot marry or function in society. The fashion exaggerates the smallness of a feature that is already smaller in women than in men. Women typically have smaller feet than men, and yet they're supposed to have very tight shoes or high heels. Women typically have smaller waists than men, and yet are supposed to wear corsets, and women typically weigh less than men. And the medical establishment endorses the practice as health promoting, while at the same time treating large numbers of women for medical complications resulting from the practice. And so hopefully you can also see how weight fits into these characteristics as well.

Also, I want to mention Mary Daly, who is a feminist theologian, and among her numerous books, she wrote a book in 1984 called *Pure Lust: Elemental Feminist Philosophy*. She talks about what she called "plastic" and "potted" passions. Plastic passions are things we are not born loving, but we are told have high status, like certain clothing designers, for example. Potted passions refer to the fact that women are allowed to do things in very, very small spheres. If you put a plant in a very small flowerpot, it cannot grow any larger than that flowerpot. It's constricted.

I want to give you an example of how I see Mary Daly's work being applied. A book was reviewed in the *New York Times Book Review* in 2008 called *The Day I Ate Whatever I Wanted*. On the back cover it says, "What would you do if you could do whatever you wanted for just one day? Every now and then don't you wish you could do something impulsive, like eat an entire pint of ice cream, or call an old flame out of the blue? Or tell your mom what you really think? In *The Day I Ate Whatever I Wanted*, women are rebelling, kicking up their heels and finally breaking free." Now, first of all, notice the book is called *The Day I Ate Whatever I Wanted*, not *The Month* or *The Rest of My Life*. And what do you do if you could eat whatever you want? You eat a pint of ice cream and yell at your mother. This is a great example of potted passions. Do you do something about antiwar activism? Do you dismantle the patriarchy? No, you focus on a very small thing. That is what women are allowed to do.

Also in 1981, Kim Chernin wrote a book called *The Obsession: Reflections on the Tyranny of Slenderness*. And she has this quote: "In this era, when inflation has assumed alarming proportions and the threat of nuclear war has become a serious danger, when violent crime is on the increase and unemployment a persistent social fact, five hundred people are asked by the pollsters what they fear most in the world, and one hundred ninety of them answer their greatest fear is 'getting fat.'"

So let me talk about the history of fat. In *The Fat Studies Reader*, Laura Fraser wrote about the fact that from the 1880s to the 1920s, in the U.S., the image of fat as pleasant and prosperous began to change. People had to do less to produce food, the U.S. economy switched from being mostly agricultural to being mostly industrial, and there was a huge wave of immigration. People of Northern European descent, who tended to be taller and thinner, wanted to distinguish themselves physically and racially from immigrants, who tended to be from Southern Europe and therefore shorter and heavier. Fitness was a sign of morality. And the medical profession switched with great difficulty from advocating weight gain to advocating weight loss. So again, this is kind of a more recent historical trend.

Now the 1960s, which usually refers to 1968 to 1972, was a time of liberation movements, particularly the civil rights movement. Out of that came the gay liberation movement and the women's liberation movement. Bill Fabrey in 1969 founded NAAFA, the National Association to Advance Fat Acceptance, which still exists. There was also a group of women in Los Angeles who formed the Fat Underground. They wrote what they call *The Fat Liberation Manifesto*, written by Judy Freespirit and Aldebaran, in 1973. *The Fat Liberation Manifesto* was based on *The Communist Manifesto*, and had the phrase "Fat people of the world unite, you have nothing to lose."

Currently, and this should not be a surprise to anyone, there is a tremendous obsession with thinness in Western nations, especially for girls and women, and there's a rise in eating disorders. And this is a really interesting area to me, because if you are studying racism or sexism or ageism people are reluctant to say they are racist or sexist or ageist, even on anonymous questionnaires, but they will tell you they hate fat people. In other words, it's still an area where it is appropriate to discriminate quite openly, rather than in a more coded way.

I also want to point out that the U.S. likes to fight wars, for instance, in Afghanistan and Iraq, and there's a war on cancer. And so in 1995 the Surgeon General at the time declared "War on Obesity." Again, it's important to follow the money. The War on Obesity was funded by a number of weight-loss, dieting companies.

Weight rose in the U.S. in the 1990s, but in the first decade of 2000 it remained the same. According to Katherine Flegal, who works for the Centers for Disease Control, the weight for boys, girls, men, and women was pretty much the same. What is usually not mentioned when people talk about changing weights is that we are living so much longer. We are outliving our grandparents by almost 20 years, or a whole generation.

I also want to bring up the vast power of the pharmaceutical industry in this country. If you're putting out a drug, let's say to treat cholesterol, it would help if more people had high cholesterol; you would make millions more in profits. So what do you do? You argue that the cutoff for what is high cholesterol should be lower.

A lot happened here in the 1990s. First of all, body mass index, BMI, for overweight changed in 1998, from 27 down to 25. Overnight, over 30 million people went to bed "normal weight" and woke up "overweight." The glucose threshold for diagnosing diabetes went from 140 down to 126, which meant there were 1.7 million new cases of diabetes. Also, this new category of "prediabetes" started, which was defined as 110 and then went down by 2003 to 100. The threshold for high blood pressure went from 160/100 down to 140/90, resulting in 13.5 million new cases of hypertension. And then this new category of "prehypertension" was defined as 120 over 80. The cholesterol threshold went from 240 down to 200, resulting in 43 million new cases of high cholesterol.

People often say to me, "Well, isn't this based on science?" If your blood pressure, glucose, or cholesterol goes way up, you're going to probably have health problems, but what is subjective is the cutoff. Think about this: at Syracuse University, the admissions committee probably has a certain grade point average below which they will not take a student even if they're the daughter of the president, or a varsity athlete, but that cutoff is subjective. Every university has a slightly different one. They don't tell you what it is, but it's there. The cutoff itself is subjective. You might even say "Well, what's the problem with giving everybody cholesterol drugs from birth or at age 10?" The problem is that these drugs have side effects. A drug for diabetes was causing heart risks. And of course, Lipitor, the most commonly prescribed drug for high cholesterol, also has a lot of negative side effects.

One more thing about health that I want to talk about is mortality. I know it's probably a beautiful day out there. But I have to warn you again that everybody will die; the mortality rate is one per person. When mortality rates go down, if you read about that, that doesn't mean that some people have eternal life. And healthy countries have high rates of cardiovascular disease and cancer. I just want to repeat that: healthy countries have high rates of cardiovascular disease and cancer. Why? Because they have people who live to an old age. When people die of infant mortality, war-related deaths, natural disasters, accidents, malnutrition, and infectious disease, they are not going to live to an old age. That means that cancer and cardiovascular disease are the major causes of death in healthy countries. If you read something in the media like "Nepal has an increase in cancer," that's actually good news; it means that people are not dying at a younger age. Also, because cancer and cardiovascular disease are the two most common ways of dying, that means that if you cure cancer, let's say breast cancer is cured, then people are going to die of something else. If somebody has died in their sleep, it doesn't mean they've died of sleep.

I am very intrigued by how few fat people have organized, so, again, those of you here are really in the vanguard of that. My university has probably 15 organizations for students who are LGBTQ+, which is wonderful. There's a Pride Center, a Queer Student Union, a gay fraternity, a lesbian sorority, a faculty group, lavender graduation, LGBT studies, and so on. And yet, I would argue that on our campus 80% of students, especially women, feel bad about their bodies or feel too fat, and there isn't a single organization about that. How come? Well, I think fitness is one of the major criteria determining physical attractiveness in the U.S. It's difficult for women to violate appearance norms; they are not trivial. Fat people, especially women, tend to be poor in the U.S. and have less political power. Fat people are blamed for their weight. Most people believe that diets are effective if the dieter has willpower. And I think most importantly, a multibillion-dollar economy would collapse if people stopped focusing on their weight, including the diet soda industry, the diet cookbook industry, the diet food industry, the number of people who join fitness clubs to lose weight, and so on.

Regarding the creation of fat studies: Marilyn Wann says she was not the first to use the term, there was somebody before her, but I think she was the first to write about it. She wrote a book, *FAT!SO? Because You Don't Have to Apologize for Your Size.* Fat studies has made tiny inroads in the academy. The Popular Culture Association and the National Women's Studies Association have fat studies groups, and the Association for Women in Psychology has a size acceptance group.

What can we do to throw our weight around? I would urge you to read original research articles about weight, not the media summaries. Follow the money. As Rachel Maddow, the newscaster, has said, "If you're not scared, they're not making money." Speak out about oppression. It's not okay to discriminate against any group based on appearance. Ask ourselves and other people what we would be thinking and talking about if we weren't focused on weight loss and dieting. Follow the lead of other civil rights movements and organize.

And of course, I want to talk about submitting your scholarship to academic journals, not just the journal *Fat Studies,* which I edit. I want to say, you can see in the last three volumes, just the last three years, we've published articles from authors from many different disciplines. This is really an area you can do in many different disciplines. And also, we've published research from people in many different countries. Additionally, *Fat Studies* does book reviews, and in the last three years we've included 27 book reviews of new fat-affirmative books, focusing on such topics as the intersection of fat and the Black body, cultural history, embodiment, girls of color, health, Islam, media, medicine, memoirs, motherhood, politics, psychotherapy, rhetoric, social justice, television, and yoga. There's a lot of books out there that are fat affirmative.

And finally, as Marilyn Wann has said, "Weight discrimination will continue to thrive so long as efforts to end it focus on changing people's bodies, rather than changing people's minds."

Thank you very much.

The video of the entire excellent presentation
"Critical Fat Studies: From the Academy to the Community"
can be found at https://www.youtube.com/watch?v=4sBhc2dQdl4&t=66s

MAUDSLEY PARENTS, WEIGHT STIGMA, AND DIET CULTURE

HARRIET BROWN

SOMETIME IN THE SUMMER OF 2006 a small group of like-minded mothers met online. We lived up and down the East Coast of the U.S., and came from a range of backgrounds and situations, but we had two crucial things in common. Each of us had a child with anorexia nervosa. And each of us had realized that the usual treatments for eating disorders were not helping, were in fact hurting our daughters, and that something different was needed.

That something different was a relatively new (in the U.S.) treatment protocol known, variously, as the Maudsley method, the Maudsley approach, and Family-Based Treatment (FBT). Each of us had found our way to some version of FBT and either had used it or was still using it to facilitate her daughter's recovery. Laura Collins was one of the first to come across FBT and had written a book, *Eating with Your Anorexic*, that described her family's experiences. I'd stumbled on that book in the library one night early in my daughter's illness, and FBT immediately made more sense to me than the treatment that had been recommended to us.

Traditional eating disorders treatment then and still sometimes now relied on a psychodynamic approach, where patients were encouraged to develop insights about the causes of their eating disorders and to use those insights to help themselves recover. Families were believed to cause eating disorders, so they were excluded from treatment and recovery; providers often prescribed what they called a "parentectomy," where even young patients were encouraged to separate themselves emotionally, if not physically, from their parents.

Much of this approach grows out of the work of Hilde Bruch, an American psychiatrist and psychoanalyst who, according to Wikipedia, was "known foremost for her work on eating disorders and obesity," which pretty much says it all. EDs and "obesity" were and still are seen as analogous disorders, two sides of the same illness. Both have been viewed as issues of personal responsibility, lifestyle choice, laziness, and vanity. Those perceptions have hobbled the field of eating disorders treatment and research, have contributed to the primacy of diet culture, and have literally hurt and even killed people in larger bodies.

The relationship between weight stigma and eating disorders is fairly clear, once you let yourself see it. In our culture, anorexia nervosa often manifests as a fear of fat—both dietary and body fat—and often involves distorted thinking and compulsions focused on getting and staying thin. People with anorexia literally can't see themselves as they really are, and usually aspire to levels of thinness that would be fatal. While anorexia has strong genetic and neurobiological roots, its form is clearly associated with our cultural obsessions around thinness and unrealistic body ideals. (Joan Jacobs Brumberg's book *Fasting Girls* takes a fascinating look at how eating disorders presented during the Middle Ages, when holiness rather than thinness was the aspirational ideal.) Research and my own experiences tell me that many of us have internalized a terror of fatness, and many of us build our lives around that fear. People with anorexia think and say many of the same things the rest of us do when it comes to bodies; the difference is that they are compelled by the disease to take those thoughts and behaviors to extremes.

Weight stigma is also pervasive among people who treat eating disorders—unsurprisingly, since they're human beings who live in this culture, too. And many providers have a history of or still suffer from eating disorders themselves. I remember one of my daughter's doctors telling her, "Don't worry, I won't let you get fat," a comment that reinforced her anorexia-driven fear of weight gain and so impeded rather than facilitated her recovery. Here was a doctor we trusted validating her terror of fatness, so it must indeed be something to fear and avoid.

I'd been aware of weight stigma before this, of course, but like many women I struggled to see it as a societal or institutional issue, instead blaming myself for gaining weight and for any negativity that came my way when I wasn't thin. Parenting my daughter through anorexia opened my eyes to weight stigma as a much bigger societal problem. In the months when my daughter was at her sickest, for instance, when she looked like a concentration camp victim, friends and strangers would stop her on the street to compliment her. "You could be a model!" they'd crow. "What's your secret?" These interactions disgusted and enraged me. They also made it stunningly clear just how disordered the entire culture was when it came to bodies and weight. Once my daughter began to gain weight and looked healthier—once she started wearing sizes over a 00—the compliments abruptly dried up.

But I couldn't unsee reality. As that small group of parents created a non-profit, Maudsley Parents, to support families and disseminate better information and research on eating disorders, I went down the rabbit hole of weight and health, spending hours reading scientific literature, hoping to better understand the relationships between them. The more I dug in, the more I realized that the assumptions I'd made for so long—that thinness is always better than fatness, that fatness is unhealthy and will kill you prematurely—were for the most part not supported by the evidence. I also began to see how those assumptions shaped the research itself as well as the ways in which the media presented those findings. I reported a series of stories for the *New York Times* on weight stigma and related issues, and to my horror (though by this point I was no longer surprised) they got enormous pushback from readers and media commentators. A 2010 story I wrote, "For Obese People, Prejudice in Plain Sight" (I didn't write the headline!), garnered more than 800 reader comments; many were variations on the trope "Eat less and exercise more and you won't be fat!" but put much more crudely and judgmentally. "We could all use a little anorexia!" was another popular comment. My in-box began to fill up with hate email about how I was killing people by telling them it was OK to sit on the couch and eat bonbons all day, about how disgusting I was personally, and so on. It seemed like people couldn't let themselves question the assumptions and associations between weight and health they'd come to believe, even if that questioning reassured them. They couldn't let go of their own internalized bias.

I got similar responses to my 2015 book *Body of Truth: How Science, History, and Culture Drive Our Obsession with Weight—and What We Can Do About It*, which set out to illuminate the complicated connections between weight and health and help shift our cultural understanding of those connections. It puzzled me; I thought people would be happy to hear that they didn't have to beat themselves up about their weight every day, that being on a diet wasn't going to improve their health (to the contrary, usually), and that they could focus on health instead of weight in ways that were more achievable and more pleasant.

These reactions taught me just how deep that internalized bias and self-loathing goes, and how threatening it is when anyone questions it. The weight-loss industries' global worth is estimated at close to $4 billion a year, so there's a whole lot of money at stake. Late-stage capitalism is built on people's anxieties and insecurities. "Obesity" research is also a robust and growing scientific field. I've heard researchers say the way to score an NIH grant is to make sure your application includes something about "obesity" and you'll get funded. It's awfully hard to swim against such currents.

On a personal level, I came to understand that if you've spent years of your life denying yourself food, treating your body like an enemy to be conquered, forcing yourself to exercise painfully and religiously, of course you're not going to be too keen to hear that maybe you didn't need to do those things. Maybe, in fact, you'd be just as healthy, or healthier, if you'd spent your energy in other ways. I'm not surprised now when the haters start up.

The eating disorders world began grappling with its own fatphobia in the last decade or so, and more people within that space have become aware of how damaging their own and others' biases are. But those stigmas are still informing treatment, and that needs to change. They're still deeply embedded in the culture and in us, even in those of us who actively question them and reject them.

Maudsley Parents disbanded as a standalone organization in 2015, having helped thousands of families through arguably the toughest time in their lives. The four women at its core—Jane Cawley, Laura Collins, Ann Farine, and myself—all went on to other preoccupations. All the information we gathered, the resources and providers and FAQs, is still publicly available at www.maudsley-parents.org for anyone who needs it. The site is now supported by the Training Institute for Child and Adolescent Eating Disorders, which trains clinicians in FBT and other evidence-based treatments for EDs. The videos we created are also still accessible on the Maudsley Parents Vimeo channel.

In writing this history I've given a lot of thought to why Maudsley Parents dissolved. For one thing, there's a lot more information out there now about FBT and other kinds of treatments for eating disorders. Parents who look for it can find it now in a variety of places. FBT has become better known and understood in the last 16 years, as more researchers run protocols on a wider variety of treatments. The clinicians and parents who aggressively bashed FBT back then are quieter now, either because they're keeping their thoughts to themselves or because the evidence has become harder to dismiss. While there is no single treatment that will cure everyone struggling with an eating disorder, there are many more options now than there were when my daughter was sick.

The other reason, I think, is that parenting a child through an eating disorder, especially in a culture that worships thinness, is a grueling process, whatever the outcome. I still struggle with PTSD from that time. Writing this history, for instance, has stirred up a lot of anxiety, depression, and feelings of helplessness. I'm lucky; my daughter is now in her 30s, fully recovered and thriving. We're close now despite the challenges and conflicts of those years. I'm grateful for the solidarity and support I found with other families, and I still talk and email and even meet with parents who are going through the same nightmare now.

The work I went on to do around weight stigma has helped me grapple with some of that anxiety and made me feel a little less helpless. A few years ago I developed a course at Syracuse University, where I teach journalism, called "Fat & Feminism," which looks at the intersections between misogyny and weight stigma (among many other things). I get great satisfaction from helping young adults understand the cultural history of these realities and from giving them some of the tools they need to push back against them, to think critically about the status quo and reclaim some of their own power and autonomy.

I wish my daughter had had a course like that when she was younger. I wish all teens and young adults did; maybe it would spare them a little of the body image trauma so deeply ingrained in our culture. Maybe someday that will change. Maybe.

VARIATIONS ON A THEME
CHALLENGING WEIGHT STIGMA

NANCY ELLIS-ORDWAY

FOR AS LONG AS I CAN REMEMBER, I have been fascinated by the way humans use food to do things in addition to fueling our bodies. We celebrate, comfort, mourn, and gather with food. We maintain connections to ethnic and religious identities with food. We express creative artistry with food. During the course of my lifetime, I have seen enormous changes in individual and cultural attitudes about food.

When I was growing up in the late '50s and the '60s, the standard of beauty for women was well-rounded and full-figured. Weight loss programs were few and far between, and they exerted very little influence on the general public. When I started college in 1971, no one talked about "the freshman 15" because it was understood that 18-year-old kids are still growing. Sugar-free foods were rare and marketed to people with diabetes. There were, certainly, some people (primarily women) who were trying to lose weight, but they were in the minority, and weight loss was not a national obsession. That began to change over the next decade, and the increased idealization of thinness coincided with an increase in body dissatisfaction and disordered eating.

I earned a bachelor's degree in home economics, which included several courses in food and nutrition, followed by a master's in social work. It only made sense for me to track into eating disorders treatment. From 1985 to 1993 I worked at St. John's Mercy Medical Center in St. Louis on the ABtec (Anorexia Bulimia Treatment and Education Center) unit.

It may be hard to imagine, now, how limited our knowledge was about eating disorders in the mid-'80s. There were few resources, and some of those turned out to be less than helpful. Eating disorders were thought to be so rare that medical students were told, as late as the 1970s, that they might never see a case in their careers. Early treatment approaches were influenced by the now-outdated work of Hilde Bruch. She purported that early family dynamics caused both anorexia nervosa and obesity. Our understanding of the genetic, biological, and cultural effects came later.

In 1978 Steven Levenkron published the book *Best Little Girl in the World*, which was made into a movie in 1981. For many people, this was their first introduction to the idea that eating disorders could be a serious medical problem. Because she was a celebrity, Karen Carpenter's death from heart failure in 1983, linked to restricting and purging, brought more attention to the dangers of eating disorders. Even then, anorexia nervosa was often dismissed as a trivial problem that only affected over-indulged white teenage girls. A common reaction I used to get when telling someone that I worked with people with anorexia was, "Heh, heh, heh, I could use some of that for about six weeks," while patting their belly. (I guess it's a sign of progress that I can't remember the last time that happened.)

The American Psychiatric Association's *Diagnostic and Statistical Manual of Mental Disorders (DSM)* is the document that codifies and standardizes the categories of mental illness and distress. It is used by health insurance companies to determine whether and what kind of treatment they will cover. It also influences research and research funding. In the first edition, published in 1952, anorexia nervosa is listed under "psychophysiological gastrointestinal reaction," along with ulcers, heartburn, and irritable colon. The second edition, in 1968, listed it under "special symptoms not elsewhere classified" as an example of "feeding disturbances." Bulimia was not mentioned until *DSM III*, published in 1980, and the focus then was on bingeing behavior. The term was changed in *DSM III-R* in 1987 to bulimia nervosa, with more emphasis on purging behavior. Other changes at that time included the weight criteria for anorexia nervosa, which had been 75% of "ideal body weight" and was increased to 85%, which meant we could get people into treatment sooner. In addition, a "not otherwise specified" category was added, which broadened the criteria for what insurance companies could be expected to cover. It specifically listed purging without bingeing in a person who was not considered underweight. This change in criteria meant that we could expand treatment to persons who previously would not have had access because of insurance limitations.

I was working on the inpatient ED treatment unit in 1987, and the changes in the *DSM* were a big deal. I remember it clearly enough that it feels recent to me. We are still battling to have the *DSM* criteria be more inclusive so that those struggling with eating disorders can access treatment, and the battle has been going on for a long time.

Part of my job at ABtec was community outreach, which included talking with therapists outside of our setting. Even though there were very limited resources then, many of them seemed to think, "Well, I'm a therapist and I eat, so I should be able to treat eating disorders." This attitude, predictably, led to less-than-helpful treatment for many. It was particularly tricky when naturally slender therapists assumed that their own slenderness qualified them to give nutritional advice. It took a long time for the professional community to recognize that eating disorders treatment requires specialized skills and training. The debate about developing a certification for eating disorders therapists went on for years because there was no consensus as to what it should be, and limited evidence about what worked. Different groups promoted different conceptualizations and often struggled to find common ground.

One of the controversies that never seems to go away is the attempt to make eating disorders a subcategory of something else instead of recognizing them as a unique category of their own. I've seen articles trying to make the case that eating disorders are really a subset of obsessive-compulsive disorder, anxiety, depression, autism, impulse control disorders, or addiction. Most of these arguments conveniently ignore the influence of malnutrition on brain function, focusing instead on trying to treat the symptoms of the better recognized psychological diagnosis while neglecting the importance of restoring nutrition.

In particular, considering eating disorders as a type of addiction was and is problematic, dating back at least to the 1980s. My observations at the time were that 12-step treatment approaches for substance abuse were well established, often with 28-day inpatient treatment programs. This time limit apparently was linked to the fact that many insurance companies capped coverage at 28 days. Some of these programs, seeing a financial opportunity, retooled their treatment programs and marketed them as eating disorders treatment. The outpatient version of 12-step group treatment was and is Overeaters Anonymous, which focuses on weight loss.

One of these programs was The Rader Institute, which had a chain of treatment centers in cities across the country. At one of the National Anorexic Aid Society conferences in Columbus, Kelly Bemis was giving a keynote presentation called "'Abstinence' and 'Nonabstinence' Models for the Treatment of Bulimia," in which she outlined very clearly all the problems involved with using a 12-step approach with eating disorders. Dr. Rader was in the audience, and he got up and walked out part way through, followed by a dozen or more of his staff. It was very dramatic!

I think we are still dealing with the ramifications of the 12-step influence on treatment. Part of the way 12-step programs are designed is that most of the treatment providers have, themselves, a history of substance abuse and recovery. Of course, one of the problems with the addiction model is that it is based on "abstinence," which is easy to define for alcohol or other substance use, but impossible to define for eating disorders. We cannot abstain from food, and how can we determine abstinence when the behavior is subjectively defined, such as restricting or bingeing? While it may be possible to talk about abstaining from purging, this approach oversimplifies the complexities of the illness and the necessary treatment.

In a 12-step program, it is understood that treatment providers must maintain abstinence in order to be effective; lapses are recognized as potentially career-ending problems. How can that be applied to eating disorders treatment? An eating disorders therapist who is in their own recovery may be effective in part because of their own lived experience, but how "recovered" do they have to be? And who gets to decide? This is still a controversial subject and I don't have any answers, but I do wonder if part of the debate dates back to the early arguments about abstinence vs non-abstinence approaches to treatment.

We have so many helpful books and other print resources available now, but that has not always been the case. I used to recommend the works of Ellyn Satter to adults, even though they were written for parents of younger children, because she challenged the assumption that pursuit of weight loss was always unquestionably good. William Bennett and Joel Gurin's *The Dieter's Dilemma* was published in 1982 and proposed the (now widely accepted) idea of the "setpoint." At the time, it was a revolutionary concept. The book had a great deal of helpful information, but was not exactly focused on how to effect individual change. In 1988 Jane R. Hirschmann and Carol H. Munter published *Overcoming Overeating,* based on their groundbreaking work in their clinic. It was the first book that I knew of that was written for adults who wanted to change their relationship with food and give up dieting. Kathryn J. Zerbe's *The Body Betrayed: Women, Eating Disorders, and Treatment,* came out in 1993. *Big Fat Lies* by Glenn A. Gaesser didn't arrive until 1996. Meanwhile, other books about eating and weight concerns often had some good points but also carried a flavor of "If you just solve your emotional problems without turning to food, you, too, can be thin like the rest of us," and memoirs that were allegedly about recovery often read like "how to" manuals. I'm very grateful that we have so many more resources to choose from now!

In the early days when print resources were limited, conferences offered training and learning, but they were far from perfect. Usually the audiences were 90-95% female and almost entirely white, while the speakers on the stage were generally 80% or more male. In the mid '80s the medical field was still dominated by white men with advanced degrees who had been educated in the "medical model," which did not value the lived experience of the patient.

According to this medical model paradigm, for instance, just because someone had a baby, that didn't qualify them to be an obstetrician. Pushback about this devaluing of lived experience only began when people who were not white men began being admitted in greater numbers to medical school and other graduate programs, and it continues to this day.

I think it is important to remember how little we knew in those days. There weren't any "evidence-based treatment" approaches, because the work was still so new that no evidence had been accumulated yet. Sometimes the conference sessions got edgy. Once there was a treatment team from an inpatient unit presenting about their treatment model, which involved placing a nasogastric feeding tube into all their patients, regardless of diagnosis or nutritional status, on the day of admission and removing it on the day of discharge. Some members of the audience pointed out that this denied the patients the physical experience of regularly eating to fullness in order to address their fear of losing control. It was also a violation of autonomy. I remember feeling appalled, personally. Another time, a well-known researcher was presenting his findings from a study in which patients had been randomly assigned to different treatment protocols involving individual or family therapy, or a combination. Some members of the audience were incensed with him for not offering the treatment that seemed best based on individual evaluations. Researchers and clinicians do not always see eye to eye, another dilemma that continues to this day.

Conferences offered opportunities for networking as well as learning. I have a recollection of a "social hour" at the NAAS (National Anorexic Aid Society) meeting in Columbus, Ohio, and I was hovering on the fringe of a group of physicians who were comparing notes. One said something like, "I'm seeing high cholesterol levels in my malnourished patients with anorexia nervosa. Is anyone else seeing that?" It is now widely understood that the malnutrition seen in eating disorders can cause elevated cholesterol levels, but there was a time when no one knew that yet. I may have been present when it first became a topic of interest.

Part of my training as a social worker is the "person-in-the-environment" perspective, which includes understanding how individuals are affected by society and culture. As I learned more about eating disorders and their treatment, I became more interested in the way attitudes about body size influence the way we all interact with food. Although we didn't yet have the term "weight stigma," I realized that the idealization of thin bodies and the devaluing of large bodies was behind much of the dieting behavior that led to eating disorders in some and body dissatisfaction in many others. The dieting industry was finding increasing profit in pushing the narrative that higher weights were directly tied to poor health outcomes and that the only way to improve health was to lose weight. Various groups were pushing back against that paradigm, and I began to find them.

I met Claudia Clark at one of the Renfrew Center conferences, and she introduced me to the Show Me The Data email listserv. In the days before Facebook, listservs were a resource for like-minded people to connect and share information. Show Me The Data was started by Deb Burgard as a way to respond to those who unequivocally stated that being fat was bad for health. It is still a great phrase to use when someone makes that argument or tries to say that weight loss improves health: "Show me the data!" The group's primary focus, as I recall it, was on actual medical research that refuted the unacknowledged weight bias in the culture. It felt like a lifeline for me; by that time I was living in a small community with no local connections to experts in this field, and I would have been very alone without the listserv.

During the time when Lindo Bacon was writing their first book, they posted excerpts from it on the listserv. Many of us were very excited about it, to finally have so much information and wisdom all in one place. I, for one, was very eager for its publication. One of the last bits to be decided was the title. Lindo posted an assortment of possible phrases on the listserv and asked for input; this was followed by an animated discussion involving many posts, suggestions, and opinions. The members of the listserv essentially helped choose the title *Health at Every Size: The Surprising Truth About Your Weight.* When it was published, I finally had a book to recommend to clients, family, friends, and medical professionals that laid out the science in a way that was easily understood.

Some members of the Show Me The Data group met in Cleveland in 2006 for a conference/retreat that then became the origin of the Association for Size Diversity and Health, or ASDAH. The association later trademarked the phrase "Health At Every Size" to, hopefully, prevent it from being used by diet/weight loss programs. The source of the phrase goes back much further. I have a handout that I picked up at a conference, written by Frances Berg and Gail Marchessault, titled "Naming the Revolution: What should the nondiet paradigm be called?" This question was posed in April of 1999 in the *Healthy Weight Journal* and elicited quite a number of responses. One person mentioned hearing the phrase "health at any size" from Pat Lyons in 1992. That phrase was mentioned by several others, along with the acronym "HAAS." Other suggestions were "body wisdom," "good health for all sizes," "nondiet," "body size acceptance," "size diversity," "health-at-large," "fit and fat," "health centered paradigm," and "healthy at every size," along with a suggestion to replace "BMI/body mass index" with "body health index." There were comments addressing the pros and cons of the words "size" and "weight," but there seemed to be general agreement about including the word "health."

The idea was still to push back against the dominant narrative that weight loss was the key to health. We didn't have terms like "weight inclusive" or "weight neutral" yet, but the idea was the same, that individuals could improve health without pursuing weight loss. Of course, over time the conversation has become more nuanced and sophisticated, and we understand that there is no moral imperative to pursue health, and that those with chronic health conditions might feel excluded by the phrase, but back then the "weight equals health" paradigm was so entrenched and unquestioned that we had to start somewhere. While we have made progress, many conversations about weight neutrality are still met with "But what about their health?!?!?"

Jeanne Courtney summarized this nicely in a 2010 post on the ASDAH listserv, quoted in O'Hara & Taylor (2018):

> How many weight loss experts does it take to screw in a light bulb? Three. One to stand on the ladder and keep trying to screw a burned out bulb into a socket that doesn't fit, one to stand under the ladder and tell him he's doing a great job, and one to write a press release declaring that the three of them have discovered a revolutionary, completely safe and effective new way to screw in light bulbs. How many Health at Every Size experts does it take to screw in a light bulb? The light bulb is fine, the socket is fine, the switch is on, and the room is brightly lit, but it still takes several dozen Health at Every Size experts, with impeccable academic credentials, to publish independent studies proving that there is no need to change the bulb. And those three guys with the ladder still won't go away.[1]

I have another example of the way weight stigma has appropriated efforts to improve the health of fat people. I can't remember where I learned this; it was many years ago, but I think it is accurate.Somewhere I learned that Albert Stunkard, who began researching issues related to weight in the 1950s, suggested that we needed a separate branch of medicine called "bariatrics," which would specialize in treating people with larger bodies, the same way that pediatrics specializes in people in young bodies, geriatrics specializes in treating people in old bodies, and obstetrics specializes in treating people in pregnant bodies. He reasoned that medical care should be adapted for bodies of different sizes. Unfortunately the term "bariatrics" became associated with weight loss efforts, because it was and is assumed that the only treatment a fat body needs is to be turned into a thin body, even though pediatrics is not about turning children into adults nor is geriatrics about turning elderly people into middle-aged people. Medical care is compromised when it is not adapted for different populations. We know that body size can affect many medical interventions, from the size of blood pressure cuffs to the length of needles used to give Covid vaccinations to the effectiveness of emergency contraception. Maybe someday we will have a branch of medicine that focuses on the well-being of fat people without the effects of weight stigma, but it will need another name besides "bariatrics."

Pushing back against weight stigma happens on many levels, from individual to societal to political. There is a helpful analogy that I used in my book, *Thrive At Any Weight:*

> People who work in the field of public health often talk about upstream or downstream interventions and outcomes, referring to treating a problem versus preventing it. There are different versions of a story to explain this, and I would like to share mine.
>
> A group of friends were having a picnic one sunny afternoon on the banks of a river. Suddenly, someone said, "Look! There is someone in the water!" Sure enough, there was a person struggling against the current. The friends organized themselves and pulled the wet and shivering individual out of the flow, wrapped her in a blanket and asked, "What happened?" The reply was, "Someone pushed me into the water!" They looked out at the river and cried, "There is someone else! And another! And another!" Soon they all focused on pulling people out of the current. No one had time to go upstream to see who was pushing them into the river and make them stop.
>
> Weight stigma has pushed us all into the river. Promoting body insecurity allows the highly profitable weight loss industry to continue making money. Weight stigma distracts from other social concerns, such as racism, classism, sexism, and all other systems that promote a hierarchy of one kind of people as better than another. Weight stigma distracts from and interferes with efforts to promote a more fair and equitable society in which all people have access to health, security, and a better quality of life. Weight stigma is a medical issues, a public health issue, and a social justice issue.[2]

We have made much progress, and there is still a long way to go, In the early days, when people began literally dying from eating disorders, body dissatisfaction, dangerous weight loss interventions, and other effects of weight stigma, we were scrambling to pull them out of the water. It took time and effort to see the upstream influences like racism, transphobia, homophobia, economic policy, bias in research and medicine, and other systemic influences. As we move forward, we must address these dynamics at all levels of society to make ti safe for everyone to live in the bodies they have.

And we still need to pull people out of the water.

FOOTNOTES

1. O'Hara, L. & Taylor, J. (2018). What's Wrong With the "War on Obesity?" A Narrative Review of the Weight-Centered Health Paradigm and Development of the 3C Framework to Build Critical Competency for a Paradigm Shift. SAGE Open, 8(2), 1–28.

2. Ellis-Ordway, N. & Brown, H. (2019) *Thrive at Any Weight: Eating to Nourish Body, Soul, and Self-Esteem.* Praeger, p. 101–102.

TO TELL OR NOT TO TELL
A LOOK AT THE ISSUE OF
RECOVERED PROVIDERS IN
THE EATING DISORDERS FIELD

CAROLYN COSTIN

WHETHER OR NOT A THERAPIST with a personal history of an eating disorder should treat patients with eating disorders and disclose that history has long been a subject of debate. I have been at the forefront of this controversy since 1979, when I first started treating people with eating disorders and disclosed that I was recovered from my own.

I recovered from anorexia nervosa in the mid-1970s, and for the last 45 years I have been a therapist, clinical director, and author in the field of eating disorders, promoting the fact that being recovered from an eating disorder can be a significant asset when trying to help others with eating disorders recover. Over the last four decades I have trained countless clinicians and am now training eating disorders recovery coaches, providing special training and supervision for any provider who is recovered from their own eating disorder.

In this chapter I briefly review some history and literature on the topic of clinicians with an eating disorder past, explore the values and pitfalls of clinicians or coaches disclosing or not disclosing their history, the need to clarify terms in the field, define the word "recovered" in the eating disorders context, and delineate guidelines for recovered providers. A two-part article I co-wrote with Alli Spotts Lazar titled "To Tell or Not to Tell: Therapists with a Personal History of an Eating Disorder,"[1,2] has all the citations readers might want to further investigate regarding studies or articles mentioned in this chapter.

Despite what some may think about it, research articles and surveys show that a significant number of eating disorders treatment professionals have personally experienced an eating disorder, whether they disclose it or not. Early reports suggested about one out of three or four providers had an eating disorder history, while more recent reports indicate perhaps even higher percentages, even up to 55%.

Over the years, some have suggested that clinicians with eating disorders histories should not disclose this to clients, while others have suggested they should not even work with eating disorders clients, should be banned from doing so, or should be subjected to periodic eating disorders assessment tools, weight checks, ovary scans, and more, which I find disturbing.

Though this does not happen as often anymore, I have experienced colleagues in the eating disorders field tell me that:

- I should not share my history of an eating disorder.
- I should choose between being a recovered anorexic or an eating disorders therapist.
- I think I am better than other therapists because I am recovered.
- People who have had an eating disorder have no business treating eating disorders.
- No one is ever really recovered, so I could not be.

In 2003 the European Council on Eating Disorders debated the issue of clinicians with a personal eating disorders history; however, an agreement could not be reached. What are people so afraid of when it comes to this topic, and what keeps our field from some kind of reasoned consensus on this issue?

COMING OUT OF THE CLOSET BEFORE I KNEW I WAS SUPPOSED TO STAY IN

I always joke about the fact that I was "out of the closet" before I knew I was supposed to stay in. When I saw my first eating disorders client I told her I was recovered, and told her "If I recovered, so can you." It did not even cross my mind to keep it from her. Why would I not share this and give her hope? She recovered and referred another eating disorders client, whom I shared my story with, and she also recovered. I've been saying the same thing to all clients ever since. Referrals kept coming in and I was successfully treating eating disorders, thus I made a name for myself early in the eating disorders field, about four years before Karen Carpenter's death in 1983 acquainted the world with anorexia nervosa. As I started speaking out about eating disorders, going to conferences and using the term "recovered," colleagues questioned my self-disclosure. I was comfortable with my stance and responded with this question, "If you had been hit by lightning and a client came to you who had been hit by lightning, would you reveal it?" That is how unique it felt at the time.

Helping others, I realized that I had the unique value of having lived with a brain that was once hijacked by an eating disorder and then had successfully gotten back in control. I could explain to clients, as well as other clinicians, from a personal perspective the mindset of someone with an eating disorder. I could confront and challenge clients while empathizing in a deeply connected and personal way with the client's fear of giving up the disorder. I did not have to deal with the resistance that comes in the form of "You just don't get it" or "Unless you've been there, you can't understand."

To this day sharing my own recovery helps me establish understanding, rapport and trust, reduces shame, and instills motivation and hope. I can provide empathy as a survivor of an eating disorder and can challenge and persuade clients as someone who once did not believe I could change my behaviors or get well.

My fundamental bias is that it is in the best interest of clients to know that I am recovered. I have yet to find a reason to keep this from clients or why it would not be in their best interest to know. Now, though far less than before, I still get clients who say they have never heard they could be fully "recovered" and/or have never met anyone who was "recovered." My disclosure is often the first time clients get an up close experience that being recovered is even possible, which is sad and unfortunate. Imagine being treated for something and having no example of someone who has completely recovered from it.

I have no doubt that sharing my eating disorder history and serving as a role model and guide for others has been a huge aspect of my success as a therapist in the eating disorders field.

Over the last four and a half decades I have hired and trained countless recovered clinicians and now coaches, all the while receiving consistent reports from clients and families that working with a recovered therapist, dietitian, or coach was a significant factor in the treatment success. One early astonishing testimonial said, "The way I think about using a recovered provider is that I wouldn't go skydiving with someone who had not done it before and survived."

This made a big impact on me, and though I don't think you need to be recovered to be a good eating disorders treatment provider, I do think clients should be exposed to someone who is recovered as a part of their process.

My being recovered informed and guided my practice at a time when there was no other guidance available, no journals, no books, no Academy of Eating Disorders, and no eating disorders trained dietitians to help out. Gleaned from my own experience:

- I made up a detailed assessment asking about all kinds of eating, weight, food, purging and exercise behaviors.
- I asked clients to write everything they ate and circle what

they purged, and to write their thoughts and feelings before eating and or engaging in an eating disorder behavior. This is now a big part of what we call CBT (cognitive behavior therapy).

- I asked clients to bring food to sessions, and I ate with them and sometimes their families. This is now a part of FBT (family-based treatment).
- I had clients write what their eating disorder self was telling them to do, and then to write back from the part of them that would know what to say to someone else (their healthy self, or what DBT—dialectical behavior therapy— now calls Wise Mind).
- I had clients reach out to me rather than their eating disorder behavior, e.g., before engaging in a binge or purge. (I discovered this is similar to what 12-step sponsors do for addicts.) In the early days this would mean calling and leaving a message with my exchange service. I would call back and try to help them put a pause between the thought and the behavior and maybe even abstain altogether. Now this is accomplished through texting.
- I had clients leave a message when they accomplished things like adding a snack to their day.
- I weighed clients with their backs to the scale, and got them to give up the scale and the need to value themselves based on a number.
- I made grocery lists with clients, and even ate at restaurants with some of them.
- I asked clients all the good things their eating disorder was doing for them and did not make an enemy with that part of them, but rather worked to learn from it and integrate it back into their whole self so they were no longer split into two parts.
- I told clients not to refer to themselves as "anorexic" or "bulimic" or an "overeater" because this only concretized the label as an identity. And similarly, I did not refer to their eating disorder as a disease.
- I told clients they could be fully recovered from this—and that the eating disorder could not be more powerful than they are because they give it its power and they can take it back.

All these things came from my own lived experience and recovery; they are all things I still use today and all things I teach recovered providers to say and do.

THE DOWNSIDE OF NOT DISCLOSING

Clients often directly ask their eating disorders therapist whether they ever had an eating disorder. Not disclosing can cause problems. Andrea Bloomgarden, PhD and Mark Warren, MD are eating disorders providers who have been public about how, when they were treating eating disorders patients and actively withholding their own eating disorders recovery, a barrier was created that negatively affected their integrity and working alliance with patients. Countless providers have come to me and expressed the same sentiment. Furthermore, without disclosing, no guidance, supervision or support can be given.

WHAT RESEARCH SAYS ABOUT THE ADVANTAGES OF PROVIDERS WITH PERSONAL RECOVERY

Though there is little research on the topic, informal surveys and interviews point out that eating disorders patients feel that exposure to people with recovery—those who understood the illness or have recovered—was or would have been beneficial. In "Been There, Done That"[3] Craig Johnson and I wrote the first article on this subject, where we delineated both the advantages and disadvantages of clinicians with personal recovery. The advantages included:

- Empathy and trust
- Understanding, hope and motivation
- Shame abatement
- Greater license to confront
- Ability to frame the need to stop behaviors *while* dealing with underlying issues

Though there were some disadvantages (see next section), we concluded that the advantages outweigh the disadvantages, and thus "organizations need to acknowledge the useful contributions these clinicians can make to the field." Eleven years later another study by Warren, Schafer et al., using qualitative and quantitative methods, revealed many similar benefits of utilizing therapists with eating disorders histories. Two years after that, de Vos, Netten, and Noordenbos examined both patients' and clinicians' experiences of treatment when the therapist was a self-disclosing, eating disorder-recovered clinician. Of the 205 out of 357 patients who responded, 97% indicated that the experiential knowledge of recovered therapists was beneficial in the therapy. Advantages included: the patient's feeling attunement, acceptance and hopefulness, and the therapist's authenticity, and enhanced knowledge and insight into the eating disorder. Overall, 93% of the patients indicated that the therapy provided by a recovered therapist positively influenced their recovery. 100% of the responding therapists endorsed the same advantages as those reported by patients and additionally listed the following benefits: quickly bolstering therapeutic trust and cooperation in the working alliance, reducing fear and feelings of shame, providing a positive example, having high empathy, and motivating positive change.

POTENTIAL DISADVANTAGES OF CLINICIANS WITH AN EATING DISORDERS HISTORY

Along with potential benefits, a few articles point out potential risks, limitations and pitfalls that might arise when therapists have an eating disorders history. The most cited are: risk of relapse, countertransference, having narrow views of how recovery takes place, over-involvement or over-identification, boundary problems, and the provider being triggered.

It is important to note that most of these problems were listed as "potential" issues that might arise, rather than real experiences cited. To really assess "potential pitfalls" important questions need to be asked:

- Were the therapists really "recovered;" did they describe themselves as *recovered*?
- Did the therapists have two years of being recovered before working in the field?
- How many of these therapists kept their personal histories concealed from colleagues and/or patients?
- How many of these clinicians received guidance or supervision in how to appropriately use their history in their work?

I have worked with recovered clinicians and coaches in various treatment settings for over 40 years and developed strategies that significantly curtail not only the potential pitfalls but the relapse rate. I have found that when hiring/training those who are recovered there are four very important guidelines:

- Be open about hiring recovered staff, so that potential providers feel comfortable disclosing their personal history. This means you know up front and can then ask further questions and be thorough in your assessment of their suitability.
- When a clinician or coach discloses an eating disorders history, ask if they meet the definition of "recovered." (See

definition below.)
- Ask specific questions about their relationship with food and comfortability eating various foods, meals etc. with clients, and to identify any restrictions.
- Provide consistent training, guidance and supervision related to transference, countertransference, boundaries, and other best practices in terms of using one's lived experience.

Following these guidelines has proven successful in using recovered providers and resulted in only one known case of relapse out of 26 years of my running inpatient and residential programs, and only two relapses out of over 200 coaches who are in training or have been certified as an eating disorders recovery coach at The Carolyn Costin Institute to date.

DEFINITION OF TERMS

Part of the confusion and resistance to using people with lived experience in the eating disorders field is the problem with not knowing if someone is well enough to work with others. Various terms such as "recovery," "recovering," and "recovered" are all used, and how we define these terms is important and not just an issue of semantics. These terms can be confusing, misunderstood, and sometimes even misleading.

Early on in the eating disorders field, professionals and patients started applying the 12-Step program disease model of addiction, and corresponding language, to the treatment of eating disorders. 12-Step programs widely use the terms "recovery" and "recovering" in ways that are not so easily transferred to the eating disorders population. To say "I'm a recovering alcoholic" or "I'm in recovery from alcoholism" typically means the person is *not* drinking due to a lifelong disease/addiction in which they come to accept the fact that they can never drink again. These individuals must eliminate alcohol from their lives. A person with an eating disorder cannot eliminate food. When a person with an eating disorder history says "I'm a recovering anorexic" or "I'm in recovery from anorexia," what does the person actually mean? What and how are they doing with food and weight? Furthermore, being "in recovery" or "recovering" can be used to indicate any number of things such as: one is in residential treatment, has just discharged from a treatment program, or has been well and at a weight that is appropriate for them for 10 years. These terms are too vague to have any real meaning in terms of an individual's wellness status.

I believe we must use the term "recovered" to indicate that the eating disorder is completely gone. However, the eating disorders field has yet to come up with a concise and accepted definition of "recovered" that could be unifying and helpful to clients, practitioners, researchers, and caregivers alike.

DEFINING AND DETERMINING "RECOVERED"

Though there is no consensus, most people would likely agree that to be "recovered" from an eating disorder there must be an absence of clinically diagnostic behaviors. However, this alone is insufficient. What if someone's only symptom is purging once or twice every other week? Even though the person's behaviors would not meet diagnostic criteria, most could agree that calling such a person "recovered" would be incorrect. Likewise, a person who is abstaining from overt criteria while still restricting calories, fighting the urge to purge, weighing and body-checking multiple times a day, and is unable to eat with others or in restaurants, does not seem to be "recovered."

At some point in my career I knew it was important for me to define what I meant by the term. My definition, stated here, can be found in my book *8 Keys To Recovery From an Eating Disorder:*

> Being recovered is when the person can accept his or her natural body size and shape and no longer has a self-destructive relationship with food or exercise. When recovered, food and weight take a proper perspective in your life and what you weigh is not more important than who you are; in fact, actual numbers are of little or no importance at all. When recovered, you will not compromise your health or betray your soul to look a certain way, wear a certain size or reach a certain number on the scale. When you are recovered, you do not use eating disorder behaviors to deal with, distract from, or cope with other problems.[4]

I show this definition to clients and say, "That is where we are going." To anyone with an eating disorders history who wants to work with eating disorders I say, "Do you meet this definition and have you met it for at least two years?"

RECOVERED ENOUGH

Who gets to determine the "recovered" status of a provider? When is someone "recovered enough" to safely work with clients who have eating disorders?

Even if the field reaches a consensus on a definition of "recovered," how would we verify a recovered status? Could standardized measuring and monitoring happen? When substance abuse facilities hire individuals who identify as recovering alcoholics or drug addicts, drug testing can verify if the person is clean and sober or "using." There is no similar test to determine if a person is "using" their eating disorder symptoms. As previously mentioned, some have suggested that therapists with personal eating disorder histories be subjected to clinical eating disorder assessments and even ultrasound checks for ovarian size to determine if they are at a healthy weight. Without stooping to discuss the actual merit of this, would these tests be administered to *all* therapists who wish to work with eating disorders, or just those who say they once had an eating disorder? Anyone with an eating disorder history could avoid such testing by simply not disclosing.

Other suggestions have ranged from ongoing assessments of the recovered clinicians' relapse potential, how they conduct therapy, and a myriad of other "indicators." Some have recommended regularly assessing absence from work, inability to make decisions or cope in emergencies, seeking therapeutic relationships with colleagues, potential risks to patients, and potential to collude with the patients and their illness. It is noteworthy that with my extensive experience, I have not seen higher incidences of problems in any of these areas with people who are recovered from an eating disorder vs. those with no eating disorders history. It is perplexing that there is so much attention and caution on clinicians who have recovered from an eating disorder, but not for clinicians who have histories of depression, anxiety, obsessive-compulsive disorder, post-traumatic stress disorder, or some other diagnosis in their past. Why the overconcern about those with an eating disorder past while little to no attention is paid to other past diagnoses a provider might have?

The truth is we might not know if a provider who wants to work with eating disorders has an eating disorder past or is fully recovered from it, but we are in a much better position if we encourage and promote self-disclosure, thus allowing for further exploration and specific training and guidelines geared to using their lived experience in the most appropriate way.

GUIDELINES FOR AN EATING DISORDER PROVIDER WITH AN EATING DISORDER HISTORY

Recovered providers are uniquely suited to share personal perspectives on the journey of eating disorder recovery along with what it takes to be recovered, but guidelines for how best to accomplish this have not been officially established. Over the years, through trial and error, I developed my own guidelines that offer specific parameters and suggestions to help prevent relapse, avoid pitfalls and break down self-disclosure into appropriate, usable, hands-on practices, all of which have proven successful. To read about these in detail see the article "To Tell or Not to Tell Part 2."[2]

GUIDELINES

1. **Meet the definition of "recovered" for at least two years.** Providers need to agree to have been recovered for at least two years before working with eating disorders clients. (I use my own definition of "recovered" provided earlier.)

2. **Tell clients what you mean by "recovered" and how it might differ from other terms such as "recovering" or "recovery."**

3. **Focus self-disclosure on empathy, understanding, and "how" you got better.** Share specifics on how you got through things rather than specifics on why you got an eating disorder or details of your eating disorder behaviors.

4. **Never discuss horror stories of how ill you were or give detailed specifics of your eating disorder behaviors.** Let clients know you had a real, legitimate eating disorder without giving them details.

5. **Don't discuss numbers (weight, calories, miles run, laxatives taken, etc.).** Discussions involving numbers nearly always fuel competition and do not serve a purpose.

6. **Disclose information based on the client's issues that arise in therapy.** Share things when it matches something the client is dealing with or has mentioned.

7. **Disclose based on who you are disclosing to.** Take into account the client's diagnosis, age, cultural background, religious beliefs, gender identity, relationship status, and, of course, their basic sensitivities and personality traits.

8. **Don't discuss any limiting behavior you have regarding eating.**

9. **Be comfortable in your body.** Be prepared to deal with and respond to scrutiny about all aspects of your body.

10. **Accept that you are a role model, and be the best one you can be.** It is important to be a good role model at all times, even when you don't feel like it.

11. **Be prepared to deal with increased scrutiny about what you eat, how much you exercise and other behaviors.** Comparisons and scrutiny from clients should be expected and accepted.

12. **Be clear that recovery can mean many different things and take many different paths and phases.** Be careful about over-identifying with a client's story, or thinking they can heal how you did.

13. **Know your boundaries and how to explain them to clients.**

14. **Do not share things that make you uncomfortable.** You have to know *how* to say "no" when asked to disclose information you don't want to share.

15. **Check for feedback.** Ask clients about their experience of you as a recovered provider.

16. **Repair any disclosure that has gone wrong.**

17. **Get well-rounded training; don't go directly from having an eating disorder to treating eating disorders.**

18. **Have ongoing supervision where any issues can be discussed.**

CONCLUSION

Providers with a personal history of an eating disorder should be able to make their own decision about whether or not to work with eating disorders clients and whether or not to disclose their personal history. Some practice a "tell only when asked" policy, sharing only if asked by patients or colleagues. Some choose not to share at all, and some share as a routine part of their work. It's obvious by now that I feel strongly that recovered providers have something very important and unique that only they can offer. This does not mean that one has to be recovered themselves to be a good eating disorders clinician or coach, but it does mean that if someone is recovered they should not be discouraged from appropriately disclosing it and using their lived experience appropriately.

REFERENCES

1. Costin, C., Spotts Lazar, A. (2016) To Tell or Not to Tell: Therapists with a Personal History of an Eating Disorder, Part 1. *Gürze Eating Disorders Resource Catalogue.*

2. Costin, C., Spotts Lazar, A. (2017) To Tell or Not to Tell: Therapists with a Personal History of an Eating Disorder, Part 2. *Gürze Eating Disorders Resource Catalogue.*

3. Costin, C., & Johnson, C. L. (2002) Been there, done that: Clinicians' use of personal recovery in the treatment of eating disorders. *Eating Disorders,* 10(4), 293-303. doi:10.1080/10640260214506

4. Costin, C., & Grabb, G. S. (2012) *8 Keys to Recovery from an Eating Disorder: Effective strategies from Therapeutic Practice and Personal Experience.* New York, NY: W. W. Norton Company.

I Love You, Too
The Radical Work of
Susan C. Wooley

Carmen Cool

I'M SITTING HERE LOOKING at a piece of yellow legal pad paper that I've been holding onto for 35 years. I had once filled out a post-treatment questionnaire and my therapist at the time sent back a letter responding to what she heard, reflecting back to me where she saw me inside of my own recovery.

Written at the bottom in black pen, in her typically hard to read handwriting, it's signed, "I love you."

I remember the first time I read those words.

I remember that I smiled.

It was unexpected, and it moved something in me.

The letter was from Susan C. Wooley, PhD, a psychologist specializing in eating disorders. The field of psychology has become medicalized and sanitized in its boundaries, and so to many, it feels unprofessional or unethical for a therapist to say or write those words. But Susan was willing to be busted loving someone.

Let's go back. How did we get here?

Doorways

I have been a psychotherapist for 23 years, moving with the politic and commitment to body justice, anti-fat bias, and liberation. When I reflect on the experiences I've had in my own body in relation to my clients as an eating disorders clinician and activist, I think first about my experience with my eating disorders therapist when I was in treatment.

The people who change us, encourage us, and expand our work are doorways we pass through. The analysis I hold has been shaped by a vast number of teachers, therapists, writers, poets, and colleagues—all of whom I have been deeply impacted by. The person who first picked me up and sat me on this path was Susan Wooley: Psychologist. Researcher. Activist. Author. Teacher. Mentor.

When I met Susan, she was a professor of psychology and co-founder and co-director of the eating disorders clinic in the psychiatry department at the University of Cincinnati. Susan published extensively, and she was a founding member of the Academy for Eating Disorders. She mentored my mentors. And she dared to love her clients out loud.

Susan wrote academic journal articles, many along with her husband, Wayne Wooley, opposing dieting.[1,2] She questioned "obesity" as a disease, pointing out the risks of treatment, the physical and emotional harm that comes from dieting, and highlighting the flawed assumptions underlying the dominant belief that thinner equals healthier.

In 1983 Susan began calling for an end to the suffering that dieting causes, particularly when no benefit to health and well-being could be pointed to, and instead asked, "should obesity be treated at all?"[3] She called out health professionals for contributing to the suffering, and highlighted the hypocrisy of the applause she would receive when presenting her work, without any subsequent changes in action, policy, or behavior.[4]

She called for an end to shame being used as a tactic to drive behavior change, saying "if shame could cure obesity, there wouldn't be a fat person left in the room."[5]

Her work was radical and urgent, and was the early underpinnings of what would become Health At Every Size. Much has changed since the early '80s (and some things have not changed nearly enough). Language has shifted, and the work has grown into a contemporary set of concerns and deeper understandings.

EVERYTHING I WANTED TO BE

I was 22 years old when I arrived at the University of Cincinnati in February 1987 for the Intensive Treatment Program for bulimia. I was shy, quiet, and focused on my (then) music career, something my eating disorder had begun to threaten. I had been undone by bodily self-consciousness for much of my life and had firmly believed that I needed to be thin to be successful, beautiful, powerful. I was driven, ambitious, and a hot mess. My eating disorder served many functions, but was primarily the result of me trying to be not-fat.

When I arrived at the program, she greeted me politely. She wore a long purple dress, had short gray hair and round glasses, and spoke with a warm voice. And she was fat. I felt my stomach sink and a wave of pure panic crash over me. I was so afraid that she wouldn't be able to help because she wouldn't understand my feelings or my fears.

But she did understand. And she did help me. She was my first relational image of a large woman who was solidly inside of her own life. She was powerfully in her own body, so there was the possibility that I could be powerfully in mine. Her presence had a profoundly destabilizing impact on who I thought I wanted to be.

It was an unapologetically feminist treatment program, one that allowed us full agency. We prepared our own meals. We weren't monitored or under surveillance at mealtime or in the bathroom. We were trusted with our process and our recovery. I remember that I described in one group having only eaten bread the day before, because it was all that I wanted. Susan let me know that she was impressed that I followed my cravings, rather than what I thought I "should" be doing.

She put me on the path to finding fat liberation and what would become HAES. She introduced me to the work of people who are now my dear friends and colleagues, leading the way for me to grow up in the lap of fat activists. It was the early stirrings of my own activism.

She catalyzed my feminist awakening and my critical thinking. After 30 days I left treatment, went back to school, and took my first women's studies course and continued questioning everything I had absorbed, calling back in feelings that were unclaimed.

Because of who Susan was, fat positivity had everything to do with my recovery. And it made sense to me. It made sense *of* me.

THE DISCOVERY OF OUTRAGE

I still remember sitting on the floor of her office along with seven other women towards the end of our month-long treatment, listening to Susan share her body story with us. She did not shy away from self-disclosure. The bigger element of secrecy surrounding eating disorders bumped up the value of her self-disclosure, particularly for someone who was not going to recover into a thin body. I withdrew into myself as I listened to her, and she asked me if I wanted to share what was happening. I was moved by her story, touched by the generosity of her sharing, and I was thinking about all of the wasted time I had spent trying to perfect my body instead of all the other things that mattered to me. And I remember asking "what THE HELL am I doing?" It was then that

I felt indignation and grief begin to enter my body.

In the three decades that have followed, I have let myself continue to be guided by anger. As I wrote recently on a blog about eating disorders recovery, someone asked me once what the single most important factor was for me in my recovery from bulimia. I thought about it and I really wanted to say something like: Compassion. Or love. Or kindness.

But that's not what it was. It was anger. More specifically—it was outrage. For me, recovery began when I felt my spirit begin to up-roar. The fury was necessary. I couldn't move forward without it. Anger is so valuable; it is such an immediate source of information and wisdom in the ways it lets us know what needs to stop. I remember sitting in a women's studies class, learning about the patriarchal demands and prescriptions of how my body was supposed to be, and starting to get angry. When I think of how much energy gets poured into the project of perfecting our bodies instead of the project of fighting injustice or in service of the things that light us up, I feel angry. This is a rigged game, and I'm pissed.

To be angry is an act of self-definition/revolution. It pushes back on messages that tell us we can't be angry. It's where we feel our edges, and our boundaries. We feel what's OK and what's not.

Here's the truth: I love a good fight. Outrage propelled me into activism, where I wasn't just subject to forces acting on me. Activism showed me that I could act and take part in reshaping the culture and feel my own agency. Activism has been deeply healing in the ways that it lets my actions become an extension of my heart.

Anger helped me stop locating the problem as inside of me and identify the problem that was out in the world that affected me. Eating disorders are a reasonable response to a disordered world. Recovery couldn't happen for me without a social justice lens—until I could situate eating disorders in a bigger frame of social justice. Until I could uplift and affirm fatness, I could not recover. I needed to recover my own relationship with my body.

Susan saw me and cradled that small quiver of my anger. She knew that I was onto something. I didn't yet know the cruciality of having fat providers working in the field of eating disorders treatment. I didn't know yet the vital role that therapists in diverse bodies offer to those in treatment. I didn't know yet that they are living invitations to celebrate all of us and investigate what we think we are looking for to feel a sense of belonging.

But it was also these words she spoke to me once when I was in graduate school that had the most profound impact: "You can help a fat person learn to love themselves, but they still walk out of your office into a world that hates them." Those words laid dormant for quite a few years, then came back to remind me that individual healing work, while important, is not enough without cultural transformation. And I, as a therapist, need to work at that level also. It became one of my ethical imperatives.

THE BODY KNOWS ITS OWN TRUTH

I talked with her again in 2000 when I was in graduate school, asking her some questions for a paper I was writing. She planted seeds during that conversation, ones I didn't even know had been planted until years later, when I began learning about liberation psychology. She told me that body image is not our own. It was the beginning of my understanding that we need to examine where we locate the problem. Are eating disorders individual illnesses, or do they signal a greater cultural pathology? Perhaps the problem is not located inside of people's bodies at all.

At the time she expressed concern about binge eating disorder (BED) being included in the *Diagnostic and Statistical Manual of Mental Disorders (DSM)*, worrying that people would diagnose it by looking at someone's body. And indeed, eating disorders of all kinds are still diagnosed by someone's size, while others can't get the help they need if their body doesn't align with diagnostic categories. Believing the truth that others tell us, "especially when they have been forced into the habit of being habitually unbelieved,"[6] is so necessary.

At the time of that conversation with Susan I was still a year away from graduating and beginning to work as a therapist. She expressed her trust in me, and again, told me she loved me. What she nurtured in me was the restoration of self-respect.

HUMAN TO HUMAN

In the 1994 book *Feminist Perspectives on Eating Disorders* Susan wrote a chapter entitled "The Female Therapist as Outlaw"[7] in which she boldly, bravely, and radically made a case for ways of working that were contrary to the accepted ethics of that time. Self-disclosure. Emotional response. Touch. Letting authenticity move out in front of authority. Moving away from sterile diagnoses, when what was needed was not just a move away from pathologizing something that millions of people were suffering from, but also when those ways of conceptualizing the problem obscured the humanity of the two people in the room. We companion our clients to be whole human beings, and yet we demand, expect, and regulate therapists to be less than whole. And there's loss in that. Full range of human emotion is necessary and vital to practice with integrity. I am not interested in any way of working, as a therapist or as a client, that tells us we have to constrain our humanity. Healing happens human to human, and body to body.

It was Susan who first taught me to break with convention and become an outlaw, not allowing the status quo to go unquestioned and pushing back on harmful patriarchal models that refuse to yield. She beautifully and skillfully broke from the mainstream ways of thinking and of working with her patients/clients. She taught me that relational responsibility is more important than ethical respectability.

TEARING DOWN THE WALL

Susan taught me that the wall between the personal and political does not serve. She acknowledged that "there is the disrespect for 'the law'—the law, for example, that what 200 patients tell you is less valid than a paper-and-pencil survey at a mall; the law of therapist neutrality; the law that science is value-free."[8] Most of us were trained (indoctrinated) into the myth of neutrality, and are realizing that we lose something essential inside of this myth. Susan wrote this nearly 30 years ago, and we are still arguing in Facebook groups about if we should hug our clients. Where did we stop trusting experienced practitioners to manage their emotions, politics, and passions in relationship to clients?

I used to read research articles and before reading I'd look at the bibliography to see if the Wooleys were quoted, and if not, I didn't trust the article. I told Susan that once, and she cautioned me to be careful about that, because they hadn't done research in a while.

I think what I was actually looking for was: does this article have a feminist analysis? A fat liberation framework? Because if not, I don't trust it.

Susan was a real human being, which is messy—which might have been her point. Lives are messy, and her life was messy. She struggled with physical illness, and illness often reshapes bodies. Susan was a therapist who dared to say no to a way of working dictated by men in suits. She broke free of multiple prevailing paradigms and ushered so many of us through the threshold of trusting our ways of knowing and working. She reminded us that "we need to take good care of one another because the work is hard, because it is essential, and because it requires us all."[9] She taught us that we are necessary, and the world needs us whole.

RETURN TO SENDER

In my 23 years of practice, I have written many notes to many clients, and they have written beautiful notes to me. But that original letter I got from Susan all those years ago continues to inspire and invite me forward. So today I offer one back:

> Dear Susan,
>
> For the centrality of your place in the lineage of how I came to this work, for helping me set out on the path of genuine self-love, for your trust in my appetites, for the permission to work in a way that aligns with who I am and what I know to be healing, for the radical kindness that shaped my thinking and the ways I now support my clients—thank you from the bottom of my heart.
>
> I love you,
> Carmen

FOOTNOTES

1. Wooley, S. & Garner, D. (1994) Should Obesity be Treated? Dietary Treatments for Obesity are Ineffective. *BMJ* (Clinical research ed.). 309. 655-6.
2. Garner, David M. & Wooley, Susan C. (1991) Confronting the Failure of Behavioral and Dietary Treatments for Obesity. *Clinical Psychology Review, 11* (6).
3. Wooley, Susan C. & Wooley, Orland W. (1984) Should Obesity be Treated at All? In A.J. Stunkard & E. Stellar (Eds.), *Eating and Its Disorders* (NY: Raven), pp 185-92.
4. Fraser, L. (1997) *Losing It: America's Obsession with Weight and the Industry That Feeds On It.* NY: Dutton, p. 247.
5. This quote has been widely attributed to Susan Wooley, but it does not exist in any published work. It may have been passed down through stories from those who knew her.
6. O'Tuama, P. (2015) *In the Shelter: Finding a Home in the World.* London: Hodder & Stoughton, p. 146.
7. In modern context we see the limits of language available to us at the time. I imagine that Susan would not just use more inclusive language but would bring a more intersectional frame to her work.
8. Wooley, S. (1994) The Female Therapist as Outlaw. In P. Fallon, M.

Katzman, S. Wooley (Eds.), *Feminist Perspectives on Eating Disorders.* NY: The Guilford Press, pp 318-338.

9. Wooley, S. (1994) Sexual Abuse and Eating Disorders. In P. Fallon, M. Katzman, S. Wooley (Eds.), *Feminist Perspectives on Eating Disorders*, pp 171-211.

A 45-Year Journey in the Eating Disorders Field

Amy Baker Dennis

I HAVE WORN MANY HATS in this field—researcher, advocate, clinical psychologist, professor, trainer, consultant, conference planner, board member, clinic owner, supervisor/mentor, writer and co-founder of many eating disorders organizations and programs.

I started out in the field in 1973, working for the Franklin County Mental Health Association in Columbus, Ohio as a substance abuse educator and trainer. Then in 1975 I was hired as a counselor and community educator at the Bridge Counseling Center. I was promoted to assistant director in 1976 and then became the executive director in 1978. Some of my major goals at the community mental health center were to increase community awareness of our services, hire and train new clinicians, and recruit and train volunteers to staff our crisis line.

I accidently backed into the field of eating disorders in 1977. Patricia Howell, a journalist for the *Columbus Dispatch*, contacted me and inquired about using one of our group rooms for a monthly support group for individuals recovering from anorexia nervosa. She had been running the group in her living room for a year but had outgrown her space and needed a new location to accommodate everyone who wanted to attend. I must admit, I had little or no knowledge of this mental illness. I do remember that there was a paragraph about it in one of my graduate school textbooks, but it was a rare condition and I had never met or treated anyone with this disorder. I asked her to fill out a "request form" and told her I would take it to the next board meeting for approval. It was just standard procedure, and the board had never turned down a community group that asked to utilize the facility. However, they did turn down her request because one of the psychiatrists on the board stated, "Anorexia nervosa is a life-threatening illness with no known treatments." He did not think the organization should take on that liability—as someone could "code" in the building. I very quickly realized I had not done my homework and was unable to adequately defend her request.

As a young professional, I was stubborn and did not like to hear the word "no." After the board meeting I met with Pat and told her that the board meeting ran long and they had to "table" the request until our next meeting. But in the meantime, I needed to learn everything I could about this eating disorder. She also revealed that she was spearheading an organization called the National Anorexic Aid Society (NAAS) and producing a quarterly newsletter that was sent to hundreds of people all over the United States.

A professional friend of Pat's, Helen Botell, wrote the long-running, nationally syndicated advice column "Helen Help Us!" in the 1960s and 1970s. Helen had received a letter from a woman who was suffering from anorexia nervosa and struggling to find treatment. Helen knew that Patricia had received treatment and asked her to craft a response. Once the response was printed in her column, Helen got hundreds of letters from around the country and sent them all to Pat. Initially, Pat tried to respond to each letter, but it became overwhelming. That is when she created NAAS and began publishing newsletters that addressed all the issues presented in the letters. She was able to identify small patient and family advocacy organizations in several other states and began building a network.

So in my pursuit of a better understanding of anorexia nervosa, she invited me to join her at Johns Hopkins Medical School, where she and her psychiatrist, Arnold Anderson, MD, were presenting at a weekend conference on her treatment and recovery from anorexia nervosa. I was able to attend the conference and grand rounds and had a tour of their inpatient eating disorders clinic and met many staff members. I returned to Ohio with "fire in my belly" and a game plan to convince the board to reconsider Pat's request.

During that month I did a central Ohio and statewide needs assessment to see if there were any medical or mental health providers treating anorexia nervosa. There were none in central Ohio, but there was one NIMH (National Institute of Mental Health) funded study being conducted at the medical school at Ohio State University. The Cleveland Clinic was treating anorexia in their inpatient psychiatric program, and the University of Cincinnati medical school was creating a residential treatment program for eating disorders, headed up by Susan Wooley, PhD. I met with Kathrine Dixon, MD and her chief psychiatric resident, Randy Sansone, MD, at Ohio State Medical School, to discuss their study. They were looking at the family demographics, family characteristics, and environments of adolescents with anorexia nervosa. I shared with them my vision of creating an outpatient treatment program in the Center and they both were interested in supporting its development.

In preparing for the next board meeting, I invited Drs. Dixon and Sansone to attend with me. I outlined how we could not only allow the support groups to meet monthly at the Bridge, but that we had a large volunteer staff that could assist with producing and mailing out the NAAS newsletters. I also proposed that since there was a significant treatment gap in Ohio, we should create an outpatient eating disorders program at the center. I requested funds to explore how we could do it, and they said "yes!" I had the board behind me, my clinical director, two staff members, and two outside consultants who were interested, but there was nowhere to send the staff to get training. By 1979 the Bridge took over NAAS and began preparing to open a treatment program for people with eating disorders. This was when I began to realize how much I enjoyed starting new programs.

I had spent a considerable amount of time talking with researchers around the country, and decided that I should ask them all to come to Columbus to train my staff. We decided to hold a 1½ day training session. To defray the costs of bringing in these professionals, we invited everyone in the mental health system in Ohio to attend. We needed 50 registrants to cover the cost of the conference. Much to our surprise, we had 110 people from five different states attend our first conference in 1982. This was also the year the Center for the Study of Anorexia and Bulimia in New York City ran their first conference, and several months after our conference the *International Journal of Eating Disorders* sponsored their first conference in New York City.

With the support of Harding Hospital, NAAS hosted an additional seven "Columbus Conferences," and professionals came from around the U.S. and Canada. I am proud to say that we brought in speakers from all over the world that were on the cutting edge of research and treatment at that time, and for some of them, it was their first time speaking to an eating disorders audience in the United States.

In 1983 The Bridge Foundation was created and took on the responsibility of running NAAS and the conferences. Simultaneously the Center for the Treatment of Eating Disorders opened and was the first dedicated outpatient treatment facility in Central Ohio for individuals with eating disorders. I became the founding executive director of both organizations. During this time I was in graduate school and knew that I wanted to conduct my dissertation on eating disorders and borderline personality disorder (BPD). I was able to connect with Craig Johnson, PhD and his post-doc intern, Dave Tobin, PhD at Northwestern and Michael Reese Hospital in Chicago. They were looking at the clinical characteristics of patients with bulimia nervosa, and I was able to add the BPD questionnaires to the project. This was my first experience with multisite data collection, and led to a great dissertation and my first published journal articles.

The next important project I was involved in was the development of "Eating Disorders Awareness Week." We launched EDAW in 1984 to coincide with our third national conference. Forty-five secondary schools and five colleges and universities in the community were provided posters, information flyers, and speakers on eating disorders. Staff members were interviewed on TV and radio, and the mayor of Columbus and the governor of the state of Ohio each declared it "Eating Disorders Awareness Week."

Meanwhile, there were other exciting things happening in the field. Gürze Books published their first book catalog that was exclusively dedicated to eating disorders literature in 1980. In 1985 the International Association of Eating Disorders Professionals (IAEDP) was founded with the mission of developing a curriculum to train and certify therapists as eating disorders specialists. Also in 1985, the Renfrew Center opened the first free-standing eating disorders residential treatment facility, in Philadelphia, PA. In 1991, under the direction of Judi Goldstein, MMS, LSW, the Renfrew Eating Disorders Conferences were launched. This year they celebrated 32 years of providing outstanding professional training.

Then in 1986 Mary Pabst, MSW (founder of the Maryland Association for Anorexia Nervosa and Bulimia) and I decided to invite 35 representatives from self-help, support and advocacy organizations from around the country to a weekend retreat in Baltimore. Our goal was to see if we could merge our programs and create one organization for families and sufferers. However, after nearly a day of debating, it became clear that very few participants were interested in giving up their programs to create a national organization. However, everyone was interested in working together to make "Eating Disorders Awareness Week" an ongoing national program. By the end of the weekend we had created a new organization, Eating Disorders Awareness and Prevention (EDAP), and appointed a board of directors. I was delighted to serve on that initial board. The United States was divided into 12 regions, and coordinators for each region were identified. A plan for a National Eating Disorders Awareness Week (EDAW) was developed, and it was launched in 1987. It has been running annually for the last 38 years, and is now an ongoing program of the National Eating Disorders Association (NEDA).

In 1988, my husband was transferred to Detroit, MI. I left the Center for the Treatment of Eating Disorders and NAAS in the very capable hands of a new executive director, Laura Hill, PhD, but continued as a consultant for the conferences for the next few years. She continued the conferences, expanded our services, and created the first partial hospitalization program for ED patients at Harding Hospital.

Detroit had very few ED providers, but I was lucky to connect with Alexander Sackeyfio, MD and Ann Moye, PhD, who had attended my conferences in Ohio. At the time, they were the predominate ED specialists in the community. Eventually Dr. Moye and I opened a private practice together, with a majority of our clinicians working with ED patients. I also joined the faculty at the Wayne State Medical School and worked with the team at Children's Hospital. This is where I met Arthur Robin, PhD, who was the chief of psychology. He had received a seven-year grant from the National Institute of Mental Health to conduct a randomized-controlled treatment study comparing family therapy to individual therapy for adolescents with anorexia nervosa. This was the first study of its kind in United States, and our first paper was published in 1995.

The next organization I helped to found was a professional organization for eating disorders researchers and treatment providers. In 1992 Craig Johnson, PhD (the psychologist who started the *International Journal of Eating Disorders*) and Pat Santucci, MD invited 33 researchers and clinicians to Laureate Psychiatric Clinic and Hospital in Tulsa, Oklahoma. We spent the weekend together and created a multidisciplinary professional organization for eating disorders specialists. After hours of debate about what we should name the organization, it was agreed that it should be called the Academy for Eating Disorders. By the end of the weekend we had created a structure for the organization, agreed on membership recruitment, and invited colleagues who were not present to become charter members. We identified Ken Schonberg, MD (Montefiore Hospital at Albert Einstein College of Medicine) as the executive administrator, and selected our first board of directors (Pauline Powers, MD—president, Amy Baker Dennis, PhD—secretary, John Levitt, PhD—treasurer, and Susan Wooley, PhD—past president). We watched this organization grow from 33 American members to an international organization today, with close to 2000 members from all over the world. I sat on the board of directors for the first 11 years and served as director of education and training for regional teaching days and the international conferences, and have chaired and participated on numerous AED committees over the last 29 years.

I am also a founding member of the Eating Disorders Research Society. Initially we had envisioned a robust research division within AED, however, because the founders of AED were from the United States, researchers from the United Kingdom, the Netherlands, Germany, Spain, and Italy were reluctant to join an American organization. In 1995 James Mitchell, MD invited researchers from North America, the U.K., and Europe to meet at the University of Minnesota to discuss developing an independent organization specifically for researchers that would support AED but be separate from AED. We decided that it would remain a "closed organization" with limited membership. Prospective new members would be invited to apply and would be accepted if they were sponsored by a current member and met certain research criteria and standards. The membership remains very small, and there are only approximately 150 of us worldwide. However, these are the premier researchers that have dedicated their lives to better understanding what eating disorders are, and what treatments work. Our biggest struggle is disseminating these findings and training clinicians to utilize evidence-based interventions in their practices.

In 2000 my husband was transferred again, this time to Orlando, Florida. We knew it would be a temporary position, so I did not want to give up my clinic in Bloomfield Hills, MI. I was able to make monthly visits back to Detroit to run the practice, continue my training program, and see patients. This also gave me the opportunity to teach graduate students at Hamilton Holt School at Rollins College in Orlando and medical students at the University of South Florida Medical School with Pauline Powers, MD in Tampa.

It was during my time in Orlando in 2000, the founders of NEDO (the National Eating Disorders Organization, formerly NAAS), the American Anorexia and Bulimia Association (AABA), and EDAP met in Seattle to create the National Eating Disorders Association (NEDA). A founder's council comprising 30 members from around the country was formed to acknowledge their many years of dedication and service to the field and to insure, going forward, their continued support and engagement in the organization. With a generous grant from Don and Melissa Neilson, NEDA was launched, our first CEO (Lynn Grefe) was selected, and National Eating Disorders Awareness Week (NEDAW) was adopted as one of the ongoing campaigns to promote awareness, support patients and families, and disseminate educational information about eating disorders. I had the privilege of sitting on the NEDA Board for nine years, and served on the NEDA conference committee from 2004 until 2016. Recently, I was invited to chair the new clinical advisory council for NEDA.

In 2000 another very important organization was created. Through contributions from eating disorders treatment facilities, eating disorders organizations, and private donations, the Eating Disorders Coalition (EDC) was established. In those days, eating disorders received very little research funding from the federal government, and many insurance policies did not pay for treatment or even recognize eating disorders as mental illnesses. EDC worked with members of Congress to conceptualize and draft the Federal Response to Eliminate Eating Disorders Act (the FREED Act), which was a comprehensive bill on eating disorders addressing research, treatment, education, and prevention. Since then the EDC has been instrumental in the passage of several bills, including the Anna Westin Act, the creation of the Centers of Excellence for Eating Disorders, and the compliance and enforcement of the Mental Health Parity and Addiction Equity Act, and has significantly increased eating disorders research funding on a federal level.

In 2008 Chevese Turner founded the Binge Eating Disorder Association (BEDA), a national organization focused on increasing prevention, diagnosis, and treatment of BED and associated weight stigma. Through outreach and education, BEDA was committed to facilitating awareness, excellence in care, and recovery for those who live with and those who treat binge eating disorder and its associated conditions. In 2018 BEDA joined forces with and became an important program of NEDA. Then in 2010 Diane Mickley, MD, Leah Komar Harris, and Rebecca Parekh founded the Global Foundation for Eating Disorders. The primary mission of this organization was to raise money to fund research programs submitted by young investigators. They have been a major contributor to independent research grants, and in 2022 merged with the NEDA Feeding Hope Fund to continue their research efforts.

There have been significant changes in the ED field over the last 45 years. When I first came into the field in the late '70s the only eating disorder that was mentioned in the *Diagnostic and Statistical Manual of Mental Disorders, Second Edition (DSM-II)* was anorexia nervosa. There was no mention of either bulimia or binge eating disorder in the *DSM*. The term "bulimia nervosa" was coined by Gerald Russell, MBChB, PhD, and with the publication of *DSM-III* in 1980 it became the second eating disorder. In that volume binge eating was first mentioned as a condition and criteria for bulimia nervosa. In the *DSM-IV*, published in 1994, binge eating disorder was still not known as a distinct disorder, but was placed in the "study section" (appendix) of the manual as an "eating disorder not otherwise specified," or EDNOS. It wasn't until the publication of *DSM-V* that eating disorders were moved from "Childhood Disorders" to its own chapter and BED was fully recognized as a major eating disorder. This legitimized the disorder, and individuals with BED could finally receive treatment and insurance reimbursement.

When I entered the field, there were very few female role models. My academic role models were Katherine Halmi, M. (Cornell), Regina Casper, MD

(Stanford), and Elke Eckert, MD (University of Minnesota). My clinical role models started out with Marlene Boskind-White, MA (White Plains, NY) and Susan Wooley, PhD. (University of Cincinnati). At that time men dominated most of the leadership positions, research studies, professional publications, and speaking/training programs. For a primarily female mental illness, that did not seem quite right. As a young researcher and clinician I was hungry for knowledge and skills, and running the early national conferences in Columbus and attending any available training gave me the opportunity to meet and collaborate with many of the experts in the field.

In the 1970s there were no evidence-based interventions or treatments for eating disorders. Hilde Bruch, M.D. had published *The Golden Cage: The Enigma of Anorexia Nervosa* and *Eating Disorders: Obesity, Anorexia Nervosa and The Person Within*. Coming from a psychodynamic point of view, she suggested that individuals with anorexia nervosa had problems with emotion processing, body perception, and interpersonal relationships, and most of our early treatment approaches evolved from her works. The dominant belief was that eating disorders were caused by unhealthy environments, family dysfunction, and the influence the media exerted on women to conform to certain standards for weight, shape and appearance.

However, in the '90s and 2000s, with the explosion of technology and a focus on understanding brain-based mental illnesses, there was a growing body of literature that supported a very different etiological hypothesis. Today we know that genetics contribute approximately 50-80% of liability to the development of an eating disorder. This knowledge has moved the field to develop several different treatment approaches.

In the mid-1980s there was a growing emphasis on utilizing evidence-based interventions for depression in the mental health field. Our ED patients also suffered from high rates of both depression and anxiety, so a few researchers/clinicians in the ED community sought training/certification in cognitive behavioral therapy (including me). The predominant researcher who explored the use of CBT with bulimic patients was Christopher Fairburn, PhD, MD, and his team from Oxford University. He has dedicated his career to identifying what treatments work for what disorders, and CBT-E (CBT for Eating Disorders) was the first and probably the most utilized intervention in the field.

In 1989 James Hudson, MD and Harrison Pope, MD from McLean Hospital at Harvard University published a book called *New Hope for Binge Eaters*. The premise was that binge eating could be a subcategory of depression, because clinical trials using antidepressants demonstrated a significant reduction in binge episodes and obsessional thinking in patients who did not have significant depressive symptoms. This was a significant finding at the time; however, as soon as patients stopped the medication, those who were not receiving ongoing talk therapy tended to relapse back into binge eating.

Today we have several evidence-based talk therapies for eating disorders where once there were none. After our study on family vs. individual treatment for adolescent anorexia nervosa was published, researchers James Lock, MD and Daniel LeGrange, PhD from Stanford created and manualized Family Based Treatment (FBT) for anorexia nervosa. Denise Wilfley, PhD from Washington University in St. Louis reported that Interpersonal Psychotherapy was an effective intervention for patients with BED. Christy Telch, PhD, Debra Safer, PhD, and Eunice Chen, PhD, published studies and wrote a book, *Dialectical Behavior Therapy for Binge Eating and Bulimia,* that demonstrates the efficacy of DBT with eating disorder patients. Stephen Wonderlich, PhD and his colleagues at the University of Minnesota and the University of North Dakota have also demonstrated that Integrative Cognitive-Affective Therapy is as effective as CBT-E in the treatment of bulimia and BED.

Although numerous psychotropic medication trials have been conducted over the last 40 years, to date, fluoxetine (Prozac) is the only FDA-approved medication for bulimia nervosa and lisdexamfetamine dimesylate (Vyvanse) has approval for the treatment of binge eating disorder.

I guess for me, one of the most exciting things that has happened over the last several decades is the development of several exceptional treatment facilities with all levels of care, professional organizations to support researchers and clinicians, an effective legislative arm, and an organization that is dedicated to patients and families. Individuals with eating disorders now have a strong infrastructure to support them in their journey to recovery. The field is now filled with talented women in leadership roles. There is a much stronger focus on treating "the whole person" and all the comorbid conditions in an integrated fashion instead of just attempting to eliminate the eating disorder symptoms. The field has become much more attuned to meeting the needs of the LGBTQ community as well as underserved and ethnic populations. I think we are doing a better job at bridging the "research-practice gap," and many more clinicians in the field have access to good training not only at conferences but through online webinars and mentoring programs.

I have grown up in this field. The friends and colleagues I have made along the way remain my "work family," and we still delight in spending time together. We have gone through marriages and divorces, raising families, and losing parents and loved ones. Many of my generation's leaders, researchers, and clinicians are semi-retired or planning to retire in the near future. However, I believe we have left the next generation of leaders in the eating disorders field with resources, a wealth of knowledge, and the skills to eventually eradicate eating disorders.

"It Can't Be Looking Like This"
Thoughts on the Evolution of Diversity and Inclusion in the Field of Eating Disorders Treatment

Gayle Brooks, *as told to* Dalia Kinsey

I GRADUATED WITH MY PhD in clinical psychology in 1982. At the time I was doing a psychology residency at a hospital that was opening a women's unit, and I was very interested in personality disorders. On this unit, in the early '80s, they started identifying neating disorders. There wasn't a lot of attention to eating disorders in the early '80s. It was kind of a new era.

After I finished my residency, my first job was in a clinic. When patients with eating disorders came in, I was somebody who had at least a little bit of experience and so became the resident expert. My perceived expertise was, I believe, way beyond what I really knew. I went from there to be a director of an outpatient eating disorders clinic in Wisconsin and then came to the Renfrew center in the late '80s. I've been to at Renfrew since then.

The field has evolved so much over time. It's a very dynamic field. When you look at eating disorders, there's so many things that impact someone who is having a struggle with an eating disorder or having those types of symptoms. And whether you're looking at family issues, whether you're looking at cultural issues, whether you're looking at identity issues, or trauma, there's just so many aspects of it. And individuals with eating disorders are so multifaceted that I found it was just very stimulating as a clinician to be working with that population. I found that to be something that was really professionally very interesting.

At the time, working with women in particular was important to me. I'm talking about women because at the time the thought was that women get eating disorders and very few men may get eating disorders. Gender diversity beyond a binary construct wasn't even thought of at the time, so we talked about either men or women. As the time, very little was being done to really deal with the psychology of women. Things were starting to come out of the Stone Center, saying that a relational approach is really how women psychologically evolve and that these relationships need to be at the heart of it, and then it sort of moved into culture needing to be at the heart of it. All of that made a lot of sense to me, and I never felt like there was a dull moment. I mean, even now, the field is evolving in some very important ways.

Initially, what I experienced in the field was that I found myself having to suddenly learn a lot. What I knew in the beginning wasn't what I was coming to understand in terms of looking at the field, looking at the patients that were out there, looking at who wasn't there seeking treatment. I have to say, I, not one time, thought about it in terms of cultural issues. I sort of made the assumption that Black women didn't have eating disorders so that I'd be working with white women primarily.

I was certainly trained in the notion that while eating disorders were culturally based, they were culturally based in a sort of white female culture, and that's why individuals who had eating disorders were white girls and women. All research in the field was very limited in the beginning, and a lot of it was focused on that demographic. And if you looked at who was doing the research, it was young college-aged white women. At the time, I don't think that we understood how much who was studying it, and the population that they were studying, impacted the outcome and findings of the research. We didn't acknowledge the bias there.

In the early '90s I was asked to do a closing keynote at a conference. One of the areas that I could pick from was diversity. And at that time I thought, hmm, how is it that I've been in the field for six years now, but never really asked myself the question of why are we not seeing diversity? I just assumed that this was what it was.

I think it was at that time that Becky Thompson's book, *A Hunger So Wide and So Deep,* came out looking at multicultural, multi-racial issues. It just really got me thinking, and I had to do a very deep dive into the very limited resources on the subject at the time. But I also had to do a very deep dive internally, just to be thinking about how is it that I've come to believe that this is not something that would be impacting me in any sort of significant way?

We were also starting to look at the role of the trauma of racism and seeing all the -isms and how they impact psychological health. That's taking more of a center stage these days than it was back then. Becky Thompson was really one of the first to address diversity, and she's actually a Caucasian woman with, I think, a background in sociology. There were also people of color who were writing about diversity from a variety of cultural backgrounds, too. I found myself gravitating toward the work that was coming out of the Stone Center about relational cultural theory.

I remember at the time having a conversation with my mother about racial issues and eating disorders. "Oh, yeah," she said, "I had a girlfriend when I was in college who abused laxatives, she was taking laxatives all the time, and we just couldn't quite understand why." This would have been in the '40s. Bulimia back then, you know, I hadn't even really thought about that.

It became a source of tension for me, because I began then to question a lot of stuff—our theories we use, that it's about issues of separation, individuation, things like that. I had made assumptions about what was at the root of eating disorders, but then I started thinking, okay, but that doesn't really fit everyone outside of the more dominant culture perspective. I did end up doing the keynote, but took a very personal perspective with it about invisibility. I addressed the fact that at this conference I had never really had anybody of color talking about this, and I challenged the audience to think about what that meant about us as an organization and as a professional field. I had more questions than answers at the time, but that was a real jumping off point for me.

Another moment that really opened my eyes around that time was when *Essence* magazine did their survey of Black women around weight control behaviors. It identified a high use of laxatives as a method of weight management. I thought, oh my God, how could I not know this kind of thing?

I've been at the Renfrew Center for 30-some-odd years now, and the issue of weight stigma and how that manifests itself is still a very relevant issue. It impacts everything in terms of the environment that you set and how you understand weight medically. We're still dealing with a medical model that a person's weight inherently means something, that if you are this weight it must mean this about you. How we approach weight, medically or health-wise, impacts what we do in terms of nutrition and what kinds of interventions we do. There's tension in the field around how to approach weight, and it's a very big focus right now.

I think a big portion of time what was influencing the thinking about weight was the research that was being done. We went through this period of evidence-based treatment, and we're probably still using that as the gold standard. But what defines evidence? What research strategies have been deemed to be helpful versus other things? That has influenced how the field has evolved, but now we're developing more understanding of the limitations of research and how that has its own biases. We think about science, and we think "oh, it's unbiased." Well, no, it's not unbiased. We clearly can understand that.

There's this tension, as I see it, of do we throw the baby out with the bathwater? Do we say, "That evidence stuff, let's smash it all down, because it hasn't been created on solid footing." I definitely understand that perspective. I think, being a treatment provider in our organization, the idea of tearing it down without anything necessarily to build it all back up again right away is unrealistic. We've got to look at how we adapt some of what exists while staying very understanding of its limitations, with an understanding that there may still be something there that is also of help.

A more individualized approach would be less potentially harmful than a focus that hasn't really been based on diverse backgrounds. For example, when you think about cognitive behavior therapy for eating disorders, which has really been considered the gold standard for many, many years, it addresses certain things about the factors of an eating disorder, such as a drive to thinness being a part of it, or the thinness culture being a part of it, that sort of thing. Those aren't necessarily going to work with people from diverse backgrounds as what made an eating disorder for them. You end up using a model that is based on factors that are not necessarily helpful.

For example, when you look at body image issues with women of color, people of color, people from different diverse backgrounds, those concerns may not be what's really driving their eating behaviors. Those aren't necessarily the values of those communities; overvaluing of thinness might not be what's at the core of that. We can understand cognitions play a role. However, whatever those cognitions are, that person's emotions also play a role. If we're going to look at what's fueling those cognitions, we need to have a model that is done within a cultural context, understanding what causes those emotions, what causes those thoughts, and how living in the world that we live in has had an impact on us.

One of the ways we are seeing more professional development opportunities for those in the field to consider diversity is via the increased attention to discussing race at conferences. Just about my whole professional career has been at the Renfrew Center, and very early on we started having professional conferences. We were probably one of the first, and it's gone on years and years and years. I've been involved, from the very beginning, in giving talks. What is different now is that I'm involved in putting on the conference itself. It has been an important shift, because I get to help define how the whole conference is going to be, versus somebody just inviting me to give a talk.

One of our missions for our conference, and I think not just for us but for all the major eating disorders conferences, is that issues of diversity cannot be peripheralized. I used to give a talk and I had the same audience each and every year. I was preaching to the choir each and every year, because it wasn't embedded within the whole understanding of what should be presented. When you're talking about eating disorders, and I don't care what you're specifically presenting on about eating disorders, you need to be looking at how it impacts diverse people, and not just one particular perspective. What has evolved over time is that conferences are starting to prioritize more about diverse issues, particularly from professionals with lived experience. They are being positioned much more front and center at these conferences.

It's taken a real push from professionals of diverse backgrounds saying, "Enough is enough. The diversity talks need to be more centralized. I don't want to just come and give this one little talk that will come to you on a Sunday evening. If you're going to do a conference, you've got to pay me and make this subject a keynote now." That is where I see a lot of the energy right now in the field. It is really kind of calling to task, rightfully so, the community of organizations to be embracing this and not just sort of taking it on as "oh, yeah, we do diversity as well."

I definitely think new people are coming into the field with this understanding of the importance of identity and diversity because they were exposed to it in college and in their graduate programs. They have little tolerance for lack of inclusion. Older folks like me have come to understand it and to also know that this has been missing for a long time, but I really appreciate the young people that are in the field, because they're pushing the whole field to say "You know what, it can't be looking like this." There has to be representation.

I'll tell you one of the other areas that I think really impacts things: marketing. Being a treatment facility, do you market yourself to very thin white girls, because that's who was coming into treatment, that's who had access to treatment? I think there was the belief that those are the ones who needed our services. We have to step back and say, "Okay, they're not really the only ones who suffer with eating disorders, and we can't just be marketing to them." We have a responsibility for opening up access into treatment. If your whole patient community is white, you have to ask yourself why?

There's the shift in the way we define eating disorders as well. Our thinking about eating disorders is evolving. When the field first started, it was focused on anorexia. That was the big thing and that's what we understood. And then bulimia came along, and then binge eating came later. As the field has changed, I think we're also understanding size differently; when you look at all the eating disorders, size does not necessarily dictate which eating disorder you have. You can be in a larger body and be dealing with anorexic tendencies. That is what you're experiencing, maybe as well as bulimia and binge eating. Understanding this today means breaking a lot of the molds in terms of assumptions that we made about size, and how that fits within an eating disorder.

The flip side of it is that size doesn't indicate an eating disorder. One of the other intentions in the field is about this whole issue of obesity and the word "obesity" and is it a disorder? Is it something to treat? The thinking about this is in transition, I would say.

We have to be intentional in understanding emotional distress, and in understanding that what is causing emotional distress can be lots of things, and it can show up as an eating disorder. If we want to heal people, we have to look at what the heck is distressing them! A lot of that distress can be internal things, because certainly people will have internal kinds of psychological issues going on, but distress also comes from the context that one lives within and how a person experiences the world. I think we are coming to understand that we have to be dealing not only with the internal, but within context as well, to really be able to truly make a difference.

It's a very tall order, maybe one that will never be fully realized, but we are starting to understand that context has to be considered. Because clinicians can be thinking about cognitive strategies that we can do to help a person look at some of their distorted thinking, and we can teach somebody these principles, and it can help with depression, but if we don't understand that if they live life in a way where they are marginalized there is a lot of microaggression that goes on in their daily lives, that in and of itself is going to continue to fuel a lot of internal struggles. It's not enough just to give a person the tools, we've got to also look at acknowledging what is sick in their environment and in the greater culture.

I also know that a lot of my work is within a white institution and still within a pretty white field. I think as I grow I see more of the struggle for myself than maybe even in the early days, when I thought people of color didn't really have eating disorders, even though I was very much in the field. It was like there wasn't a lot of dissonance right at that point. Now there's probably much more dissonance that I have to deal with and come to terms with.

In the field today, there is more of a sense of community responsibility, a practice in which people understand that you can't just be doing your own thing, you have to be thinking about the larger world. People see the importance of having a voice and making a difference, not necessarily just in eating disorders, but in other areas as well. I'm thinking in particular of a book I recently read by Maureen Walker, who was a part of our last Renfrew conference. Her work discusses race and gender, how we can improve racial relationships. She and others like her are thinking about how we deal with diversity in treatment, in therapy, across mental health fields. I just really appreciate a lot of that kind of work that's being put out there these days.

I started in eating disorders in the early '80s, and I've stayed with it the whole time. If there was anything I might have done differently, I would have maybe attempted earlier on to be more active in the field outside of my role at Renfrew. That's what I see a lot of young people doing, and I'm thinking, gosh, I would have liked to have done that at the time. My attention was on my work environment and making a difference there. In the end, things have pretty much fallen into place for me. It has really been my field of choice. The field has evolved in ways that have kept me very much engaged and interested. I feel like there's space to be able to talk about these things and to try to be in a process of growth myself. In another profession, I don't know that I would necessarily have those resources to be able to do that. I feel like the eating disorders field was a good fit for me. It has really been a good fit.

THE POWER OF TRUSTING MY INTUITION

ELYSE RESCH

M Y FIRST ENCOUNTER WITH coming up against a belief system opposed to mine arose during graduate school in the late 1970s. I was taking a nutrition therapy course and was asked to write a paper about a topic I now have forgotten, but at the time felt counter to my understanding of the subject matter. What a dilemma. I scratched my head about how to handle this situation and came up with a solution that resolved my discomfort: I wrote two papers! One paper addressed the issue as it had been taught in class, and the second spoke my truth about this issue. I believe it had something to do with treating a health problem, but I don't remember the specifics. And right there, the professional maverick was born! I believe that this was a defining moment for me. I internalized the understanding that I couldn't be complacent with everything I was taught from any "authority figure." I didn't know then that this experience would be the template for me as my career and commitment to change in the world would evolve.

After my course work was finished, I did my traineeship to become a registered dietitian through the American Dietetic Association (now the Academy of Nutrition and Dietetics) at the University Affiliated Program—Center for Child Development and Developmental Disabilities at Children's Hospital Los Angeles. This was a multi-disciplinary approach to treating children with developmental disabilities, and it was a wonderful opportunity to be trained by professionals in many fields, including psychology, social work, and psychiatry. This training was foundational in my understanding of the psychology of eating and, of course, psychology in general. I even learned how to set up a room for counseling—where was the best place for my chair and where would be the most optimal place for my client to sit. This training encouraged me in later years to pursue the understanding of the psychological underpinnings of diets, disordered eating, and eating disorders—a critical piece for the foundation of intuitive eating (more to come on that later).

After finally passing my RD exam and receiving my master of science degree, I was ready to start working. I was fortunate to be hired into the program where I had trained, and I continued to run the feeding clinic as I had during my training. Eventually I knew that my journey needed to progress into beginning a private practice as a nutrition therapist. My intention was to devote my work toward treating patients with developmental disabilities, as I had in my traineeship, but best-laid plans often go awry.

I rented an office, bought furniture and equipment, but didn't have a single client. Fortunately I had made many connections at the clinic and finally received my first client. It was both terrifying and exhilarating. As time went on more referrals came in. One day I saw three clients in a morning, and then went out to lunch with a friend. I remember thinking "how could I ever do this day in and day out?" Now, 40 years later, there have been many days of seeing nine or ten clients in a day, leaving me tired but so satisfied.

Although hoping to receive referrals for those with developmental disabilities, many of the referrals that I began to receive came from medical doctors, asking me to help their patients lower their cholesterol or blood sugar or blood pressure. What came with these requests seemed to be steady recommendations to help these people lose weight. To be fair, the world of dieting was rampant, and there was no external voice that refuted this goal. But my inner voice began to emerge, leading to a cognitive dissonance that would ultimately need to be resolved. Somewhere in my inner wisdom I knew that there was something terribly wrong with the focus on weight loss. I couldn't put my finger on it, so I proceeded with what I had learned in graduate school—give people meal plans, weigh them, and expect them to comply with the plan. I never called these plans "diets," but in reality that's exactly what they were, as I was the one who wrote them, with the unfortunate goal of weight loss. And comply with the plans most of them did. Their blood work showed a benefit from the self-care changes they were making—moving their bodies, eating in a consistent manner. What didn't show up, however, was their inner turmoil, leading to the rebound that resulted from following an externally created plan. Sometime after they would leave my office, feeling triumphant, I'd receive a call telling me how embarrassed they were for "falling off the plan," gaining back weight, and feeling defeated. They blamed themselves—never me.

I had a powerful reckoning one day when a young woman came back for a second visit and told me that not only could she not follow the meal plan I had given her, but she was also uncontrollably bingeing. I was stymied, distraught, and lost.

This was the beginning of a transformation in my work. Around this time I found some literature on what was then called "the non-diet approach." Reading about this new concept gave me both hope and panic. The literature, which was based in psychological theory, was suggesting that the right path was to tell people to eat whatever they wanted in whatever quantity—with no regard to nutrition. The goal was to eliminate the feeling of deprivation brought on by forbidding certain foods and the subsequent rebound eating beyond fullness as they uncontrollably sought what they hadn't been allowed to freely eat. But here is the source of the panic: How could I, a registered dietitian with a master of science degree in nutrition, take off the reins and let clients run wild with their eating!

Back to the drawing board. I quickly realized that I was thinking of things in a very all or nothing way. Advising people to merely eat just what they wanted, at all times, neglected many psychological underpinnings that were not as simple as "go wild" with your eating. These psychological explanations would need to be learned and taught to clients to comfort their fears of being out of control. One powerful concept was that of habituation, an experience that occurs only after having full permission to eat what you want, as much of it as you want, forever and ever. Habituation can best be defined as "the greater the stimulus—the less the response." By giving clients the go-ahead to figure out which foods they truly enjoyed and promise themselves that they would never again deprive themselves of these foods, something magical took place. Their initial fear that they would never stop eating foods that had previously been forbidden just didn't happen. After a while they either realized that they didn't really like that food as much as they thought, or they didn't crave it in the uncontrollable way they did when it had been forbidden. Making peace with this food and every other food led to a deep sense of security that any food chosen would be there when they wanted it and that it would taste even better once habituation wore off. They realized that eating the same thing over and over, often in large quantities, did not give the satisfaction that is derived by having it when they truly craved it. Getting in as much of it as they could to make up for past deprivation and fearing that they'd never have it again never led to pleasurable eating.

I quickly realized that I needed to be a detective to notice when clients were giving themselves pseudo-permission to be fully free with their food choices. If there was some hidden (or not so hidden) agenda of "oh, I'll give this making-peace-with-food thing a try, and if it doesn't work I'll try the latest, greatest diet," disaster would lie ahead. I began to understand that even the slightest perception of future deprivation would negate the emergence of the habituation factor.

While doing this deep-dive into the psychology of eating permission, another light bulb went off. As I studied about the development of the human psyche, as presented by Erik Erikson, a Danish-German-American developmental psychologist and psychoanalyst, I began to understand the power of the human drive to assert autonomy. This drive, which is one of the defining indications of one's healthy personality and ego, struck me as a significant reason that diets and meal plans and external eating direction were bound to fail. Erikson proposed a model called "The Eight Stages of Man." Each stage included a psychosocial task that, when accomplished, would lead to the next stage on the way to full psychological maturity.

The stage that stood out to me as most significant was called "autonomy vs. shame and doubt." This stage arises around 18 months of age and continues through about three years old. This is the time when the toddler realizes that they are their own little being, separate and apart from their caregiver. They can walk; they can pick toys with which to play, and learn which foods they like and which they don't. They can also begin to use language, with the word "no" being their favorite. Rebellion emerges at this developmental stage as a sign of the assertion of autonomy in the quest of developing a healthy ego. This stage is replicated in a significant way during teen years. Accepting the concept that each human retains the feelings of their inner child that are carried within through their development led me to appreciate the power of inner child work.

I then had another tool for teaching my clients that honoring their inner intuitive wisdom about hunger, fullness, food preferences, and sense of their body's response to different foods would be the way that they could express their autonomy. This was confirmation that so much of their inability to stay on the meal plans I had given them or to maintain the rules of any diet they would undertake was all a sign of their healthy ego, instead of a sign of their personal failure.

With the psychological understanding that people were garnering, they became willing to take the risk to tune into their body to notice how a particular food felt when they ate it or when they ate it in a great quantity. They discovered that eventually, self-care took over and eating became finely aligned to well-being.

By serving these new understandings to my clients, rather than directing their eating, I guided them to an acute connection with their inner signals and the trust in their body that comes with this.

As I began to see the profound changes in my clients, I knew that I had to write a book about this so I could share it not only with the general public, but with other health professionals. Their goal, as mine had been, was to do no harm, but because they had not as yet become enlightened they kept their clients and patients trapped in their old mistrust of themselves. By telling them what to eat, what not to eat, and how much to eat, rather than listening to their bodies, clients tended to feel infantilized and incapable of taking care of themselves.

I sat down at my computer and began to list chapter headings and possible titles. I first thought of calling the book *The Tao of Eating*, because I was very intrigued by one of the main principles of Taoism—the understanding that the more we try to control our world, the more out of control it becomes. The more we allow a process to unfold in all the twists and turns it might take, the more learning that occurs along the way, and the more healing that ultimately takes place.

Now here is where synchronicity took place in my life. I have frequently found synchronicity to play a big role in my life. Often two things would happen at the same time, one not causing the other, but together creating a positive occurrence. It often feels like magic, so I know that there is something spiritual about it when it happens.

I had been renting some space in my office to Evelyn Tribole, another dietitian, who happened to live an hour away and needed to have an office to use once a week to see her patients in Los Angeles. One day Evelyn and I were passing by each other in the hallway when I looked up and saw some distress in her face. I stopped her and asked her what was wrong, and she responded that she was trying to write a book with a psychologist who "didn't know how to write" and she was very frustrated, not knowing how to proceed. Another lightbulb went off in that moment. Because I knew I was a good writer and that I had some deep understanding of the psychology of eating, I said, "Evelyn—I'll write that book with you." And then it began.

We shared ideas and found that there was a great deal of similarity between her intention for her book and my intention for mine. Thus began the writing of the first edition of *Intuitive Eating*, which was published in 1995. Each of us had specific strengths that came together to create a unique approach to healing disordered eating.

This book was revolutionary, as it was the first "non-diet" book to be written by two dietitians and to offer a detailed pathway toward the healing of one's relationship with food and body. Over the 27 years since that first book was released we have updated it, edited it, and brought in new important information for each edition. The fourth edition was published in 2020. There are now over 170 scientific studies validating intuitive eating as an evidenced-based process for achieving higher levels of physical and emotional health.

Intuitive eating is now a movement that challenges the profoundly toxic message that comes from diet culture. Diet culture is a phenomenon driven by a multi-billion-dollar industrial complex in which economic activity affects and is shaped by social and political institutions. Businesses that promote diets create or support a profit economy from these systems. Diet culture pursues its own financial interests regardless of, and often at the expense of, the best interests of society and individuals.

Although the concept of dieting has been around for centuries, I had not heard the term "diet culture" until a few years ago. I had always known how toxic dieting could be, but until I became acquainted with diet culture, I didn't know about the roots of it, nor the extent that its tendrils were strangulating people. Diet culture idolizes thinness as the ideal, driving people to pursue a multitude of diets in an attempt to achieve this goal—over and over! Diets fail for physiological, neurochemical, and psychological reasons. The system of dieting is destined to fail, while the dieter blames themself for the failure.

Diet culture also assumes that thinness is a sign of health, which is not substantiated by research. In addition, it brings moral virtue into the picture. One is elevated in society if they are thin and subjugated if they are larger. In addition, it denigrates certain foods, making them "bad," while putting other foods on a pedestal. But the piece of it that opened my mind to a different dimension was how it creates and perpetuates fatphobia, weight bias, and weight stigma, leading to the oppression of people in larger bodies.

A very sad example of how damaging fatphobia can be occurred with a teenager I was counseling. She did not have an eating disorder, had stellar labs, and had a level of self-confidence rarely seen in girls her age. She liked her body and wasn't interested in losing weight. Her biggest problem was her mother's view of her. She was somewhat larger than the size her mother wanted her to be, and the mother told her that she wanted her to lose weight for "health reasons." Although this girl saw through her mother's explanation, knowing her mother's internalized fatphobia and that she wanted her to lose weight for appearance reasons, she couldn't help taking in the health fears. When the teen told her mother that "Elyse said that my weight was not equated with health," the mother fired me. It was heart breaking to me to know that I was forbidden from contacting this girl because of my "collusion" with her body acceptance and my assurance that her weight was in no way implicated in her health.

As a result of the messaging of diet culture, I began to see the damage that was being done all around me, and ultimately understood that weight stigma was an oppression as powerful as other oppressions in the world. I have acknowledged my privileges each day and have felt pain for people in marginalized communities who are regularly oppressed—whether due to their race, religion, gender, sexual orientation, disability, or age, to name a few. I also knew that people attempting to be politically correct would never make a negative statement about any of these groups. Yet I heard many comments denigrating larger people, with an entitlement to make these comments, justified by an ill-informed belief that weight is a causative factor in ill health. But once again, I believe that the ostensible worry about health is just a way to hide their stereotypical beliefs about fat people and their terror of gaining weight, driven by their own internalized fatphobia.

My desire to learn more about weight oppression took me even deeper into learning about the racial origins of fatphobia and how entrenched it is in slavery, race science, and white supremacy. I learned how the medical community adopted anti-fatness and perpetuates the myth that weight is equated with illness, especially designating "obesity" as a disease even though most doctors in the American Medical Association didn't approve of this diagnosis.

I finally understood that the true essence of my work was to fight for social justice for people of all sizes. My mission went far beyond helping people reject dieting and find the freedom that comes with intuitive eating. It brought me to the goal of fighting weight oppression by promoting the concept that all bodies deserve dignity and respect, regardless of size, shape, or disability.

To carry out my mission, I accept most invitations I get for press and radio interviews, podcasts, and talks. Each time I am interviewed I make a point about social justice and how anti-fatness, weightism, weight stigma, or however it is framed, will be heard by the audience. I know that I've opened the eyes and ears of many people. As a Jewish woman I am committed to the Jewish principle of *tikkun olam*, which is Hebrew and translated as "repairing the world." It is thought that if one person can be healed, that person can "touch" another person and help them heal, and on and on.

I have continued to write or co-write books that put words to my beliefs, in the hope that those whom I can't personally help will be able to have their eyes opened by reading and utilizing these books. There is an *Intuitive Eating Workbook*, an *Intuitive Eating Workbook for Teens*, an *Intuitive Eating Journal*, and an *Intuitive Eating Card Deck*. I have also consulted with the authors of *How to Raise an Intuitive Eater* in the writing of their book and wrote the book's foreword. If children are consistently nurtured and protected from the damage that diet culture pours into the world, they can go on to trust their inner wisdom about eating, which was a gift they brought into this world when they were born.

Another way in which I work toward getting my message heard is to speak to as many people in the medical community as I can reach. When I have a personal doctor's appointment, I bring them a copy of *Intuitive Eating*. I speak to them about how unfair it is to people in larger bodies to have gowns that are so small that they don't fully cover their bodies. I give them data about the "obesity myth." When I have a client who is a physician, I strive to have them take their own healing that has come from their intuitive eating treatment and spread the word among their colleagues. Recently a surgeon who is my client told me that I have drastically changed her belief about people in larger bodies, and that she is telling her colleagues that rather than believing that people need to lose weight, doctors must learn how to treat people in all size bodies. She believes that medical tools must be adjusted for all sizes, and surgical techniques must be honed to fit people in all sizes. It is my hope that she is powerful enough to make a difference in the hospital in which she works.

And then there are my friends and family—often astonishingly resistant to changing their beliefs. I once was at a dinner party of six very successful women in their 50s through 70s who were doing important things in this world to help and benefit people. Four of them were talking about how bad they felt about their bodies, or what diet they were going to start (after this dinner), or how much weight they needed to lose. I stood up and forcefully spoke to them about how sad it made me feel that their sense of their worth was tied up in their body size. How much happier they would be if they radically accepted their bodies and let go of trying to change them. How much more room in their thoughts and creativity there would be if they could open up their mind space by letting go of diet culture. Maybe I made an impact, but at least I directly spoke my truth, and it may have given them something to think about.

And, finally, I supervise and teach students, younger dietitians, psychotherapists, nurses, and other health professionals about how to help people heal from their dieting, disordered eating, and eating disorders by incorporating the principles and essence of intuitive eating. I must pass on the torch, after 40 years of private practice, so they can all make a significant impact on healing and repairing the world.

In most recent years, as a result of the awakening that has come from the Black Lives Matter movement, I have added to my anti-diet work by committing to learning about the injustices that have been dealt upon BIPOC (Black, Indigenous, and People of Color) individuals. I have done extensive reading, have made contributions to important anti-racist causes, and have joined a number of groups committed to reparation of the damage that has been done historically by systemic racism. But that is not enough. I have hired an anti-racist coach to teach me how I have inadvertently caused harm and to guide me into action that I can take in my own anti-racist work.

Looking back at my career, I believe that I've been a professional maverick from the time I was in graduate school through the many years of working with people in my office, in an eating disorder treatment center, and in other professional settings. The status quo has never felt right to me, whether disagreeing with the professor, or with a colleague or a physician or a friend or family member. I have strived to push myself to unlearn old ways of thinking and learn new, more equitable ways to think. I have made many mistakes, and as I try to heal the damage of these mistakes, I give myself grace for having not known and for changing when I have learned better ways of being.

MOVING BEYOND
A SHADOW OF A DIET

JUDITH MATZ

IN THE LATE 1980S I co-led a support group for participants in the Optifast® program, a medically supervised fasting plan for weight loss. I thought that "helping" people to lose weight, even if it didn't work for everyone, was worthwhile. I didn't realize at the time just how much harm I was causing. I didn't know any better.

But my sister, Ellen Frankel, did. She had struggled with an eating disorder as a teenager, which led her to embrace the non-diet approach (as developed by Jane Hirschmann and Carol Munter, authors of *Overcoming Overeating*, and Geneen Roth, author of *Breaking Free from Compulsive Eating*) in her later work as an eating disorders therapist. As I prescribed diets and she rejected them we had numerous heated discussions about our dad's weight. I suggested low-fat eating and exercise, which was Optifast's recommended "lifestyle" approach; she suggested we just leave him alone!

As I continued working with people who had completed the fasting program, my sister's words started to sink in. I began to see that the members of the program who kept the weight off and were considered to be "successful" were engaged in the very same disordered behaviors I had seen during my postgraduate training on an eating disorders treatment team: counting calories or fat grams, measuring or weighing their food, over-exercising, and a constant preoccupation with food and weight. As my discomfort grew, I turned to Ellen for advice. She recommended I read *Overcoming Overeating*, and that book was pivotal in changing the direction I took as a therapist.

Overcoming Overeating resonated not only professionally, but personally as well. I had gone through a dieting phase of my own from high school through my early 20s, partly because I was afraid of getting fat, but also because it was a way for girls to connect. My attempts to restrict food actually led to a lot of out-of-control eating that left me full of angst and took the pleasure out of food. I was fortunate to realize on my own that the deprivation of dieting was the trigger for my binges, and with that "aha" moment came a promise to myself to never restrict foods again for the purpose of weight loss. And yet it never occurred to me to bring that epiphany to my early professional work. As I now reflect on why that is, I understand that my own fatphobia made me believe that "helping" people at higher weights get thinner was necessary for them to live a good, healthy life. It wasn't until I read the work of Hirschmann and Munter that I began to deeply understand the harm of my beliefs and regret my participation in the Optifast program.

Now that my philosophy had shifted, I decided to develop an introductory workshop to teach the concepts of ending the diet cycle and becoming a "demand" eater, which was the phrase used in *Overcoming Overeating* to describe the concept of responding to physical cues for hunger and satiation (Ellen and I would later use the term *attuned eating* to describe this concept). This workshop evolved into an ongoing group that I led for over 25 years. Every Wednesday evening I gathered for 90 minutes with women who were taking a journey to let go of the shame they felt around food and weight. By sharing their struggles with each other within a safe, non-judgmental space, members became empowered to reject diet culture and embrace a nourishing and pleasurable relationship with food. As members healed their relationship with food and left the group, new participants would join. It was always an honor to witness the moments of excitement as these women found freedom from the tyranny of dieting.

I want to note that when I created my non-diet workshop in the late 1980s, it was before the time of the internet, and I existed within my own bubble. I relied on a book written by two New York therapists, the advice of my sister, and my own experiences as an ex-dieter. I didn't know about the other mental health professionals who were also rejecting the diet mentality. I had absolutely no awareness of the fat activism by Black and gay women or about the existence of the National Association to Advance Fat Acceptance (NAAFA), a civil rights organization formed in the 1960s.

It was when I advertised that first introductory workshop that I learned there were others in my local area who had already reached these same conclusions about diet failure. After seeing my workshop flyer posted on a bulletin board at a women's center, Nancy Guenther contacted me about her similar work. Nancy, along with Carol Coven Grannick, another local therapist who previously worked with Carol Munter and was now using the non-diet approach with her clients and in workshops, were in the process of forming a Chicago Center for Overcoming Overeating that would be affiliated with Jane and Carol's National Center for Overcoming Overeating. I remember the excitement I felt sitting at Carol Coven Grannick's kitchen table as Hirschmann and Munter interviewed me by phone about how I came to do this work and my commitment to moving it forward. In their search to work with people who would help spread their social justice agenda, they wanted to feel confident that I would advance their approach beyond my own private practice. I assured them I would.

I jumped at the chance to be part of a bigger movement, and together Nancy, Carol (Grannick) and I went to New York City to meet with Jane and Carol (Munter) and begin our collaboration. For personal reasons Nancy had to withdraw from our partnership, so Carol G. and I formed the Chicago Center for Overcoming Overeating, Inc. Then in 1994 Jane, Carol M., Carol G. and myself launched the *Overcoming Overeating Newsletter* with the intention of creating support and community for people rejecting the diet mentality. Our newsletter was subscription-based and mailed to people all over the country, promoting the following philosophy:

- Compulsive eaters are people whose hands or minds move toward food when they are not at all hungry. Compulsive eating has nothing to do with the size of your body. Compulsive eaters come in all shapes and sizes. Compulsive eating has to do with how many hours you spend preoccupied with thoughts about what you are eating and what you look like. The Overcoming Overeating approach does not address eating disorders; it addresses dieting disorders, the casualties of the diet industry.
- Compulsive eating may seem self-destructive, but it is always an attempt at self-help.
- Diets never, ever solve eating and weight problems. Diets cause compulsive eating.
- Significant change flows only from self-acceptance, never from self-contempt
- Food is not the compulsive eater's problem; **it is the solution.** The Overcoming Overeating approach teaches people how to eat their way out of an eating problem.

Given that these principles were developed almost 40 years ago, imagine how radical they were at the time. Rejecting diets and body hatred were met with ridicule by just about everyone. My daughter now tells me that when she was in elementary school her friends' mothers would actually laugh at her when they asked what kind of work I did and she told them that I helped people stop dieting. They told her that couldn't be true, and that she must mean I help people *stay* on their diets. When Jane and Carol M. were in Chicago for their

When Women Stop Hating Their Bodies book tour in 1995, a radio show host told Carol Munter that she was way ahead of her time. "I hope not," Munter replied. "I've already been doing this work for a decade." Sadly, the radio host was right.

At the time of our original writings, "compulsive eating" was the commonly used term for eating that was either deprivation-driven or used to manage emotional distress. Binge eating, as a discrete eating disorder, was still decades away from recognition. There was no such thing as Instagram, Facebook, blogs, podcasts, or listservs to connect around these ideas and terminologies.

It's important to recognize that the use of language changes over time. Recently there's been some criticism of the term "overeating," which I've used for most of my career to refer to people eating past fullness or feeling out of control with food. While I've always rejected the term "overweight" because it is stigmatizing and suggests that there's a "correct" weight for someone to be, I considered "overeating" to be subjective, based on a person's own experience of eating past the point of comfort. However, as I recently worked on *The Making Peace with Food Card Deck* with my co-author, Christy Harrison, she explained that she also rejects the term "overeating" because it can be stigmatizing, and because some people with eating disorders believe they are "overeating" when they're actually not eating enough. In response to this feedback, I've now abandoned the term in favor of other ways to describe the experience of eating past fullness.

A thread in a Facebook group recently attacked Hirschmann and Munter for their use of the term "overeating." I hope that when people look back at all of us in the earlier stages of what are now referred to as anti-diet and weight-inclusive frameworks, they will do so with compassion and respect for the learning that takes place over time. Wherever any of us are in our process of doing this work, we must continue to listen to others—and especially those with lived experience. We must realize when we've made errors and be willing to change our thoughts and actions so that we don't continue to do harm. I have no doubt that the ways we approach these topics and movements at this moment will also change over time.

While we ended the publication of the *Overcoming Overeating Newsletter* in the late 1990s, our philosophy still has merit in its understanding of how diets are causal in rebound or binge eating, and how the reach for food in times of emotional distress is an attempt at self-help that deserves to be met with compassion and curiosity, not self-blame. The belief in helping people accept their bodies and reject conventional standards equating "thinness" with health, beauty, and happiness was at the core of Jane and Carol's *Campaign to End*

Body Hatred. This campaign was rooted in social justice concerns *as we understood them at the time.* Our more recent understanding of the importance of frameworks such as being trauma-informed, cultivating self-compassion, using the lens of intersectionality, and acknowledging our privileges offers opportunities to reconsider and/or deepen the work of early anti-diet pioneers.

My journey as a speaker and writer began when, through our affiliation with Hirschmann and Munter, Carol Coven Grannick and I were invited to participate in and present at our first AHELP conference (the Association for the Health Enrichment of Large People) in 1992. What a thrill to meet more like-minded colleagues across the country—some of whom became and have remained my friends—and to attend the presentations of so many wise and knowledgeable researchers, clinicians, and activists. I'll never forget Esther Rothblum giving a talk in which I thought she made an error in the title: *I'll Die for the Revolution, But Don't Ask Me Not to Diet.* Didn't she mean, "Don't Ask Me to Diet?" But I was the one who had it wrong as she spoke to the continued bias against fat people within the feminist movement.

The AHELP conference was the first of many conferences I would attend over the years where I continued to present my own work, learn from others, and build and become part of a wise and vibrant community. While AHELP dissolved—and again, in these early days of the internet there were no easy ways to stay in touch other than email—I continued to work with my clients to make peace with food and feel at home in their bodies, to collaborate with Carol under the umbrella of the Chicago Center for Overcoming Overeating, Inc., to offer workshops throughout the Chicago area, and to write for and edit the *Overcoming Overeating Newsletter.*

Writing is my most effective way to support people who have already rejected diet culture. But more important, I believe, is my ability to get people entrenched in the diet mindset to question the impact and harm of diet culture on themselves and others in their lives from a place of compassion. In the early 2000s I was acutely aware that members of my own profession—therapists—were perpetuating harm by supporting weight loss methods and strategies with their clients. Given that there was very little training in graduate school about the treatment of eating disorders—and certainly none about the dangers of dieting and weight stigma—I wanted to teach mental health professionals about a non-diet, size-accepting approach, which is how I conceptualized it at the time. My sister, Ellen, and I were standing in the kitchen of my parent's home when the idea came to me: together we could write a book for professionals about how to integrate the non-diet approach into their clinical practice. Ellen and I have always loved coming up with clever titles, and at some point she had

thought of *Beyond a Shadow of a Diet.* I suggested we use her title and collaborate on a book. She agreed, and we navigated our way through the process of
publishing, eventually signing a contract with Routledge, who released *Beyond
a Shadow of a Diet* in 2004 (we published a second edition in 2014). We've
heard from many professionals over the years that our book was their introduction to a non-diet approach and that it transformed the way they worked with
their clients.

During the process of writing our manuscript, when it was still more difficult to connect with others who were like-minded, I interviewed Cheri Erdman, a colleague in the Chicago area and author of *Nothing to Lose*, about
some of the information in her book that we wanted to incorporate into ours.
She suggested that Ellen and I join a listserv (a what?!!!) to connect with other
people who were engaged in similar work. Joining *Show Me the Data*, a listserv
started by psychologist and thought leader Deb Burgard, was life changing.
Now there was a way to discuss ideas and issues and to ask questions in real
time. Or to take research from prestigious journals that promoted weight loss
for health and have brilliant minds from around the country and the world
to critique these studies. This listserv gave me opportunities to share my own
work, and to use the work of others to support what I wrote and talked about
in presentations. This connection via my computer was energizing and exciting.

But even more energizing and exciting was attending conferences and meeting the people whose names were now often in my inbox. Deb Burgard, whom
I quoted most recently in my 2022 article for the *Psychotherapy Networker* entitled "Unlearning Weight Stigma," and with whom I presented a workshop
called "Dismantling Weight Bias in BED Treatment: Using the HAES® Model
for Stigma Resistance" at a major eating disorders conference. Jon Robison,
an early reader of our first book, whom I met in person for the first time at a
Renfrew conference. I remember Ellen kicking me under the table when Jon
stood up at the presenters' dinner and praised our soon-to-be released *Beyond
a Shadow of a Diet*—a moment of great pride. Lindo Bacon, who collaborated
with me on an article about diabetes and intuitive eating for *Diabetes Self-
Management* that offered people an alternative to traditional recommendations
for weight loss. Carmen Cool, who models over and over how to incorporate
activism into the healing work of psychotherapy. Too many more to name, but
the shared mission, respect, and joy in these relationships has truly enriched
my work and life.

Following the release of *Beyond a Shadow of a Diet*, an editor who had seen
our proposal for *The Diet Survivor's Handbook* invited Ellen and me to submit

our manuscript to their acquisitions team. In 2006 Sourcebooks published *The Diet Survivor's Handbook,* used widely by mental health professionals to work with their clients and by the general public.

Many people writing about rejecting diets and, instead, using cues of hunger and fullness to guide eating often implied that weight loss would follow. I'm proud that in the two books we co-authored in the early 2000s, Ellen and I understood from the outset that weight loss as a goal of making peace with food was counterproductive, harmful, and promoted weight stigma. We believed from the beginning that bodies of all shapes and sizes are worthy and deserving of respect.

Over the following years I remained dedicated to helping people unlearn diet culture and weight stigma through my private practice, writing, and presentations at conferences and other workshops. In 2018 my association with PESI, a non-profit organization that offers trainings and continuing education to mental health/health professionals, allowed me even greater reach to teach about the harms of diet culture, the anti-diet and Health At Every Size (HAES) frameworks, and most importantly, to ask participants to examine their own explicit and implicit anti-fat bias. I continue to offer trainings throughout the U.S. and Canada on a regular basis, and I've also collaborated with PESI to publish *The Body Positivity Card Deck* with my co-author Amy Pershing, and *The Making Peace with Food Card Deck* with my co-author Christy Harrison.

The formation of the Association for Size Diversity and Health (ASDAH) in the early 2000s, which gave more shape to the mission of weight inclusiveness and became the home of the HAES paradigm, is written about in other chapters in this book. As happens with all movements, the tenets and needs of the community have changed over time. While I attended ASDAH conferences for many years to learn and to network, I never took on a position of leadership. But through the ongoing learning that happened in this organization and others, I've become more aware of the need to look at the intersections of other marginalized identities with that of body size, and how my many privileges (e.g. white, cisgender, able-bodied and thin) affect what I've put out in the world. I remain on a journey where I continue to learn, even as I feel gratified that I've contributed to the greater understanding of the need to dismantle diet culture and challenge systems that uphold weight stigma within my profession, as well as for my clients and the general public.

Over the years I've lost touch with Jane Hirschmann and Carol Munter, my original mentors. But I've never lost touch with our mission. In our first conversation, they asked me to do more than expand my private practice. They asked me to make a difference in the movement to reject dieting, promote peace with food, and encourage body acceptance. I believe that with the support, wisdom, and collaboration of a vibrant community, I've lived up to the challenge.

THE ORIGINS OF EDAW AND NEDA
THROUGH THE LENS OF THE BOLDER MODEL

MICHAEL P. LEVINE *and* MARGO MAINE

BASED ON THE VISION and mission statements at its website, "envision[ing] a world without eating disorders," the National Eating Disorders Association (NEDA) "supports individuals and families affected by eating disorders, and serves as a catalyst for prevention, cures and access to quality care." NEDA has been the United States' foremost non-profit organization providing information, support, and various sorts of services and programs to people with eating disorders, their families and concerned friends, educators and coaches, the media, policy makers at the state and federal levels, and a vast contingent of local, regional, and national advocates.

Its earliest program, and still one of its most prominent, began as Eating Disorders Awareness Week (EDAW). Now known as NEDAwareness Week, in the USA it takes place the last week in February. This chapter is our experience of the origin stories of EDAW and the major forerunner of NEDA, a nonprofit organization called Eating Disorders Awareness & Prevention (EDAP). We conclude with a brief statement of some of the many important lessons we learned—and were not available in our doctoral training—in the course of being involved, somehow, in the beginning. Thus, this chapter is also, from each of our perspectives, the story of "somehow."

MICHAEL LEVINE AND EDAW

I (ML) am six months shy of 73 years old. Between 1974 and 1979 I earned an MA and a PhD in experimental psychology, with an emphasis on personality theory, at the University of California at Santa Barbara. My graduate training, beyond my exposure to various "schools" of thought in psychology and psychiatry, was extremely narrow. I obtained my PhD with only one course outside of the psychology department: a speech pathology course focused on single-subject designs in applied behavior analysis. Under no pressure otherwise, I naively, indeed immaturely, considered three statistics courses to be the equivalent of "having to take"—actually "not having to take"—what my peers and I blithely referred to as "some foreign language." I did know for certain that what I was doing "empirically" as an "*experimental* psychologist" was superior to "social studies" such as anthropology, sociology, and political science. I received my doctorate having never heard of public health, media studies, or community psychology.

My first feminist role model was my wife. In 1981, two years after I be-came an assistant professor in the psychology department at Kenyon College in central Ohio, she joined a small advocacy group that eventually established a domestic violence shelter for our very rural county. Their consciousness-raising efforts included speaking to civic groups and training law enforcement officers. Consequently they formed a speakers' bureau, which to no one's surprise ini-tially consisted entirely of women in the advocacy group. After a while my wife volunteered me to join this bureau, because my doctoral dissertation addressed learned helplessness, a theory that featured prominently in the first edition of Lenore Walker's influential book *The Battered Woman* (1979, Harper & Row). My initial presentation, to a business group, marked the first time I had ever spoken, let alone to non-college students, about psychology, gender, culture, prevention, social change, and—although I didn't know it—social justice.

My visibility in speaking and later writing newspaper articles about domes-tic violence led to my being recruited by Norma Fladen to serve as an educator and advocate on the education committee of the Knox County Mental Health Association (MHA), of which she as director was the only full-time employee. I discovered that I loved this volunteer work, a good deal of which was consis-tent with my teaching abnormal psychology. Soon I found myself immersed in it when I wasn't teaching. But it created dissonance, at least in me, with what I perceived to be my department's and my "field's" expectations for laboratory-based "empirical" research: "I like education and advocacy, in person, on the radio, in print" clashed with "This is not what we rigorously *empirical* ex-perimental psychologists, who are *not* social scientists, do," which conflicted with "But I resonate with so many aspects of this mental health work," which clashed with (repeat various versions of this sequence as Levine's characteristic rumination requires).

One late afternoon in early 1983 I was sitting quasi-comfortably (see "various versions" above) in the midst of our group of education committee volunteers at the MHA office, preparing for a meeting. One of the volunteers said conversationally, "You know, maybe we ought to stop doing our piecemeal, one-shot programs for a while. Instead, let's do a set of integrated newspaper articles, radio shows, a training session for professionals, a presentation to the public, that sort of thing." Another person responded, "We should have something for students, too!" We all smiled when our designated curmudgeon added, "Please. You don't mean one of those silly 'awareness weeks,' do you?" After we all agreed that of course we wouldn't have to call it that, someone interjected, "Fine, but what would be the topic?"

Just then the Kenyon College physician, Tracy Schermer, MD, who was not a member of our committee, stopped by the office to pick up some flyers for the college's health center. He must have overhead the conversation, because right away he filled the ensuing silence with "anorexia nervosa." While the other education subcommittee members just looked at him perplexed, I seriously thought he was joking. As Nancy Ellis-Ordway alluded to in her chapter, I too was told, in this case by several prominent abnormal psychology textbooks, that anorexia nervosa (AN) was a controversial diagnostic construct that one would likely never encounter. Indeed, these books proclaimed (now laughably) that, like "multiple personality disorder," AN might not even be a "real" psychological disorder. When Dr. Schermer enthusiastically followed up with, "I know an organization in Columbus that specializes in treatment and public education," I wondered for more than a moment whether the past 15 minutes was an elaborate prank at my professorial expense. As the others in the group began excitedly to work with these facts, I thought (fortunately not out loud) this direction might be a *really bad* idea for the Mental Health Association and its tiny budget.

Several weeks later Norma and I drove to Columbus to meet the leaders of the Center for the Treatment of Eating Disorders (CTED)/National Anorexic Aid Society (NAAS). They were enthusiastic about working with us, agreeing for $1,000 (an embarrassingly large proportion of our yearly budget in 1983) to come to Mt. Vernon (the county seat of Knox County) in October. In the course of a single day two experts would appear on local radio, be interviewed by our hometown newspaper, do a two-hour professional training session at the local YMCA, and give a public lecture in the evening at the beautiful auditorium at the Nazarene College located on the edge of town. Informational flyers would be available at that lecture, covering topics such as warning signs of "eating disorders." Of course I was totally unfamiliar with that phrase, and with the diagnostic category "bulimia nervosa," even though I was teaching about the *DSM-III*, which had been published three years earlier.

As our conversation with the CTED/NAAS leaders was ending, I remembered to ask for their educational materials for middle school and high school students. This was met with a question: did I mean a "curriculum guide"? As my father had been a high school teacher and a reluctant, sometimes cynical, member of "curriculum committees," I tentatively replied, "Yeah, I guess." The director smiled at me and said "No. Why don't you write one? That would be great." Norma and I were halfway back to Mt. Vernon when I realized that despite my father's work, my nine years of post-secondary higher education, and my four years as a professor, I had no idea what a curriculum guide looked like. More to the point, I asked myself, why did I agree to write one in order to educate middle school and high school students, whom I had never taught, about a subject about which I knew nothing apart from skepticism?

I spent the summer of 1983 reading all I could about eating disorders, including some of the books mentioned in other chapters in this volume. With feedback from the CTED/NAAS leaders and one of my MHA colleagues who was a middle school social studies teacher, and with some guidance from an extensive nutrition, exercising, and eating disorders curriculum guide kindly sent to me by Dick Moriarty, PhD of the Bulimia and Anorexia Nervosa Association (of Canada; https://bana.ca/), I was able to craft what became *The Psychology of Eating Disorders: A Lesson Plan for Health and Science Courses, Grades 7–12*, published eventually by NAAS (Levine, 1984). In early October 1983 we held our week of education and events, which was successful and invigorating for our community and for the MHA. I will never forget hoping that maybe 25 people would show up to the YMCA for our professional training session, and then being frozen with amazement at, before scrambling to accommodate—more chairs, more handouts, more coffee, more snacks—the nearly 120 eager and grateful clinicians and educators who participated.

This was the foundation of the first Eating Disorders Awareness Week in the USA. And the entire exciting, humbling, confusing process was a key moment in the "long strange trip" that transformed my life. The director of the CTED/NAAS was Amy Baker Enright (now Amy Baker Dennis, PhD), my first professional role model. Amy was and is a dynamic leader whom I later recognized as a Bolder Model (Irving, 1999), a person of substance who takes up space in the world and acts passionately and courageously on the personal, professional, and political levels to prevent and reduce mental disorder, while promoting biopsychosocial health. Amy was the catalyst—the driving force to be reckoned with—for the yearly "Columbus eating disorder conference" mentioned several times in other chapters in this book. It was at the conference held in 1984 that I presented my first in-person paper, a description of our EDAW and my curriculum guide, the rights to which we had sold to the NAAS to cover the cost of their essential participation. And it was through my work with Amy, NAAS, and the first EDAW that I met two of the three other early Bolder/Role Models for me and my prevention/advocacy work, Niva Piran, PhD of Canada (see, e.g., Piran, Levine, & Steiner-Adair, 1999), and Margo Maine, PhD.

Margo Maine, EDAP, and the Origins of NEDA

"Somehow," as Michael suggested, we both became instrumental in developing ideas and organizations that would serve the needs of those affected by eating disorders. How did we get here from there?

While Michael and his colleagues were educating and advocating about eating disorders in Ohio in the early 1980s, I was in the midst of practicum and internship placements as a master's level provider in the psychology department at a tertiary care children's hospital in Connecticut, finishing my graduate courses and in need of a dissertation topic. During an otherwise uneventful first meeting, my dissertation advisor suggested that students should pick a topic we loved for our research. While that may sound elementary, it was big news to me. I had only heard people complain about their dissertations. It never occurred to me that I had a choice to not hate it. Thank the goddesses for that advice.

I had always been drawn to the interplay of culture, self-esteem, family dynamics, adolescent development, and gender, and eating disorders seemed to be a great example of this. At the children's hospital most of our early cases were teenage girls with anorexia nervosa, but soon enough some presented with bulimia nervosa, and then younger children and a few boys. The field was just emerging, and research was in early gestation. The literature about recovery and outcome was sparse and not very promising. I decided to conduct in-depth interviews with women who had recovered. I learned so much, and their words still inform me. Graduate education provides a framework of information and theory, but falls far short of lived experience. The most important lesson was learning to listen while encouraging these women to describe their experience of the illness, the recovery process, and what life has been like since. Now, four decades later, I am still mindful of listening to my patients and not simply to the theory or research or what I as an "expert" already know. Understanding the narrative of their eating disorder always empowers patients and gives clinicians a roadmap for treatment.

Despite my passionate interest, my clinical supervisors and others ahead of me professionally advised me not to specialize in eating disorders, stating that they were "just a fad" and I would have nothing to do in a few years. *Somehow* I knew that what I was seeing in my office and in the hospital hallways was just a preview of what was to come in response to the powerful, toxic, and contradictory messages girls were receiving from our culture. Constant objectification, sexualization, and gender inequity were distorting their identities and their desires. Right before our eyes, women's bodies were becoming a form of currency, and the young women I was meeting were caught in this unprecedented and little understood biopsychosocial storm. I assumed it was only going to get worse—and it has.

The pain and suffering of my patients, their families, and of my "dissertation subjects" soon convinced me of the need to work on prevention, education, and outreach. Parallel to Michael's network of activity in Ohio that created the original EDAW and other efforts, I was on the ground in schools, community and professional organizations, and college campuses, discussing the growing problem and creating educational materials and programs. The hospitals where I worked in the 1980s and 1990s had firm commitments to community and professional education and supported this mission. *Somehow* I did as many as 40-45 presentations a year in addition to creating and overseeing hospital-based treatment programs for eating disorders and treating patients directly.

Looking back at my curriculum vitae entries in those years, you can see that I tended to look at systems, not just at individuals, for answers. A sampling of the titles of my presentations include:

- College Campuses as Catalysts for Social Change: Your Role in Prevention of Eating Disorders
- The Body, The Culture, The Self: A One-Day Course on Eating Disorders
- Eating Disorders, Body Image, and the Performing Arts
- Food, Self, and Systems: A One-Day Course on Eating Disorders
- Body Wars on Campus
- How To Prevent Eating Disorders: Curriculum Ideas
- Addictions Because of Culture: Dieting, Exercise, and Food

Michael and I were not the only pioneers in this new territory. Across the USA others were doing similar work, and suddenly we began to meet like-minded souls. I met Leigh Cohn and Lindsey Hall of Gürze Books in 1987 at the American Association of Marriage and Family Therapy conference in Chicago, where I spoke about the role of fathers in female development and eating disorders. While Leigh and Lindsey were not interested in turning my dissertation into a book, Leigh did encourage me to focus on a topic from it, and in 1991 we published *Father Hunger* (revised in 2004). I met Michael in

April 1988 when, along with Catherine Steiner-Adair, EdD (see Piran et al., 1999), we both gave talks at a conference sponsored by Anorexia Bulimia Care, a small organization founded by parents of young women with eating disorders in the Boston area. "ABC" is now MEDA, the Multi-Service Eating Disorder Association (https://www.medainc.org/), a larger organization that provides group support, educational programs and services, and an annual professional conference. The founder of ABC, Patricia Warner, was an inspiring advocate for patients and families and helped to organize the New England states to coordinate Eating Disorders Awareness Week activities and sponsor some joint programs.

I thank Pat Warner, now deceased, for her heart and tireless energy, and especially for bringing Michael to Boston that spring day. Meeting him has changed my life and brought out the best in me as an advocate and a human being. *Somehow* this field is full of those moments, and I am grateful for these gifts.

These collaborations of small groups of people were happening across the country. *Somehow,* after several painful attempts, we came together to form one national organization we named Eating Disorders Awareness and Prevention (EDAP) (circa 1987), which later morphed into National Eating Disorders Association (NEDA). Leigh and Lindsey were central characters in our early organization; EDAP was housed in their garage for a couple of years as we grew and raised funds to support an office and staff.

To keep myself going as a clinician, facing the heartbreak and devastation caused by eating disorders day in and day out, I had to believe we could do something to stop what the media erroneously labeled "this fad." To Michael, me, and many others, prevention was absolutely an essential core ingredient of eating disorders work. While we ascribed to the biopsychosocial nature of eating disorders, we were convinced that the sociocultural environment was a key toxic factor and should not be underestimated, while others were more inclined to stress the biogenetic factors. Nature needs nurture, and nature is very unlikely to be explanation for significant increases in the incidence of eating disorders over time measured in decades.

By 1993 *somehow,* due to significant support from the Nielsen family, EDAP had an office in Seattle, a staff, and a comprehensive mission statement vowing to increase the awareness and prevention of eating disorders by pursuing the following goals:

- To challenge cultural attitudes and values that promote the development of eating disorders;
- To advocate the importance of self-esteem based on inner

beauty and personal strengths, rather than on appearance and weight;
- To promote attitudes and behaviors toward food, body image, and exercise that will encourage psychological and physical health;
- To eliminate the **3Ds**: Body Dissatisfaction, Dieting behavior, and Drive for thinness;
- To enhance public and professional awareness of the signs and symptoms of eating disorders and specialized treatment options;
- To emphasize that early detection and prompt treatment are likely to speed the recovery process;
- To encourage public understanding of eating disorders to facilitate compassionate, supportive attitudes.

In addition to EDAW (now NEDAW), we sponsored Fearless Friday (a holiday from dieting), national conferences and local workshops, educational materials, and programs. To address our prevention goals we developed the EDAP Puppet Project, an interactive prevention program with life-size puppets (Irving, 2000). The scripts addressed family, social, and relational issues that affect young children's self-esteem and body image, potentially contributing to eating disorders. For older children we created the GOGIRLS! program, blending media literacy, activism, and advocacy with extensive input from Michael, Niva Piran, and Lori Irving, PhD, as well as EDAP staff members (see Piran et al., 1999). The program included research so we could evaluate its effectiveness along the way.

Our Media Watchdog initiative was also impressive. The EDAP National Media Advocacy Campaign employed two strategies: to *attack* advertisements that promote negative body image, dieting and disordered eating by letter writing campaigns and media statements, and to *reward* positive messages by giving awards and recognition through media statements. EDAP watchdog members would write letters, or sign onto ours, directed to those with the power to change the messages. Many companies withdrew ads and indicated a change of approach after hearing our concerns. This program excited and energized so many.

These enormous projects were part of the pioneering work done by EDAP board members, staff, and volunteers, all of whom were creative and generous believers in our cause. EDAP survived due to the support of one family—Don and Melissa Nielsen and their family—and an army of EDAP supporters, too many to name. The energy was electric. The commitment was inspiring. The results were amazing.

EDAP leadership included many familiar names as president, including

Michael and myself. Craig Johnson, PhD did not join our efforts immediately, concerned that prevention efforts, if not done well, may increase the problem, but our track record impressed him. When he joined the board and served as president (circa 2001), he observed that the eating disorders field was somewhat disjointed and confusing to people outside it. Consequently he advocated for bringing the smaller organizations together under one roof. The Ohio organization NAAS, so central to training professionals through its conference and the inspiration for EDAW/NEDAW—and such an integral part of Michael's professional and personal development—was one of the groups that merged into EDAP. The two largest organizations, EDAP and AABA— the American Anorexia/Bulimia Association—agreed to consolidate in order to improve our effectiveness. I was on both boards and recognized the many advantages of merging. One voice and united efforts would both simplify and empower our efforts to educate and engage leaders and decision makers who can advance the causes of preventing eating disorders and improving the care and support available to those suffering, all the while maintaining that vision of a world without eating disorders.

NEDA was incorporated in 2001. Many of the founders stayed involved, serving as advisors or on committees. It continued to consolidate and welcome other organizations under its roof, most recently BEDA (Binge Eating Disorder Association) and NAMED (National Association of Men with Eating Disorders). And like many other large nonprofits, NEDA is now a different organization than what emerged from its homegrown, organic roots, having left behind its childhood and adolescence and moved into adulthood. Still, the moral of this story is that, *somehow,* energy, dedication, and collaboration can achieve great things. Not that long ago, no one advocated for recognizing the extent and seriousness of eating disorders and for addressing prevention, treatment, and recovery in a systematic organized manner. NEDA helped to change this. Let us all continue to give voice to those affected by eating disorders and do everything we can to create that world without eating disorders.

How does our *"somehow"* potentially apply to others who are committed to preventing the spectrum of body image problems and disordered eating? We hope that the adverb *"somehow"* implies not sheer or pure luck, but that we might never completely understand a set of processes of which we are often in awe.

MICHAEL'S CURRENT INTERPRETATION

My personal, professional, and political development through the fields of body image and eating disorders has hardly been linear, so I will start with the importance of Bolder Models in my life (Irving, 1999), beginning with Amy Baker Dennis and flourishing in the presence of Linda Smolak, PhD, Margo Maine, and Niva Piran. Lori Irving, PhD and I chose that phrase as a feminist extension of the Boulder Model of scientist-practitioner training in clinical psychology, developed in the late 1940s under the guidance of the American Psychological Association's president Carl Rogers. Arguably the most influential psychologist of the 20th century, some of Rogers' work (e.g., the actualizing tendency, the self, person-centered therapy) has deep roots in Gestalt psychology. One well-known Gestalt method for studying "aha moments" in problem-solving is the "matchstick challenge": using six matchsticks of equal length, make four equilateral triangles. It turns out that the solution requires the brain/mind/person to be open to synthesizing the individual sticks into a pyramid in three dimensions.

Thanks to my parents, personality, and privileges, I had a number of "matchsticks," but I did not know, let alone understand, what to do and be with them. These included a Jewish sense of obligation to learning and community, an interest in the lack of distinctions between "normal and abnormal," a knack for teaching, and a sense of humor and showmanship (arguably histrionics). It took my Bolder Models such as Margo to enable me to experience the passion, possibility, respect, and substance necessary for my Self, limited by conditions of worth, to form all the matchsticks into a larger, more capable, more assertive, and more open self with direction and purpose. My message, at least to those like my younger self: seek out those Bolder Models, be open to the "psychological matchsticks" that emerge, and pursue your commitments in collaboration with others whose lives are moved in that direction. They are both, *somehow*, nearby and somewhere out there.

MARGO'S CURRENT INTERPRETATION

I love Michael's matchsticks metaphor. I always learn from him. Now, over 35 years into our collaboration and deep, abiding friendship, I am still learning. Message to students: find people who make you think and help you to see the bigger picture. It helps if those people, like Michael, not only teach and challenge you, but also make you laugh.

My matchsticks emerged from a family that instilled: the need to make the world a better place; the importance of relationships and caring for others; an appreciation of the systems around us and how they shape our experience, values, and behavior; the critical role of teaching and sharing knowledge; the power of standing up for what is right; and good old Irish determination and stubbornness. That dogged determination really does help, although it may "get old" to those around me.

My formative years intersected with the civil rights movement, the Vietnam war, and the feminist movement, all critical catalysts for social change. I came to see that the wars we were waging against women's bodies (and soon against men and all genders) were as wrong as the Vietnam war and racism. *Somehow* we must fight back, first by raising consciousness and then by working together in systematic ways to chip away at the wrongs and to transform our culture to one that wages peace with our bodies instead of profiting from our self-hatred. EDAP, EDAW, NEDA and all the offshoots of these initiatives have helped, but we must move forward fast and furious to do more, to catch up with this rapidly changing world and challenge the toxic messages now directed to people of all ages and all genders, races, ethnicities, classes, and abilities.

As Michael suggests, we all need to find our matchsticks and the people who bring out the best in us and help us to synthesize it into self-as-purpose-meaning-direction. Allow yourself to be passionate and to follow those passions. I am so grateful for the simple advice to study something I cared about at that dissertation meeting back in 1980.

My simple advice: listen to your passions, follow them, and find people who inspire you with their passion. In this respect, Michael and I agree with the encouraging quotation—attributed to Margaret Mead but without a discernible source—with which the late Lori Irving used to close her emails:

> "Never doubt that a small group of thoughtful, committed citizens can change the world. Indeed, it's the only thing that ever has."

REFERENCES

Irving, L.M. (1999). A Bolder Model of Prevention: Science, Practice, and Activism. In N. Piran, M.P. Levine, & C. Steiner-Adair (Eds.), *Preventing Eating Disorders: A Handbook of Interventions and Special Challenges* (Routledge).

Irving, L.M. (2000). Promoting size acceptance in elementary school children: The EDAP Puppet Program. *Eating Disorders: The Journal of Treatment and Prevention, 8*, 221-232.

Levine, M. P. (1984). *The Psychology of Eating Disorders: A Lesson Plan for Health and Science Courses, Grades 7–12.* Columbus, OH: The National Anorexic Aid Society.

Maine, M. (1991). *Father Hunger: Fathers, Daughters and Food.* Gürze Books.

National Eating Disorders Association (2022). https://www.nationaleatingdisorders.org/

Piran, N., Levine, M. P., & Steiner-Adair, C. (Eds.) (1999). *Preventing Eating Disorders: A Handbook of Interventions and Special Challenges.* Brunner/Mazel.

My White Fat Activism

Marilyn Wann

WHEN I LOOK BACK ON MY FAT ACTIVISM, which began in 1993, there are things I'm proud of, things that I hope did people good and were useful in the world:

- With the print 'zine and book versions of *FAT!SO?*, I brought a light hearted, joyful style of rebelliousness to the fat freedom fight.
- I worked with other fat activists (Sondra Solovay, Carole Cullum, Frances White, and Jo Kuney) to organize support for passage of the San Francisco height/weight anti-discrimination ordinance in 2000.
- I organized a street action in San Francisco on February 15, 1999 that garnered widespread media attention and motivated those legislative efforts. (A gym's billboard showed a space alien with the slogan "When they come, they'll eat the fat ones first." I invited fat community people to gather outside the gym's location on a major thoroughfare, where we frolicked and waved signs that said, "Eat me!")
- I showed up to help various fat lib performance projects get started in the late '90s: Big Moves dance, the Bod Squad cheerleaders, and the Padded Lilies synchro swim troupe. (The Lilies performed on *The Tonight Show with Jay Leno* as part of media coverage after the SF law passed.)
- I did a lot of media interviews and public speaking and got to meet fat positive people on college campuses. In June 2004 I invited 63 such contacts to join a fat studies email list, an early gathering place for people in this academic field.

- I made Yay! Scales™—bathroom scales that give appearance-based compliments instead of numbers—and used them in public interactions, inviting people to find out what they Yay! instead of what they weigh. (Thanks to Nomi Dekel and her VoluptuArt website for making this merch available.)

These stories and others from my fat activism are likely documented elsewhere. Here's my real reason for wanting to contribute to this anthology:

In my fat activism, it is disappointing but true that I have also brought along unexamined racism and white supremacy. (I mention white supremacy because white people inevitably participate in and reinforce societal systems that promote this worldview, in addition to the white privilege that we benefit from.) These harmful dynamics have been present in my activism even if I don't intentionally do or say racist things. I've done harm while I meant to do good. Acknowledging this distressing reality and trying to do better doesn't guarantee that I won't still do harm. I must keep expanding my awareness and learn how to better approach activism with a real commitment to intersectional justice.

I'm no expert. In this piece, I'll discuss some examples from my activism in the hope that they offer useful prompts for further reflection and growth for other white people in fat community. I'm also glad that many white people in fat community are already engaging whole-heartedly with these issues and showing up for activism that avoids doing harm.

Black people, Indigenous people, Latinx people, and people in the Asian and Pacific Islander diaspora are the authorities on these topics. Here are a few crucial books from fat-positive authors who address these topics: Da'Shaun L. Harrison writes about powerful connections in the experience of oppressions that target Blackness, gender, disability, and weight in the book *Belly of the Beast: The Politics of Anti-Fatness as Anti-Blackness*. Sonya Renee Taylor shares her brilliant vision of holistic ways to heal from intersecting oppressions in her book *The Body Is Not An Apology: The Power of Radical Self-Love*. Sabrina Strings, Ph.D. documents how racism and white supremacy historically attempted to justify colonialism and slavery and also spread a fat-hating worldview in her book *Fearing the Black Body: The Racial Origins of Fat Phobia*.

As these voices and others rightly point out, anti-fatness both comes from racism and white supremacy and also falls hardest on people of color, who may also have other marginalized identities. So BIPOC voices and experience and leadership need to be central in fat activism.

White fat activists like me need to avoid the pitfalls of defensiveness or guilt when we inevitably, despite our good intentions, reinforce white supremacy and racism. I'm nowhere near perfect. I try to acknowledge my wrongs and the harm I do, and educate myself about these issues in hopes of doing better. I aim to keep trying to be trustworthy, even when—or especially when—I get it wrong.

I lacked this awareness in my early fat activism. Here's an example:

When I first connected with fat community in the mid-'90s I heard this slogan: "A waist is a terrible thing to mind." I don't know who first used it. I repeated it. For years I didn't bother to recognize that its wording relies on—and distracts from—the classic message of the United Negro College Fund: "A mind is a terrible thing to waste." For nearly seven decades UNCF has supported Black college students and historically Black colleges and universities, contributing to Black leadership in society—an answer to racism in education and other institutions. Fat community should support anti-racism movements. Instead, white fat activists appropriated wording related to the hard-fought advancements of generations of Black people as if it were ours to take and use, removed from its civil rights context. I'm grateful that at some point fellow white fat activists educated me about the problematic nature of this appropriated slogan, so I could avoid doing further harm. How distressing it must be for Black people to hear white fat activists misusing this slogan—for years. What an unwelcome conflict for Black people in fat community to face: either choosing to point out this slogan's disrespectful appropriation of Black community labor or choosing not to push back, to avoid white people's disbelief, denial, and fragility. In more recent years when I've encountered people using this harmful slogan, I have shared the awareness that others gave me. I hope that there is expanding understanding about the harms of appropriation.

My awareness about the harms of appropriation failed to carry over to another time when I should have known better and done better.

In 1998 a fat community friend and I were discussing possible fat activism events. We joked about the idea of a Million Pound March. In 1995 Black community organizers had created a highly publicized national event—the Million Man March in Washington, D.C. Two years later Black women organized the Million Woman March in Philadelphia, Pennsylvania. As far as I know, fat community—which at the time was mostly led by white fat activists—offered no support or even solidarity for these historic events. I mentioned this thoroughly wrong idea for an event name to other white fat activists. That year the large public event at a longstanding annual gathering for fat community was called the Million Pound March. I didn't organize it, but I should have recognized the idea as unacceptable appropriation from the start. At the event there was no explicit recognition or acknowledgement or thanks or respect shown to Black community or anti-racism in general, or to Black people in fat community. Thanks to this name the fat community event got more media coverage than usual that year, by taking advantage of the labor and creative vision of Black community organizing. I do not know how Black members of fat community felt about the name of the event. If they had concerns, I can imagine they felt outnumbered or expected not to complain. There were no Black people in leadership roles related to this organization or this event. If there had been, they should not have been cornered into doing the work of educating white fat activists about the wrongness of this idea. The public attention this event garnered thus spread a harmful message that event organizers should have recognized and avoided.

A full decade later I concocted a fat activist project that repeated this kind of disrespectful cultural appropriation. Again, I simply should have known better.

In 2008 the Japanese government called for Japanese adults to have their waist measurements documented. People with waists above a certain size (based on gender binary) would be advised to lose weight, with a goal of improving public health. In the U.S., cities sometimes announce weight-loss goals for the general population. The federal government has also imposed weight-loss programs under the guise of public health. None of these programs has produced lasting change in either weight or health. At the time I was not acquainted with fat positive people in Japan. It was not my place to formulate a response to this policy. No white savior needed. Regrettably, I convinced a friend to come up with a fat version of an origami crane. Then I publicly invited people in fat community to fold cranes and send them to me until we collected a thousand of them. A local newspaper wrote about the project uncritically. Even then, I felt no qualms. I had a vague plan to send the fat cranes to Japanese health officials, an idea that I later dropped when I finally met fat-positive people in Japan and they very gently shared their concerns about the idea. I regret putting them in the position of having to educate me in this way. My badly conceived project appropriated the traditional Japanese symbolism of cranes representing long life, the Japanese art of origami, and the use of origami cranes as post-Hiroshima symbols of peace, which references the life story of a Japanese girl named Sadako Sasaki. (She survived the bombing but later died from radiation-related cancer. During her life she folded more than 1,000 origami cranes, inspired by Japanese legends about the gods granting a wish for people who complete that goal.) Horrifyingly, I announced this project on the anniversary of the Nagasaki bombing. My responses to the Japanese government policy were selfish and thoughtlessly hurtful. At the time, an Asian-American fat person in fat community posted online, pointing out the problematic nature of my fat cranes project and asking why no one was willing to question my actions. She was, of course, correct. At the time I either didn't see the post or completely failed to take it to heart, adding yet another layer of harm. I deeply regret my intense disrespect to Japanese people and culture with this project. I regret encouraging other people to participate in it. I am so sorry for the negative impact it had on Asian American people in fat community and elsewhere.

I recognize in myself a desire to use what I think of as rebelliousness and humor as a response to the fat hate that I encounter. I risk doing harm when I'm not aware of how I might be punching down toward oppressed people, when I think I'm punching up at oppressive forces. That lack of awareness comes from white entitlement and privilege. Confronting these aspects of myself is an ongoing practice.

I have one more example to share.

In 2012 the children's hospital in Atlanta, Georgia inaugurated its new anti-"obesity" program with an advertising campaign timed for New Year's/diet season. The ads showed fat children of different skin colors and genders looking sternly into the camera. Large, all-caps, red letters crossed their middles: WARNING. The tag line was "Stop childhood obesity" and the program, Strong4Life. Each image had a mean-spirited and hurtful slogan. The first ad I saw was a photo of a white girl with long hair who looked a lot like I looked at that age. The slogan printed over her belly sneered, "It's hard to be a little girl if you're not." I felt such anger and such ferocious yearning to protect her, to protect fat children who would see these ads as billboards or on TV. To go back in time and protect my fat self as a child. With a particular mix of involvement in my own pain and lack of consideration about how other people might be hurting from these ads, I came up with a response. I asked a friend to help me create a template over a black and white photo of myself that I hastily took. With her help, I was able to add a bold headline in fuchsia (instead of red) that said, "I STAND…" and then, in place of the fat-joke-masquerading-as-public-health message, I added: "against harming fat children. Hate =/= health." The tag lines below said "Stop weight bigotry. Health At Every Size." I posted the photo to Facebook and offered to make similar images for anyone who sent me their photo and preferred slogan. At the time I was barely able to do the necessary photo editing and did not anticipate the large number of people who ended up sending in their photos. Over the next week or so a handful of people kindly spent long hours editing photos as they came in.

Yet again I had reacted to my own, personal pain and failed to look beyond my white entitlement. If I had taken time to review the hospital's whole ad campaign, I hope I would have noticed that it clearly targeted children of color, and that its messaging also targeted children and their families based on class. Failing to challenge the intense racism and classism of this campaign, I effectively condoned these injustices. By rushing off to invite my friends on social media to participate I also reinforced divides in fat community based on race, because my friend circles are not representative of the whole community. I didn't take time to reach out to BIPOC fat community members either, to look to their leadership in response to these racist, classist, fat-hating ads. It was their place, not mine, to devise a response, one based in their lived experience and understanding of the needs of the BIPOC families and children being targeted.

I also want to acknowledge the ableism of the slogan I came up with: "I STAND." Disabled people and their allies who submitted their photos to the project also challenged this wording, in the slogans they chose for their images. They should not have had to encounter yet more ableism from inside a fat activist project. How many people chose not to participate because my words made them feel unwelcome or devalued?

In response to the "I Stand" campaign, a group of people of color in fat community spent time and labor to write an open letter called "A Response to Fat White Activism from People of Color in the Fat Justice Movement," which was posted on the NOLOSE organization's website in March 2012 (http://no-lose.org/about/policy/fat-white-activisim-poc/). For people who have not already read it and taken its powerful and important content to heart, I strongly encourage doing so as soon as possible.

Retelling these stories is just part of trying to be accountable. When I think back on the list of accomplishments that I started this piece with, I can only begin to recognize the harms that were also inevitably embedded in those efforts or imagine the missed opportunities for intersectional awesomeness that I could have pursued in each of those endeavors. (For example: When I planned a street action, did I consider whether people of color would be safe from police violence? Did I strategize for this possibility? Did I work for representation and diversity in fat performance groups or was I comfortable with an all-white lineup? Did I push for inclusion of more BIPOC voices when I got invited to speak or do media?)

The work of noticing and avoiding harm and doing better is never finished. I hope the examples I've shared here both document this part of my fat community history and serve as points of reflection for white fat activists who seek to minimize the harm we do while we aim to be trustworthy participants in a fat community that makes ample room for everyone.

HOW I FOUND OUT
I AM HUMAN

PATTIE THOMAS

IN 1993 I WAS TRYING TO FIGURE OUT what to do with my life. Recently married, my husband and I were struggling to find work and make ends meet. I had lost my job for no real reason, and I wondered if I was just heading in the wrong direction. I sought out help from vocational rehab, and they sent me to a counselor. That counselor took an instant dislike to me. In her clinic notes she wrote about how I was overweight and didn't dress well. She used that as the basis for a diagnosis of borderline personality disorder, with little else noted to make that diagnosis.

My body size, and the fact that I was poor, equaled mentally ill. I had been to enough counseling and read enough self-help books at that point in my life to know that didn't add up. I was hurt. I was ashamed. I was angry.

The irony is that just five years before I had been a weight loss success story, complete with before-and-after pictures in an ad in the lobby of the weight loss clinic I had attended for over a year. Through the miracle of starvation, laxatives, and addiction to an amphetamine I had lost half my body weight. By 1993, however, I had kicked the addiction, stopped abusing laxatives, and gained a substantial portion of that back. In 1991 I had tried a "healthy" weight loss effort, but it was not as easy as it had been and that left me depressed and wondering if I'd ever "defeat" my "weight problem." I was 36 years old and realized I had spent my teens, 20s, and over half my 30s running up and down the scale. One friend, whom I only saw two or three times a year, said she was never sure what I was going to look like when she saw me again.

So I asked voc rehab for a second opinion.

That second opinion changed my life. My new therapist was a feminist therapist, something I had never heard about before. She told me about how I was being stigmatized for being poor and fat. She said that the problem was not me but was society's view of women like me. She helped me see that maybe all those times I tried to lose weight I was merely trying to conform. What she said made sense to me. I was so tired of fighting my own body. With her help I decided to go back to college and finish my bachelor's degree. I also decided to take courses in women's studies.

I came to realize years later, after studying sociology and receiving my doctorate, that the way I had internalized fatphobia and saw my body was typical of someone who is stigmatized.

The process of stigmatization is actually quite simple. Social psychologist Irving Goffman called stigma a *spoiled identity*. Each of us have three sources of identity: our biographies (facts about us), our social identity (the way others see us), and what we believe to be our authentic self (the "real" person we believe we are). Stigma is all about social identity. It is how others see us, and it is spoiled because instead of responding to us as individuals, our social context is determined by a *mark*, that is, a characteristic that others see as more important than anything else and that puts us in a group with others who share that mark.

Fatness is such a mark. Those who would stigmatize fat people see an individual as fat before they see anything else, and often regard anything else that person does in light of the beliefs surrounding that characteristic. So if a fat woman is sweet—well, she has to be to make up for fatness. If she is mean-spirited—well of course she is, because she is unhappy with her body. If she is unemployed, she is lazy. If she is employed, she is overcompensating for her body. The *spoiled* part is that nothing a person does will be regarded as anything other than related to the mark. It is a no-win situation and, as such, many stigmatized persons blame themselves because nothing they can do will change the perception that they belong to that group and share those characteristics.

In my first women's studies course I was introduced to *The Fat Liberation Manifesto* (by Judy Freespirit and Aldebaran, first published in 1973). I had come home. This was not the first time feminism and fatness had been introduced to me. I had read *Fat is a Feminist Issue* (by Susie Orbach) a decade before, but when I had sought to do the things I read in the book, I had not lost weight. I had regarded that as a personal failure. I had grown up in a working class family and, frankly, a lot of mainstream feminism didn't resonate with me. The women in my life worked and I did not envy the working class jobs of the men in my life. Much of feminism was presented to me as liberation from housewifery and not much else.

But fat liberation resonated with me. It was like my eyes were finally opened to the real world. My first big thought was simple: No matter what my weight, I was human. I was not a failure for being fat. I didn't deserve to be treated as less than human for being fat.

I wrote a booklet for my women's studies class project called *Before and After*. I wrote 10 essays about 10 myths about fatness and a poem to accompany each essay, along with a quote from scholars who either critiqued fatness as a social issue, not a health issue, or who critiqued aspects of criticizing women's bodies. The next year I actually self-published the booklet and sold about 20 copies, giving away about 20 more. The few people who read it gave positive feedback for the effort, and this was the beginning of my understanding that I was not alone in needing to hear that my body was something more than my weight. This little pamphlet was part of what eventually became *Taking Up Space* about a dozen years later. Two important works included in the pamphlet quotes were Rita Freeman's *Beauty Bound* (1985), and Carole Spitzack's *Confessing Excess* (1990). Interestingly, for the book I was able to update the quotations to reflect much more direct writing that critiqued fat as a health issue, such as quotes from Marilyn Wann, Glenn Gaesser, Laura Fraser, Susan Bordo and Bonnie Bernall.

Like many fat people who are introduced to the concept of being okay with variations in sizes, I didn't quite internalize the no-dieting part of the equation. All the horrific things I had done to a healthy and athletic young body started catching up to me in my late 30s. I had a melanoma in 1994. I had a hysterectomy in 1995. I had got very sick in 1997 and was eventually diagnosed with lupus. So while I understood that people should not be judged by their size, I also thought I'd feel better and be healthier if I "lost a little weight."

Two resources that helped me navigate and shed this lingering attitude about my own body were the alt-support-bigfolks usenet listserv on the then-emerging internet and my discovery of NAAFA, which at the time was basically a newsletter/magazine I received in the mail. NAAFA challenged my thinking but there were no chapters nearby, so it remained fairly abstract in my life. Big Folks, however, became a support group. Being the early internet, this group was mostly people asking and answering each other's questions and posting about new resources that might help others. Unlike later iterations of such support, there were no graphics or events or links like you might find on Facebook or Twitter. But it was a place I read and posted weekly, and some of the people I met there went on to be friends in other, more technologically advanced spaces.

The person I remember most on Big Folks was the late, great Paul Ernsberger, PhD, a researcher out of Case Western Reserve University. When I faced two cancer scares in a row he sent me research that showed that my being fat probably helped contain my cancer and helped me survive it. Every time I wrote to him and asked, "but don't you think if I lose a little weight—?" he patiently explained why losing weight would fix nothing. He spoke from authority of research and opened my eyes to the ways in which the medical information we hear about in media and at doctors' offices is biased. He is one of the reasons I started emphasizing medical sociology in my grad school studies.

It took a little bit, but slowly I realized that there was no healthy way to do intentional weight loss and that all my efforts before were probably the reason I had health issues, not the fat. It was about this time that I was introduced to the wonderful Marilyn Wann and the book *FAT!SO?* along with her online forum *Gab Café*. By the year 2000 I gave up dieting for good, and I was increasingly radicalized in my understanding of fat sociologically.

I met so many wonderful people at the Gab Café, many of whom I remain online friends with and some I have met in real life. My husband and I moved to Canada in 2001. I finished my Ph.D. dissertation there, going back to the states just long enough to defend it, and then I got a job in Victoria, B.C. I also discovered the wonderful Tish Parmeley and her blog *Fat Shadow*. She encouraged me to start blogging and even helped me create *FattyPatties*, which was originally the two Patricias writing about our lives at fat women. Her plan all the while was to get me hooked and then leave the blog to me. I am grateful to her for this. These blogs had small followings but were not widely known and were never *viral* in any way, but a devoted following read and commented. Over the years, more people read back articles. I think if these blogs had been written in the time of social media, they may have garnered more attention. I know *FattyPatties* still has some readership and occasional commenters, even though it has been close to 10 years since I wrote anything there.

Also during this time, my husband and I created a radio show on the local community radio station, CFUV-FM, called *First Person, Plural*. On that show we did several episodes on fat acceptance and fat liberation. Then in 2004, when we decided to leave Canada, we created a website called *The Ample Traveler* and a blog called *Ample Ramblings*. My brother, my husband, my cat, and I traveled around the U.S. in an RV for much of 2004, writing monthly about where we visited, pointing out what was fat friendly and accessible. We visited some of our fat friends from the web as we traveled, including hanging out in Portland and San Francisco. We were not able to raise enough funds to sustain the project, however we did meet a lot of wonderful people and discovered that the world was still not that fat friendly or accessible, but had its pockets of comfort.

It was during that traveling that we wrote *Taking Up Space*, which was published in September 2005 by Pearlsong Press. Much of what was in the book was taken from those early days in undergrad women's studies courses, from the booklet for my first women's studies course, and from the blog. In many ways the book just wrote itself. We were proud to be a part of Peggy Elam's new publishing company, Pearlsong Press, and to be among the first non-fiction authors she published. Pearlsong Press has grown over the years to be a wonderful source of poetry, art, fiction and nonfiction, promoting fat liberation. Amazingly the book continues to sell, and Peggy continues to support the book.

Before people could publish blogs and set up websites with resources, most of what one could learn about fat liberation was found in magazines and small publications. Mainstream media was never going to really pay attention to these questions about body awareness, except as novelty stories. The internet and social media has changed everything. In the years just after the publication of our book, fat bloggers and fat media producers blossomed. The rise of social media caused all this to explode. I knew this most assuredly by 2011, when I got involved in two projects.

The first started in January 2011 and was called ReVolutions. It involved a number of fat activists who were deconstructing the whole new year's resolutions trope of intentional weight loss. In addition, with a lot of help, I created a website/blog called New Year's ReVolutions Resources that had hundreds of links to blogs, nonfiction, fiction, websites, and projects that supported anti-dieting and pro-fat liberation content. It ended up being way more than I ever anticipated. The entire year ended up being devoted to this resource, and it culminated in a series of 30-second videos my husband and I did on YouTube in January 2012 that were called "31 Things to Do Instead of Dieting." Of course all these resources look like a small drop in the big fat bucket of what is available today for people like the 36-year-old me trying to understand my life in light of the stigma of fat people.

The second project was that I was invited by the magazine *Psychology Today* to write a blog on their site called *I Take Up Space*, building upon the 2005 book. This amazed me because it was so mainstream. And I was not alone on their website. Several other blog authors wrote fat positive articles and supported some version of fat acceptance or body positivity. Harriet Brown, author of *Brave Girl Eating,* probably came closest to writing about the issues I wrote about. My blog, however, seemed to be the only one dedicated primarily to discussing fat stigma and fat liberation, and more important, I seemed to be the only fat woman writing about these topics. It should be noted that some of these articles were met with anger and protest by readers. One post, in particular, where I critiqued a billboard about a local kids' weight loss and exercise program, generated well over 100 comments, with people threatening my job. Interestingly, this was the only post that generated enough hits for me to get paid. I always enjoyed the irony of being paid $112 to be yelled at for "promoting obesity in children." I didn't lose my job. Still, I could never have imagined such a popular place allowing any kind of positive discussion about fat people back in 1993 when I first read *The Fat Liberation Manifesto*.

For me, 2011 seems to be the moment that fat liberation became a movement in ways I could never have imagined in 1993. That was the year that Cat Pausé's "Friend of Marilyn" podcast began. That was the year that the *Fat Studies Journal* started preparing its inaugural issue for January 2012. The *Fat Studies Reader* had been published in 2010, and by 2011 courses were adopting it across the U.S. and beyond. This was way more than one assignment in a women's studies class. It was becoming a legitimate form of inquiry. With the publication of Lindo Bacon's book and study in 2010, the concept of Health at Every Size was garnering mainstream attention.

There have been, of course, many mistakes made along the way, and as a sociologist, I'd be hard pressed to call this a successful social movement in its own right. But I do know that it is so much more than it once was.

The women in 1973 who said "enough is enough" and declared that fat people are human. The founders of NAAFA in 1969. The early days of Big Fat Folks sharing with each other in the new frontier of text-based online forums where we shared experiences and advice and support. These early trailblazers meant a lot to me as I learned to respect the body I live in and feel at home. And, more important, I learned the tools to dismantle the social systems that reproduce these oppressions in everyday life. I am profoundly grateful for those people who touched my life and helped me navigate it.

I am now a tenured professor, teaching sociology, even with disabling chronic illnesses, and that never would have happened if I had not discovered fat liberation. I really owe my life to these brave souls who simply said, I am human.

HEALING THE WORLD ONE BOOK AT A TIME

PEGGY ELAM

FROM APRIL 2005 UNTIL OCTOBER 2011, every Monday morning I committed a radical act. I drove through the middle Tennessee countryside to the broadcast studio of the community radio station Radio Free Nashville and spent a half-hour initially, then a full hour encouraging fat people to quit trying to lose weight and non-fat people—including medical and mental health professionals—to check their privilege and jettison their fatphobia.

I played music like Big Dee Irwin's "Happy Being Fat," Abby Burke's "Built for Luxury," Candye Kane's "Big Fat Mamas Are Back in Style" and "Fit, Fat and Fine," Les Kerr's "Chubby Man Blues," Howling Wolf's "300 Pounds of Joy" and "Built for Comfort," Creamy Goodness's "Fat Girl," Mika's "Big Girl (You Are Beautiful), and Rebecca Riots's "Women's Bodies." I read The Fat Underground's *Fat Liberation Manifesto* (published in 1973, but I didn't learn of it until it was included in the anthology *Shadow on a Tightrope: Writings by Women on Fat Oppression,* edited by Lisa Schoenfielder and Barb Wieser and published by Aunt Lute Books in 1983). Initially on my own, and later with co-host Pat Ballard (AKA The Queen of Rubenesque Romances), I talked about diseasemongering and fearmongering in the weight-loss industry (which psychologist Deb Burgard, PhD has so aptly dubbed the weight-cycling industry) and the benefits of a weight-neutral, or weight-inclusive, approach to health and well-being.

I called it the "Health At Every Size show" after the approach toward health and well-being later trademarked by the Association for Size Diversity and Health. ASDAH trademarked "Health at Every Size" and its acronym "HAES" in efforts to keep the weight-cycling industry from co-opting the terms, as the industry has done with other anti-diet terminology. The clinicians, academicians, researchers, activists, and free-range fat people who developed HAES—

an approach that is still evolving—had eventually settled on the "HAES" nomenclature after using other terms, including "Health At Any Size," for a while. I thought the title of the show and its related blog and podcast could help promote the term as well as fat positivity. I also hoped to promote the fat-positive publishing company I founded in 2003, Pearlsong Press.

I earned a bachelor's degree in journalism and English back when dinosaurs ruled the Earth. Or, with less hyperbole, when *1984* was a science fiction novel set in the future. Okay, it was 1977. I then worked for several years as a newspaper reporter, editor, and columnist in my home state of Mississippi.

I had approached puberty when Twiggy was the role model for women, and can still recall the shame I felt standing in my front yard at 10–11 years old as my mother eyed my waistline critically and told me, "You'd better quit eating that second helping of mashed potatoes." Newly self-conscious of my body as somehow "wrong," I would eventually embark on decades of dieting and at times eating disordered behavior, each time I dieted regaining more than I'd lost. Gradually, though, I became aware of the misogyny inherent in fatphobia, and how the pursuit of thinness disempowered girls and women. I didn't yet realize how racism played a role, as well.

In the late 1970s and early 1980s Susie Orbach's *Fat Is a Feminist Issue* and Kim Chernin's *The Obsession: Reflections on the Tyranny of Slenderness* got me thinking about sociocultural aspects of fatphobia (although both still pathologized fatness in many ways, and neglected to address the racist origins of fatphobia). Then William Bennett & Joel Gurin's *The Dieter's Dilemma: Eating Less and Weighing More* opened my eyes to some of the science behind eating behavior and weight. I still recall Bennett & Gurin's description of psychologists Janet Polivy and C. Peter Herman's research on the relationship between food restriction/dieting and bingeing. (Short version: restricted eaters—those who were dieting—were empirically shown to eat more than non-dieters when their restriction was disinhibited.) *The Dieter's Dilemma* was instrumental in my deciding to pursue a doctorate in psychology. I enrolled in graduate school at Vanderbilt University in 1983, earned a master's in 1986 and a PhD in 1990, and became a licensed clinical psychologist in 1990.

I started a part-time psychotherapy practice after becoming licensed at the master's level, and then went full-time after completing PhD requirements. As a psychotherapist I saw adults and older adolescents and had subspecialties in eating disorders and trauma/dissociative disorders. By that time I had begun to see how mainstream attitudes toward fatness—even in the eating disorders field!—and ignorance of, or ignoring/refusing to accept, natural diversity in body size and physiological responses to food restriction/semi-starvation (or, of course, actual starvation) in pursuit of ideal body size failed to take into account the myriad biological factors involved in weight (and health) and perpetuated, even exacerbated, the harms of fatphobia. That wasn't a particularly popular perspective at the time.

Shortly before I arrived at Vanderbilt University a VU psychology professor, Martin Katahn, PhD, became a diet guru and eventually published several weight-loss-oriented books. I won't name them here, but one became a *New York Times* bestseller, and signs touting its calorie-restricting diet were displayed in local grocery stores for a while. I remember a (thin white) grad school classmate telling me she'd followed the diet for one day and then ate a box of crackers, exemplifying the restriction-leading-to-bingeing pattern. (I'm not saying eating a box of crackers is itself bad, by the way. Rather, in the classmate's case she felt she was eating compulsively in response to the previous day's restriction.)

In the early days of my psychotherapy practice, in my locale (middle Tennessee), it was common to find professionals as well as the general public conceptualizing fatness as "food addiction." In doing so they simultaneously confused a body trait (fatness) with behavior and assumed that all fat people have eating disorders—binge-eating disorder, that is, as few at that time recognized that fat people could have anorexia nervosa. Unfortunately the diagnostic criteria for anorexia nervosa included low weight, so people who were starving themselves and losing significant amounts of weight but not considered "underweight" were not recognized as having eating disorders. In fact, their starvation and weight loss were usually encouraged and celebrated!

The concept of "food addiction" applied the 12-step model employed so widely in grassroots treatment/support for alcoholism and drug addiction, as well as some behaviors such as compulsive gambling, to "treating" compulsive eating. And compulsive eating was considered to be the cause of fatness. (Later, I wrote my own "12 Steps to Health At Every Size" and "12 Ways to Love Your Body," available online at https://pearlsong.com/12-steps-to-health-at-every-size/ and https://pearlsong.com/12-ways-to-love-your-body/, respectively. I will note here that I stopped using the term "emotional eating" years ago after realizing that it is normal to eat for emotional reasons— including joy, pleasure, and celebration as well as stress and depression. Instead, I use "compulsive eating" to refer to eating that feels out of control.)

Here's a news flash: Everyone is "addicted to"—or rather, dependent on— food. We need food to survive, much less thrive. We can no more "abstain" from food long-term than we can oxygen. Viewing fatness as a problem caused by "food addiction" unfortunately leads to inappropriately and harmfully viewing the solution to the "problem" of fatness as being to abstain from eating—or, since that is actually impossible without dying sooner than one might otherwise, abstaining from eating at certain times (between meals, etc.) or from certain foods (sugar, white flour, etc.). Such food "abstinence" overrides the body's normal appetites and can result in restrictive/restrained eating that then leads to bingeing.

When running an inpatient eating disorders group in 1991 I reframed the predominant 12-step mindset there to define the problem as "dieting addiction" rather than "food addiction." Abstaining from weight-loss dieting is definitely possible, although it can be difficult in a fatphobic culture. Abstaining from weight-loss dieting is sustainable and health-promoting, whereas overriding appetites to abstain from eating (restricting eating) is usually neither.

I am not, of course, talking about avoiding or limiting certain foods or timing of certain foods for actual health reasons, such as avoiding gluten due to celiac disease, or timing and types of foods influencing blood glucose levels in people with diabetes. I will note, however, that food-related health concerns often cloak anti-fatness, with little or no understanding of how such attitudes actually harm health or how anti-fatness and anti-Blackness and anti-femaleness intersect to exponentially increase the harm for fat women of color.

A former business partner, psychologist Dawne Kimbrell, PhD, and I wrote on misconceptions about size/weight in an article in a 1995 issue of the journal *Cognitive & Behavior Practice.* That same year we partnered with Allison & Beck Nutrition Consultants (a Nashville practice) and the Renfrew Center (a residential treatment center headquartered in Philadelphia, Pennsylvania) to present "Gender, Race, & the Pursuit of Thinness," a continuing educational seminar in Nashville.

Over the next several years I gave talks to various audiences in Tennessee and, occasionally, beyond, emphasizing fat acceptance and a weight-neutral approach to well-being.

I felt a little like Cassandra.

In 2001 I presented on Health At Any Size (one of the names by which the approach was then known, before "Health At Every Size" was settled on) at a local dietetic association conference, as well as at a workshop for a local psychotherapists' association. My talk for psychotherapists was sparsely attended, but the larger room next door was packed with therapists attending a talk on a psychoanalytic case study in which a woman's fatness and apparent difficulty losing/maintaining weight loss was discussed as being psychologically driven, with no acknowledgement of body diversity or that most people who lose weight through dieting regain it as the body responds to starvation.

(Another news flash: People of all sizes/weights can have psychological issues around weight and eating, and upon resolving those issues may lose weight, gain weight, or remain the same weight.)

At another talk for a satellite branch of the local psychotherapists' association I talked about "feeling fat" (independent of the actual amount of fat tissue present) as a dissociative symptom in which one's "fat" is perceived as "other" and "bad," to be exorcised through dieting and/or exercise and/or surgery —a process which, of course, was being encouraged by mainstream society, medicine, and (unfortunately) often mental health professionals. That talk, at least, was a little better attended, as I remember.

In the early 2000s, as terminology seemed to have settled on "Health At Every Size," I offered a free HAES-related support group at a local YMCA. Over the course of the several weeks that I offered the group exactly two people showed up, on different weeks. It was discouraging.

During these outreach & education efforts, however, I met and befriended Pat Ballard, who had written and self-published four romance novels featuring what she called Big Beautiful Heroines.

Pat had grown up on a farm in Mississippi, one of six children who were all active and ate the same country foods. Two of the children were tall and thin, two were short and fat, and two were "average" size. Pat was one of the short, fat dyad. As a young girl and then woman she almost died trying to starve herself into a societally approved shape. When she started writing fiction in mid-life, she wanted to tell stories that showed fat women leading lives just as romantic and exciting as their slim sisters'. She initially self-published her romance novels because the publishers who expressed interest in them wanted her to specify the size of her heroines and limit them to size 14 or 16. Pat refused to specify her heroines' sizes, much less limit them. She wanted fat women to be able to envision themselves as the heroines of her novels if they wished, no matter what their size.

About the time I met Pat I also learned part of the story behind the publication of exercise physiologist Glen Gaesser, PhD's book *Big Fat Lies: The Truth About Your Weight and Your Health*. *Big Fat Lies* contains scientific evidence of the hazards of dieting and the shaky foundation of weight-focused approaches to health. The book was published in hardcover in 1996. Some time later I heard that Gaesser had been advised to include a photo with his book proposal in order to show prospective publishers and editors he wasn't fat. A thin person writing on the subject of weight and health had more credibility to mainstream publishers than a fat person with the same credentials. Gaesser, who is thin (and white), provided the photo and met with several publishers before accepting a contract from Fawcett Columbine.

Somewhere along the way to initial publication *Big Fat Lies* gained a section at the end of the book that basically contains a diet program. My understanding is that Gaesser agreed to add that section—which is a same-old-same-old diet contradicted by the first two-thirds of the book—in order to get the main, scientific part of the book published. So a mainstream publisher wouldn't publish a book on weight and health—even one critical of weight-loss dieting, written by a thin white man—without including a diet section. (I am disappointed that the 2002 second edition published in paperback by Gürze Books, a publisher specializing in books addressing eating disorders and body image, still contains the diet section. When I recommend *Big Fat Lies*, I recommend ignoring the diet section.)

Hearing that the publication of *Big Fat Lies* may have hinged on the author's being thin infuriated me. It was bad enough that people with bodies larger than societal and medical ideals were seeing few positive representations of themselves in literature (or popular culture in general), but to have the route to traditional print publication of health-related nonfiction barred to fat people? Not acceptable.

At that time I was already contemplating starting a publishing company that would pull together my expertise in journalism, English, and psychology to publish fat-positive books and resources that supported the Health At Every Size approach. Learning of Gaesser's experience was my tipping point. I founded Pearlsong Press, the only publishing company (to my knowledge) whose mission and vision include promoting fat-positive fiction and nonfiction, as well as health, happiness and social justice at every size.

Pearlsong Press was incorporated in Tennessee in October 2003. Its first book, Pat Ballard's *Dangerous Curves Ahead: Short Stories*, was published in May 2004. I subsequently republished Pat's first four romance novels, followed by several more over the years, and her self-help book *10 Steps to Loving Your Body (No Matter What Size You Are)*, which Selfhelp.fm named one of the top 100 best self-help books of all time. Susan Schulherr, author of *Eating Disorders for Dummies*, called it "your body's best friend in pocket form."

Other nonfiction and fiction published by Pearlsong Press include *Taking Up Space: How Eating Well and Exercising Regularly Changed My Life* (spoiler alert: not for the better) by Pattie Thomas, PhD with Carl Wilkerson MBA (foreword by Paul Campos, author of *The Obesity Myth*), *Talking Fat: Health vs. Persuasion in the War on Our Bodies* and *Acceptable Prejudice? Fat, Rhetoric and Social Justice* by Lonie McMichael, PhD, *Beyond Measure: A Memoir About Short Stature and Inner Growth* by Ellen Frankel, the *Fat Poets Speak* series edited by Frannie Zellman, the novels *FatLand* and *FatLand: The Early Days* by Zellman, *Fatropolis* by Tracey L. Thompson, *Measure By Measure* by Rebecca Fox and William Sherman, and more.

Pearlsong Press republished Lynne Murray's NAAFA-award-winning Josephine Fuller mystery series, as well as publishing two new novels by Murray (the romantic comedy *Bride of the Living Dead* and the paranormal adventure *The Falstaff Vampire Files*), and two Young Adult novels with fat heroines: Charlie Lovett's *The Fat Lady Sings* and Barbara D'Souza's *If We Were Snowflakes*.

Pearlsong has also published books that are not specifically fat positive but are healing in other ways, such as Louise Mathewson's *A Life Interrupted: Living with Brain Injury* and Félix Garmendía's *Flying on Invisible Wings, Poems of Reckoning and Hope,* and *Fire Island and Their Sister.* (Garmendía is Puerto Rican, gay, HIV+, and disabled by Inclusion Body Myositis.)

I established a fat-positive publishing company because I wanted fat people's voices and research and perspectives to be heard, especially when they challenge the status quo. I also wanted fat people to be able to see bodies similar to theirs portrayed positively in tales in which fat people live and love and have adventures and overcome challenges and thrive, providing not only a good read, but perhaps for some people the first inkling that anyone can live happily ever after (or as close to it as any of us can get) while fat.

In the two decades since I founded Pearlsong Press the publishing and bookselling world has been rapidly evolving, accelerated by the growth of the internet and advances in technology that make it easier for books to be traditionally and self-published. The past decade or so has seen several fat-positive nonfiction books published by academic presses and other companies. There is growing understanding of how fat prejudice is rooted in racism and disproportionately affects Black people, how even "smaller fat" people benefit from thin privilege, and how fat prejudice, sadly, shows up in eating disorders treatment. There are now more novels with positive portrayals of fat people besides those published by Pearlsong Press.

But I still see both mainstream and independent authors often telegraphing their fat prejudice by using fatness as emblematic of negative traits, and celebrating leanness. All of which harms fat people.

The following was published on my *On the Whole* blog on August 8, 2006:

> Paul Ernsberger, PhD of Case Western Reserve Medical School gave me permission to share the following perspective on the etiology of "obesity" hysteria, which he posted on a private e-group for fat studies scholars:

"I trace the onset of the current medical war on obesity to the marketing blitz for fenfluramine, dexfenfluramine and phen-fen. These drugs created a network of 4 drug companies to promote pills that caused only a small amount of weight loss. The only way to get physicians to prescribe dangerous drugs that cause minor weight loss was to exaggerate the health risks of high weight. They created a speakers' bureau and they sent famous obesity warriors all over the country to 'educate' physicians about the 'dangers of obesity.' These included all the usual suspects, whose careers were tremendously advanced by these lecture tours. The traveling lecturers (really propagandists) also came to dominate the talking heads on TV whenever a fat-related news story appeared.

"The companies also sponsored 'symposia' where speaker after speaker (most of them diet clinic directors) hammered on the epidemiology supporting a link between obesity and ill health. I attended many of these. As far as I recall, they never asked an epidemiologist to speak about epidemiology. These symposia took place at major medical conferences, and to draw a large crowd to fill the ballroom they included (very fattening) full dinner and often an open bar as well. No expense was spared. The odds are good that your personal physician or perhaps a senior physician that he or she trusts has been to one of these one-sided 'symposia.'

"Because of FDA rules, companies are not allowed to promote drugs that are not yet approved. So how do they advance promotion legally? By promoting the indication. The makers of subutramine and orlistat started sponsoring symposia promoting a hysterical view of obesity years before they won FDA approval."

There you have it: a first-person account of the tactics used to sell the concept of obesity as a horrible, life-threatening disease, which in turn would ostensibly justify the prescription of medications with dangerous side effects. (Read Alicia Mundy's *Dispensing With the Truth* for a closehand look at this in regards to the diet-pill combo of phen-fen).

Ernsberger's quote above was made in response to a post I made about the book *Selling Sickness: How the World's Biggest Pharmaceutical Companies Are Turning Us All Into Patients* (Ray Moynihan & Alan Cassels). That book contains a section on a New York ad agency staffer whose job was to work with drug companies to create new diseases (or rather the concept of new diseases) that could be marketed to the public in order to sell them the "solutions." (I almost wrote "cures," but the goal really was/is to develop lifelong consumers of the product, not "cure" anything.)

Selling Sickness, published in 2006, opens with an anecdote about the former CEO of Merck saying (one might think almost wistfully) in an interview 30 years previously that what he really wanted was to be able to sell drugs to healthy people—vastly increasing his potential market. As Cassels and Moynihan noted, his dream has come true.

Fat Civil Rights Activism in Washington, DC

Peggy Howell

FOR OUR 40TH ANNIVERSARY CELEBRATION, the National Association to Advance Fat Acceptance (NAAFA) convened in Washington, DC, one of the few cities in the country that has a law against discrimination based on body size (personal appearance). The leaders of NAAFA and the Association for Size Diversity and Health (ASDAH) decided that it would be a good opportunity for the two organizations to join forces and visit our congressional representatives to make a case for changing this country's anti-discrimination laws and the measures for success in the wellness programs that were becoming all the rage and had weight loss as their primary measure of success.

A great deal of energy and hard work go into creating any conference, but that is doubled when you are planning a joint conference with two organizations that each have a different focus, even when their goals are compatible. I was part of the planning committee for NAAFA.

It was proposed that the 2009 NAAFA 40th anniversary convention be held July 31 through August 3, 2009 at the Dulles Airport Marriott in Washington DC. NAAFA's and ASDAH's events would be coordinated to run simultaneously at the same hotel, with legislative advocacy training offered through both ASDAH and NAAFA and the NAAFA Size Diversity Toolkit update as good possibilities for cross-over events with a joint activism event, sending teams to Congress. Plans began to take shape for the individual conferences. NAAFA typically filled our annual conventions/conferences with learning, networking, community building, swimming, dancing and more. Being the 40th anniversary, this one was even more special! We planned many special events:

- 40 Years in Review
- NAAFA general meeting and breakfast
- Workshops—more than six different workshops each day to

choose from on Friday and Saturday
- Fashion show, dinner and fundraising Not-So-Silent Auction
- Swim parties
- Hospitality suite
- Masquerade Awards dinner and ball
- Grassroots education on how to "Educate the Hill"
- Fat Poets' Society coffeehouse
- Activism event on Capitol Hill
- "Educate the Hill" debriefing

I won't pretend co-planning was easy. There were some conflicts between the two organizations over scheduling. For example, NAAFA scheduled our "Size Diversity Super Workshop" on Saturday opposite ASDAH's keynote luncheon. The workshop included four panelists: Sondra Solovay, Esq.; Lindo Bacon, Ph.D.; NAAFA's director of programs, Lisa Tealer; and NAAFA co-chair Jason Docherty. The workshop included updates on the NAAFA Size Diversity Toolkit, which had been recently distributed to Fortune 500 companies in the U.S., along with further discussion about size diversity. We had scheduled a workshop (not a keynote session) at that time because ASDAH stated by email that they did not want their luncheon to be a joint event, but then NAAFA was publicly criticized for taking attention from ASDAH's keynote luncheon.

There was also a very controversial decision to have Susie Orbach, a British psychotherapist, psychoanalyst, writer, and social critic who was not necessarily HAES-aligned, as the keynote speaker for Saturday's luncheon event at the ASDAH conference that year. Her first book, *Fat is a Feminist Issue*, analyzed the psychology of dieting and overeating in women, and she had campaigned against media pressure on girls to feel dissatisfied with their physical appearance. Many believed that Orbach was still hanging on to the idea that fat bodies reveal some pathology in our psyches, that she saw fat people as suffering due to our fat, not as people who are everyday free-range fat people, and certainly not as people who are proud or happy to be fat. Others felt she was changing, that she was in progress on a path for HAES ideas. There were lots of highly charged emotions, and there were rumors of an organized walk-out during the ASDAH keynote address.

ASDAH officially responded with a statement, signed by the ASDAH leadership team and 2009 conference planning committee:

> ...In regard to the selection of Susie Orbach as our keynote speaker, ASDAH education co-chair Barbara Bruno has spoken elegantly and clearly as to our thinking. To add one more 'process' note, our 2009 ASDAH conference planning committee reviewed the evaluation feedback from past

conferences along with more recent verbal input from members which indicated a clear desire to 'not just talk to ourselves.' This, along with the organizational goal to reach out to potential allies as we look to expand HAES® access and advocacy, led to our approaching several possible keynote speakers who we felt might be of interest from a professional educational perspective both within and beyond our current membership... It is a long and involved process to bring together a diverse group of people and ideas from around the world in order to nurture and stimulate a new paradigm of thought. It is a very exciting and amazing thing that ASDAH as an organization is attempting to do. Do not think for one moment that those of us working on your behalf take this challenge lightly.

After further input from and discussion with their community, ASDAH made the following changes:

> In response to the issues raised, the following clarifications/ changes are being made to the ASDAH conference schedule:
>
> The timeslot for our guest speaker, Susie Orbach, has been changed to the early evening on Saturday (5:30–7:30 pm) to remove the conflict with the NAAFA keynote presentation. Since "keynote" evokes for many a presenter who would be responsible for "setting the tone" of a conference, and this was not the role we envisioned for Ms. Orbach, her designation will be "guest speaker." Ms. Orbach's presentation will include a 20–30 minute facilitated Q & A / discussion (a planned component from the onset). Any ASDAH member who would like to submit a question/concern you would like your conference co-chairs to review with Ms. Orbach in our pre-conference discussions is welcome to do so by sending an email to…no later than May 25th.

Meanwhile, prior to the convention, my sister, Darliene Howell, requested a proclamation that August 3, 2009 be declared Size Diversity Awareness Day in Washington, DC. It was suggested that even if we didn't get the official proclamation, we could self-proclaim that date to be Size Diversity Awareness Day.

NAAFA planned and executed a five-day event beginning on Thursday, July 30 with an evening of socializing and reflecting on 40 years as an organization and community with photos and stories. Friday evening's 2009 fashion show and auction dinner, organized by Darliene Howell and me, was the highlight of the day and night. Plus-size fashion designers from around the country presented their latest collections of inspired designs. And who didn't love our late-night pool parties? Having worked on the fashion show, I was really too exhausted to enjoy the pool party, but I did show up until it started to rain.

My favorite quote from Saturday's Size Diversity Super Workshop came from Sondra Solovay, Esq. She discussed fighting size discrimination in the workplace from a legal perspective, and highlighted best practices in human resources in regards to size discrimination. Sondra encouraged employers to take advantage of NAAFA›s Size Diversity Toolkit and not make costly HR mistakes. She concluded by reminding us of a lesson she learned on how to ride a motorcycle, "Don›t look where you are; look where you are going."

Saturday night was the fabulous 2009 NAAFA Awards & Masquerade Gala Dinner Dance. Whew, that was a long title, but what a special night.

NAAFA's convention committee had researched the history of Washington, DC's law that protects us from discrimination. The DC law includes the phrase "personal appearance," which is what protects us from discrimination based on our body size. The term "personal appearance" was adopted with the initial Human Rights Act of 1977 and has been in effect since December 13, 1977. The act was signed by council chair Sterling Tucker and was signed into law by then-Mayor Walter E. Washington. NAAFA was able to contact Sterling Tucker (then 85 years old) through his law practice. We invited him to join us at the Saturday night awards dinner to receive an award as a legislative pioneer in size acceptance. It was such a pleasure to honor both Mr. Tucker and Bill Fabrey, the founder of NAAFA, who received the Size Acceptance Vanguard Award.

Sunday›s breakfast speaker was Brandon Macsata, founder and president of the Association of Airline Passenger Rights (AAPR). NAAFA met and formed a strategic alliance with Brandon's organization as a result of AAPR coming out against United Airlines' declaration that they would start charging fat passengers double for seats. His talk resonated with almost everyone in the room because so many of us were flying to NAAFA conventions. Board member Frances White asked him to critique her suggestion that the airlines convert two rows of seats to two-across seats instead of three-across to be sold at a cost 1 ½ times a single seat, knowing that if there wasn't a fat passenger on the plane business travelers wanting to spread out to do paperwork would be willing to pay an extra fee. He said it would never happen because it was too practical!

That afternoon there were two legislative training classes for those convention participants who had previously signed up to make visits to Capitol Hill to educate our representatives and senators about what we as large people wanted in the healthcare reform bills working their way through the House and the Senate at the time. In order to speak with the same voice, we all attended classes to learn what language in the various bills needed to be changed.

Participants were matched by zip codes, with at least one NAAFA member to be part of each team regardless of their home location. Joslyn Smith used her set of training protocols and resources to schedule the visits. Noreen Banks provided NAAFA-specific training and advocacy efforts, alliance building, and special visits (including a White House visit), and led a letter writing campaign.

All teams carried identical packets of material to be left with the lawmakers, agencies, or organizations. All materials were co-branded, with only two focus areas: 1) health promotion and access from a HAES® perspective, and 2) eliminating size discrimination and weight bias. Packets included:

- Principles of HAES® (ASDAH to create)
- Weight/Size discrimination stats and issues (NAAFA to create)
- NAAFA informational brochure/pamphlet (NAAFA's annual report)
- ASDAH informational brochure
- CD of Size Diversity Toolkit (NAAFA)

Plans were made for teams to travel together in arranged accessible transportation on Size Diversity Awareness Day, Monday morning, August 3, 2009, to Washington, DC and return together to the hotel after the last visit in the late afternoon. Other than the scheduled legislative visits, team members would be responsible for their own additional itinerary or activities in DC during the day. Everyone would return to the hotel for a debriefing session and pizza party.

Training was led by Noreen Banks and Joslyn Smith on Sunday, August 2 from 1:00–6:00 pm, with congressional visits scheduled for Monday, August 3. Team assignments, congressional meeting schedules, legislative information, a map of Capitol Hill, and transportation arrangements were provided during Sunday's training for "Storming the Hill" on Monday.

Because of my position with NAAFA at the time and the reading I have always done to try to stay abreast of things, I felt prepared to speak to discrimination issues. However, if not for these experiences, I don't know that the training we received on Sunday would have been enough to have felt prepared to address discrimination issues. Some NAAFA members felt disappointed that only healthcare discrimination was discussed. Others felt unqualified to focus on healthcare reform and healthcare because the language of the talking points was not comfortable for them, therefore requiring them to read directly from the card and refer to notes to make their points.

When I suggested that discrimination in settings other than healthcare settings be part of the discussion the next time, I learned that the focus on healthcare was by design. Since the legislators were focused on the healthcare reform bills, to get their attention we needed to make our focus and requests relevant to what they were focusing on at the moment, then link in other aspects. As it turned out, some teams found that once the legislators saw that we were well-versed in issues they were involved with, it made it easier to emphasize NAAFA's focus. Several legislators asked for more information on other aspects of size discrimination.

More than 45 people went to see 30 different legislators as well as USDA officials. Setting up the appointments and arranging transportation, including cabs that could handle scooters, was quite a logistical undertaking. It was quite thrilling to watch all the cabs pull up to the hotel and take our members away to participate in a history making event!

Darliene Howell and I were scheduled to meet Matthew Coffron, assistant to Representative Shelley Berkley, and Carolyn Gluck, assistant to Senator Harry Reid, during our visits on Monday. The many hours the "Visits to the Hill" team put into research, planning, appointment setting, preparation of materials, and training made our appointments an awesome experience. I felt better prepared after our training. Healthcare reform is such an important issue, and one that we certainly needed to address while in Washington, DC. I appreciated the education, including the better understanding of how important a "may" and "or" can be in the writing of the new laws.

Rep. Berkeley's office was a riot. It was full of colorful flashing memorabilia from Las Vegas, and Matthew was very easy to talk with. He was a tall, thin man but was sympathetic to our cause and understood about the discrimination faced by people with large bodies. His best friend/college roommate was a man of size and he had experienced firsthand what happens to people for whom our society is not designed. We walked away feeling confident that he would do whatever he could to convince his boss to take another look at the proposed healthcare reform initiatives, with a focus on "improvement in health markers" as opposed to "weight loss" as a measure of success in healthcare and wellness programs.

The senator for Nevada at the time was Senator Harry Reid, a very powerful man in our country's government. He was a lawyer and politician who served as a United States senator from Nevada from 1987 to 2017 and was the Senate Majority Leader from 2007 to 2015. Our visit with Carolyn was not as warm or understanding as our time with Matthew had been, but in addition to making our point about discrimination in healthcare, we informed her we would also like to see Senator Reid introduce and sponsor legislation that would add height and weight to the anti-discrimination laws of our country. We told her that discrimination against people of size particularly targets women and ethnic minorities.

Monday evening after our return we all came together for a debriefing and pizza party in which we shared a slice or two and talked about our day of Storming the Hill. We also had the pleasure of a symbolic smashing and eating of a chocolate Capitol Building!

Following that historic day of our visits to the Hill, NAAFA and its members engaged in many follow-up activities:

- Members sent thank you letters to legislators
- Members participated in local town halls and demonstrations
- Board members returned to Washington DC to build alliances with like-minded organizations
- NAAFA and ASDAH sent a joint letter to senators with recommended changes, signed by Dana Schuster of ASDAH and Lisa Tealer of NAAFA.

Dear Senator _____:

Representatives from the Association for Size Diversity and Health (ASDAH) and the National Association to Advance Fat Acceptance (NAAFA) met with your staff on August 3. As a follow up to that meeting, please find our specific legislative language recommendation for the Senate HELP Committee draft of the Affordable Health Choices Act, released on June 9, below.

Page 368 Line 5: STRIKE "(i) decreases in weight" and REDESIGNATE items (ii) through (vi) accordingly.

Page 368 Line 12: STRIKE "and" after "survey;" and REPLACE with "or"

These recommended changes support extensive research stating that individuals of all sizes can be healthy and that health risk factors can improve without a loss in weight. Because up to 95% of dieters regain the weight they lost, and sometimes more, within three years, and restrictive dieting and weight cycling can be associated with poorer health outcomes, mandating a decrease in weight as a measure of community-based health prevention activities does a disservice. Therefore, we ask that these recommendations be reflected in any final version of health care reform legislation that is considered for enactment.

We understand that an amendment may have been approved that specifies changes in weight rather than a decrease in weight as a measure in the abovementioned language. Our recommendation would be to strike that language as well. If the language cannot be removed from the bill, we strongly urge you to accept the second language recommendation pertaining to the use of "or" rather than "and," as suggested above, in Line 12.

We look forward to supporting a health care reform bill that encourages health focused prevention efforts rather than one that requires communities to promote weight loss efforts.

While we were preparing to Storm the Hill, "Obesity causes $147 billion per year in extra medical costs in U.S." hit the headlines during the NAAFA convention. Reporters began calling and writing, asking for NAAFA's opinion of this announcement. Deb Burgard, PhD and Lindo Bacon, PhD agreed to field interviews with NPR and CNN. Our position on this important issue was clearly stated in a most timely manner. Dr. Bacon's interview followed the CDC's William Dietz, MD, PhD, who agreed during the NPR interview that "people can be healthy at any size"!

Media inquiries that came to us during the month following the conference included:

- Martine Powers, *Pittsburgh Post-Gazette*
- Doug Buchanan, FOX 5 News WTTG TV, Washington, DC
- Avery Johnson, *The Wall Street Journal*
- Sarah J. Hodd, ABC News *Nightline*
- Dmitry Anopchenko, INTER TV, Ukraine
- *Culture Shocks* radio with Barry Lynn
- Andrea Canning, *Good Morning America*
- Sara Stewart, *New York Post*
- Michelle for the *Dr. Nancy Snyderman Show*
- Nicole Sawyer, Fox News NY
- Kristin Graham, *Nat Geo's Taboo*

Once that year's experience was over, plans for next steps in Washington, DC began early. It had already been determined that NAAFA would return to Washington, DC in 2011. A congressional briefing was considered, but ultimately a press conference at the National Press Club was the final choice. The focus and public sentiment had shifted from healthcare in 2009 to bullying in 2010/2011. There were several anti-bullying bills being passed around. Although we had not specifically addressed it, an anti-bullying campaign was certainly something that was compatible with NAAFA's message. Fat people of all ages are bullied on an almost daily basis.

We had already learned that we would be much more successful at manipulating the legislative process and opinion on Capitol Hill if we focused on something that already had their interest and engagement. There were several anti-bullying bills working their way through Washington at the time, and not one of them mentioned body size, one of the first reasons a person is bullied. We needed to change this! Thus, NAAFA's END BULLYING NOW! Campaign was born, the brainchild of NAAFA's chair, Jason Docherty.

With a brilliantly designed visual campaign and speeches in our hands, we walked into the National Press Club on Monday, August 8, 2011. While several NAAFA members visited their lawmakers to make a case for adding weight and height to the Safe Schools Improvement Act, which was making its way through the Senate, we were pointing out that NO bill making its way through the House at the time would protect children of higher weight from bullying. Since 85% of the bullying in schools is perpetrated on children based on their body size or visible disabilities, as these bills stood, they only protected 15% of the children currently being bullied.

Jason Docherty, chairman of NAAFA and executive vice president, new media and managing director of a leading Canadian communications firm introduced NAAFA, our accomplishments, and our goals.

At the time I was public relations director and a partner in chunkEbusiness. com. I addressed how and why NAAFA was addressing the issue of bullying in schools and why the Safe Schools Improvement Act of 2010 fell short of protecting all children from bullying.

Lisa Tealer, director of programs for NAAFA and diversity specialist for a major biotech company, addressed the NAAFA Child Advocacy Toolkit and how it should be used by parents, teachers and caregivers of children of all sizes.

Brandon Macsata, founder of the Association for Airline Passenger Rights, NAAFA advisory board member and managing partner of the Macsata-Kornegay Group, Inc., explained the importance of adding weight and height to the Safe Schools Improvement Act of 2010.

If the parents and teachers cannot teach children that we come in all sizes and that diversity is a natural part of life, then enacting a law that protects all children is necessary!

Because this press conference received national coverage on C-SPAN and CNN as well as local CBS, ABC and NBC affiliates, we tracked the potential viewership and publicity value for the 30-second news clips that appeared on television alone. This does not include print media or radio. Combined local and national total television viewership potential was 119,726,576 viewers. The publicity value was a staggering $744,901.05. This was a wise way to invest $3,000.00 to get our message seen and heard. You can still see the entire

presentation on the C-SPAN website at http://www.c-spanvideo.org/program/
SafeS.

I first became aware of size acceptance when I saw an ad for NAAFA's 25th anniversary conference, which was held in San Diego, CA. In the 30 years that have followed, these two trips to Washington, DC were the only major activism events that I have attended. Because I was on the NAAFA board of directors and involved in the planning and execution of these events, I believe I have a unique perspective with more detailed knowledge than the average attendee. I hope that in reading about these events, current and future activists can see the value in visits to our congressional representatives to make a case for changing this country's anti-discrimination laws to include height and weight. I hope they can see the value of investing in a major platform like the National Press Club to reach as many supporters as possible with our message of Equality at Every Size!

The fact remains that whether or not my fat body is healthier than anyone else's body is not the point. Whether or not a fat person has healthy eating habits and moves on a regular basis is not the point. Whether or not I accept and love my fat body is not the point! The point is that the civil rights of fat people are being violated and that must stop. Whether I have blue eyes or brown eyes, am a rocket scientist or a ditchdigger, prefer Nike or New Balance, we are supposed to all be the same under the law. No one has the right to diminish my civil rights because I am fat.

IN PURSUIT OF FAT JUSTICE

SONDRA SOLOVAY
interviewed by BRANDIE SOLOVAY

Can you tell me about one case that stands out as the biggest miscarriage of justice? What are your memories from that case? What was it like to be there?

THIS HAPPENED DECADES AGO, when I was newly 30 years old, but I still remember wondering—would I make it to the courthouse, or were the police waiting outside my door? In my New Mexico hotel room I pushed the thoughts aside as I continued to search through piles of photocopied fatphobia that masqueraded as medical records, looking for the arguments that would reunite a Latinx family by returning the young, fat girl who had been removed from her parents' care.

I was worried about being arrested because the volunteer attorney for the child's parents was being threatened with contempt of court (and all manner of small-town repercussions) because *I* was accused of breaking the gag order and publicly discussing what was happening in the courtroom. (I didn't.) In fairness, I was the only fat person in the packed courtroom, so who else were they going to blame?

The parents' legal team consisted only of a local lawyer (who had heroically volunteered to help because he was worried that the family had no representation), his paralegal wife, and me, a fat volunteer from California with a law degree.

The case was getting international press coverage, which was inconvenient for the state's goal of quietly removing and forcibly dieting this child, so the courtroom was ordered closed to the press and public. The family only had six seats—three in front of the bar for their legal team and three in the gallery for their guests, even though they had many more family members who wanted to support them and witness what was happening. Nevertheless, the sizable courtroom was standing-room only. Their child had been given a dedicated state lawyer to look out for her interests. This would have been great if the lawyer was actually independent, but this lawyer sat and chatted cozily with the state's attorney who was defending the government's right to remove the toddler from her parents. The rest of the gallery was packed—many appeared to be government attorneys or staff, doctors and hospital personnel who were involved or knew someone and were able to get in for the spectacle. The medical folks were there because they were the ones who had arranged the surprise snatching of the toddler. They called the parents, ostensibly to bring the child in for a routine exam but had security waiting to take the child once they arrived.

I do not believe the removal of the child was lawful (though the court disagreed with me). Follow me—it's a bit of a ride: The medical establishment had recommended a liquid diet for the fat toddler. The family agreed to try it though no studies showed that this was a medically reasonable course of treatment. During one visit, personnel changed her diaper and found a partially undigested bean. The bean, they asserted, was evidence that the family had not followed the liquid diet, which they saw as child abuse.

Many children are abused, and it is often hard to remove them from an abusive home, so how was it so easy to remove this child?

Normally, unless a child is in emergency circumstances, due process requires a hearing during which parents present evidence before a child is removed from the home. That's in part because taking a child from a family without reason is incredibly traumatic and unconstitutional. This seizure was perpetrated by medical providers—damaging the relationship of trust between both caregiver and parent, and caregiver and patient.

Obviously, even if the child was no longer on the liquid diet, several days of normal food is not a life-threatening situation that could possibly justify violations of medical trust and due process. Why didn't the family get an emergency hearing and, if they lost, the chance to hand over the child in a less traumatic manner? The rationale was that the family was a "flight risk" to go to Mexico. This family had so many extended family members living in the area that it's hard to imagine a family more rooted to the location. It's another example of how tightly and inextricably connected anti-fatness racism and white supremacy are.

I had a "good legal education," but I learned very little about justice. I went to a top law school only a few years after Professor Kimberle Crenshaw coined the term *intersectionality*, yet we certainly did not learn about the ways racism, poverty, anti-fatness, and anti-immigrant sentiment combine to interfere in the legal process. Still, I could see from the cases I encountered how racism and anti-fat abuses go hand-in-hand. The most egregious instances of weight discrimination, like child custody issues, often target Black, brown, superfat/infinifat, and/or disabled people.

Why is this one of the worst cases?

This case was a perfect storm of complicity among the doctors, healthcare personnel, city attorneys, and the judge; it combined racism, weight discrimination, fatphobia, anti-immigrant sentiment; and, finally, it showed an eagerness to misuse legal process to thwart the constitutional rights of liberty and of freedom of speech. This wasn't the fault of any one overly powerful bad actor; it was an entire system conspiring against a low-resourced family to steal a fat child.

Despite the bad, there were some good elements—mostly how heroic people were. The extended family kept showing up no matter how many hurdles were put in their way. The husband-and-wife attorney-and-paralegal pair, who probably had no idea what they were up against, stayed and fought for this family to receive justice at risk to their own careers in this small-town-mentality jurisdiction even though they had their own family to care for. The activists, many of whom were low-resourced themselves, refused to let the system get away with disappearing this child; they protested outside the court and called and faxed the court and media to share their opinions. Expert Joanne Ikeda, MA, RD, may her memory be a blessing, volunteered her services and flew in to testify on a Friday at her own expense. Knowing she was an out-of-town expert, when the court saw she was up next they decided to shut down early and reconvene on Monday. She flew home Friday and flew back Sunday night, again at her own expense, just to testify on behalf of the family. NAAFA (the National Association to Advance Fat Acceptance) was fantastic; despite a small budget, they did everything they could to support the fight and the family, and to work with the media. There were also the dedicated reporters who broke the story and kept running with it until the judge gagged them. Add to that the heroic decision of the media to legally challenge the gag order, even though they knew that by the time the lower court's unconstitutional decision would be overturned, the story would be over. (That was the strategy—shut down the press just long enough that the issue would be resolved without public oversight.) The activists and I were not paid for our time or expertise or risk—we all did it to save a child, to help a family, and because we needed the government to understand that fat children would not be stolen in this country anymore without a real fight.

We won. The child was returned home.

What was it like to do fat law in the U.S.?

Almost impossible. Very few places have laws that clearly protect fat people from discrimination. That leaves only a few options: create laws, work within disability law, do "creative lawyering" with no roadmap, or work with a major civil rights group for a federal Constitutional challenge. I did the first three.

Creating laws is truly satisfying, because you are making something out of nothing. You are basically crafting a tool that current and future fat people can use to fight for an equal, full, and vibrant life. Making laws is something that tends to happen as a response to something bad. Someone faces discrimination and people do not want it to happen again, and they make a beautiful thing come from that bad experience—they put words on a page to empower fat people to fight for our lives.

In 2000 we passed a law in San Francisco in response to a fitness company that had created a mean-spirited billboard featuring a space alien that said: "When they come, they'll eat the fat ones first." Marilyn Wann organized a protest. Media came. The Human Rights Commission became interested in the experience of fat San Franciscans. We organized hearings where fat people testified. We had a speaker for each of many important topics, including intersectionality and the disproportionate impact on certain people of color, landlord/tenant issues, medical access and discrimination, employment, and education access. Attorney Carole Cullum and Jo Ellen Kuney, who were politically active in San Francisco politics, worked hard to help legislators understand the need for the law. We worked with the city of Santa Cruz, where a similar ordinance had already passed. After hearings, the law was passed. I was honored to contribute to the law's enforcement guidelines, which themselves were voted on and have the full force of law. Those guidelines direct businesses and organizations on what they should do, and what they must do, so that fat people are more able to participate in mainstream life in the city and county of San Francisco. This includes providing medical services to fat people, training on height and weight issues, providing adequate seating, and recognizing that one size does *not* fit all. The Human Rights Commission staff and the commissioners all received training on height and weight discrimination. Other locations used the experience in San Francisco to pass (or attempt to pass) their own laws.

Working with disability laws has been a huge challenge for many reasons. One reason is that disability law is inconsistently interpreted across different jurisdictions. Early on, some courts created an extra burden *specifically for fat people* seeking protection under disability law that they did not require of any other plaintiff. These courts essentially held that proving the person was disabled by their weight was not enough—the person had to offer *double proof*, they had to also show that *their weight itself* was caused by a disability. Of course, proving the cause of higher weight is impossible—though we know weight is not simply about "calories in, calories out," the science is just not advanced enough to explain why some people are fat and others are not. Normally, how a person becomes disabled is not a legal issue—a person could be born disabled or become disabled later. More important, even if they became disabled in a way that was totally their own fault and morally wrong, for example, by falling off a tightrope while committing a heinous crime, they are still protected by disability law. The courts seemed motivated by prejudice, as if they did not want to offer legal protection to fat people who are seen as at fault for being fat.

Another challenge with using disability law is based in fatphobia, and, to an extent, racism, within the disability community. It is disappointing that none of the numerous disability rights organizations, nor any of the general civil rights organizations, decided to advocate for fat folks. It should never have been acceptable to the traditional disability rights community to leave fat people behind. It should also have been obvious that this would disproportionately impact Black and brown disabled people. Traditional disability rights community did and continues to do amazing work, but the field has centered certain disabled experiences and left others out, especially BIPOC, fat, and gender non-conforming disabled people. Within disability community, fatphobia and anti-fat attitudes are commonplace and often unexamined, even when they impact otherwise-disabled people who are also fat.

Another problem with using disability law to fight fat discrimination is ableism in the fat community. Fat people often try to create distance from disabled people, rather than unite as a group of people who are all worthy and who all deserve accommodations and inclusion.

In order to fight these complex legal disability issues, what fat community needed were experienced and funded disability attorneys; what we had was a very small handful of fat attorneys who were largely self-taught and willing to volunteer their time, many of whom were also part of fat queer community. Within the disability legal community, there were a few individual lawyers who did help and do continue to make a difference for fat justice.

What does "creative lawyering" mean, and why is that important?

Weight discrimination and hostility toward fat people are not taken very seriously by most courts. Since it is not seen as a problem and we don't have a lot of established, powerful laws to use, we have no choice but to get creative.

Creative lawyering includes using ethical arguments and education instead of traditional law. This can be as simple as reminding people that acting ethically and acting within the law are not necessarily the same thing, and that they have the power to do the right thing even if they are not yet required to do so by today's laws. If you ask people why they behave ethically, most don't do it because it is legally required. So it's really about empowering people who are part of organizations to make ethical organizational decisions in keeping with the organization's values, without relying on a court or legislature to make them do the right thing.

Sometimes creative lawyering means using the court of public opinion instead of a court of law. Sometimes it's about inspiring people to change the law. Other times, reflecting and validating fat people's experiences and empowering them to fight is the only avenue. Corroborating that what happened was wrong and sharing in the anger that the laws haven't caught up. Strategizing with them so they can fight and connecting them to fat activist community might be the only option. When people realize they are not just fighting for themselves but for the fat people that come after them, that it might take us 40 fails before that first win, they may decide it's worth it to keep pushing.

What is something you worked on that you are very proud of?

One of the things I am most proud of achieving, and which was shockingly difficult, was *preventing* the state of California from seriously harming fat people. More than a decade ago I fought really hard for nothing to happen, and I was successful.

California was revising its disability regulations and they were trying to include a new provision that would *specifically prevent* fat people from using California disability laws to protect ourselves. It's one thing for a conservative court to refuse to protect fat people when a case is tried, but it's a whole different level of hostility and targeting for a state to go out of its way to *exclude* a class of people from using a law even if they otherwise qualify to use it.

It's really a miracle I even noticed that the proposed disability regulations mentioned weight. Of all the disability rights attorneys and advocates who, in their full-time, paid, professional capacities were reviewing and responding to the proposed regulations, not a single one called NAAFA or any other fat liberation group to alert fat community that there was an attempt to pass regulations that would prevent fat people from using disability law. I just happened to be recreationally reading the proposed regs (like a total legal geek) when I saw those couple of new words designed to prevent fat people from seeking justice, buried deep inside the redline document.

I contacted representatives of disability rights groups and asked for allyship, and I am so glad they did join us in opposing the exclusion when asked. I went to meetings and hearings where I argued, testified, implored and threatened. People were, by and large, very unwilling to hear about the plight of fat people. It was only by the grace and advocacy of one or two judges and concerned attendees that I was even able to speak in some of these meetings. There is just so much prejudice. It was impossible to know who was behind this attempted exclusion of fat people. In the end, it was lucky timing on a key federal decision, extensive research, and strong arguments that preserved the right *just to have the chance to fight* for our rights in California. Because California is a legally influential state, a loss like this could have been devastatingly contagious—many states might have adopted similar exclusionary regulations.

I am very pleased to report that California has taken a huge step forward since then. During COVID, the state initially passed very problematic Care Rationing Guidelines, but fat people along with disability and aging groups were able to collaborate to improve the initial guidelines released by the state. Now, due in part to FLARE's (Fat Legal Advocacy, Rights and Education Project) work, California's guidelines state: "Healthcare decisions, including allocation of scarce resources, cannot be based on age, race, disability (including weight-related disabilities and chronic medical conditions), gender, sexual orientation, gender identity, ethnicity (including national origin and language spoken), ability to pay, weight/size, socioeconomic status, insurance status, perceived self-worth, perceived quality of life, immigration status, incarceration status, homelessness, or past or future use of resources."

What do you see as the biggest hurdle preventing fat people from achieving justice in the legal system specifically?

Funding and friendship are the biggest hurdles.

I spent my career fighting for fat justice, but this was uncompensated work and, quite often, it cost me money to do it. I funded the work myself by doing talks, other legal work, adjunct legal teaching, and full-time corporate work in e-learning compliance. It's important to note that, as a fat person myself, I faced discrimination, from lessened opportunities to lower wages and higher costs (like paying for two airline seats, paying more for insurance and clothes, etc.)

What we need is obvious: an actual nonprofit fat legal organization that does impact cases, legislative work, and daily fat advocacy. There are numerous such organizations focused on LGBTQIA+ issues, disability issues, and other civil rights issues. There is not even one fat legal justice organization, and there never has been one. I had hoped that the FLARE Project would become the first, but I was unable to get funding or to figure out a way for the project to support itself. Today there are very different self-funding options, including crowd-sourced funding, so I am hopeful that we will get there as a community in the future, even if I am not around to see it.

When I say "friendship" is a hurdle, what I mean is that our fellow civil rights activists have not generally been great friends to fat people, nor have they been responsive to the needs of fat people within their own constituencies. The burden of antifat bias falls more heavily on Black and brown people who are disproportionately represented among higher weight people, so while this lack of willingness to embrace fat justice within progressive groups has been hard on all fat people, it has been especially devastating for many fat people of color. Time after time the ACLU sat idly by on the sidelines when fat children were taken away from loving homes. Generally, disability organizations did not embrace fat issues even when it impacted their own otherwise-disabled community members, let alone welcoming fat people who did not identify as disabled. Outrageously, most disability organizations remained silent while court decisions required fat people to meet additional legal hurdles to use disability law that were not required of their thin peers. Even when disabled groups have been willing to collaborate with fat activists, few have affirmatively reached out to include fat liberation perspectives or fat community needs. It's not been all bad—some individual attorneys and leaders within certain civil rights organizations have provided important support and allyship when called on in specific legal challenges, including Disability Rights Education and Defense Fund (DREDF), Southern Poverty Law Center, National Center for Lesbian Rights, Legal Aid at Work, and others. Some have offered moral support, but only "off the record" to protect their reputations.

Fat people are not without fault in the lack of allyship between traditional disability and fat communities. Despite needing accommodations and aids, and facing constant discrimination based on our presumed lack of physical or mental abilities, many fat people have fanned the flames of ableism, often playing the "good fatty" card to reinscribe a divide between "normal" people (which they argue should include fat people) and "disabled" people. Just as fat disabled people were sidelined in disability communities, within fat community disabled fat people were often relegated to inferior status and seen as dangerous, embarrassing, or as "bad fatties."

But good news lately! Disability Justice advocates have brought about changes. Traditional disability rights groups are starting to understand the connection between anti-fat attitudes, racism, and justice; disability justice groups are learning more about including weight in their analysis; fat community is starting to learn more about ableism, anti-Blackness, and white supremacy; and analysis by fat Black and brown activists and educators is flourishing.

What makes you angry or regretful about the movement?

That's a long list! The refusal to understand weight discrimination as an intersectional issue that impacts Black and brown people disproportionately. Unaddressed racism. Co-optation of the movement. People and organizations that simultaneously claim to fight fat stigma while actively contributing to that stigma by advocating weight loss (knowing statistically that there is no way for the average fat person to become thin). Smaller fat people who don't center the issues of superfat/infinifat people (admittedly, when I was new to the movement and smaller in size, I did not understand these issues myself). People who make money on the agony of fat people by exploiting fat people or fat hatred (such as diet programs and dangerous weight-loss surgery businesses), academic institutions taking weight-loss money, academic institutions being unwilling to challenge fat myths. Fat people who seem to adopt a fat-positive approach in order to solicit fat clients, customers, or fans, but are actually fatphobic or are actively pursuing weight-loss goals. Lack of representation of actual fat liberationists in funded movements like eating disorders, disability, and general civil rights. People who think that employment laws should take priority when fat people are literally dying due to medical discrimination (which includes blanket denials of organ transplants to all fat people even when they have a family member who wants to donate the organ and the fact that no civil rights group has ever challenged this policy, or even criticized it). The fact that diagnostic medical imaging equipment does not work for many fat people and that weight prejudice is known and rampant in the medical field. Civil rights groups that are unwilling to fight anti-fatness even though parents can legally face custody issues due to their weight or the weight of their children, fat people can't travel the way thin people can, cars are not required to have seat belts that fit fat people, etc.

You have written two books. What are the books and what led you to writing them?

Tipping the Scales of Justice: Fighting Weight-Based Discrimination was born out of research I did in law school. There were already law journal articles on weight discrimination in the employment setting and some discussion about disability law, but nobody looked at fat rights as a civil rights issue and surveyed *all* the ways fat had become a courtroom topic. My research included those and other much more devastating topics like family law, incarceration, involuntary adult commitment, and even barriers to fat people's access to justice via jury dismissals.

I had a very hard time finding a professor willing to supervise my law school research and writing. I mention this because I want people to really understand how quiet and devastating systemic discrimination is, and how it contributes to the fact that the U.S. fat justice community is still in its infancy. At that time, there was no recognized field of fat studies. There were very few fat law students at my public (more affordable) law school. I literally did not fit at school because most classrooms had affixed chairs and narrow rows. Other classrooms had chairs with fold-out desks, which I also could not use. It was so uncomfortable to be a fat person in law school, it's no wonder there were not more of us. Only one law professor was willing to support my research about fat civil rights, and even then it required a special petition to the school because he was "only" a lecturer brought in to teach sexual orientation law; he was willing to supervise my work without compensation and he was very supportive. After my book was published, inspired by that project with him, I went to a special academic job-seekers' conference focused on bringing more "women and minorities" into legal academia. The keynote speaker explained that to be competitive job seekers had to come from a "Top 10" law school and have published. I met with him for his opinion about my next steps, since I had already graduated from a "Top 10" school and actually had a book. His response was that my book did not count because it has to be a "real" topic of "legal significance."

It was my dream to eventually teach law and run the first fat legal clinic using student interns, which I thought was the best way to fund a legal rights and advocacy program for fat people and to ensure that we would be creating fat-justice-trained attorneys who could continue the fight in the future. The dean of New College School of Law (which billed itself as the oldest public interest law school in the U.S.) used to bring me in to talk to her first-year students about my book. Eventually I started teaching tort law with a social justice perspective and a few other courses there and at other schools. I also taught continuing education in fat rights to lawyers, eating disorder graduate students and professionals, and some undergrads. I came close to achieving my goal, but just as I became a member of the core faculty, the law school closed. For years I was simultaneously working my corporate job, teaching three three-hour first-year law classes (a full-time faculty teaching load) as an adjunct, running my own law office and the FLARE Project through which I did pro-bono fat rights work, and of course doing activism work.

I also tried to get funding for a fat legal organization. Against all odds I was chosen as a finalist for the highly competitive Echoing Green fellowship, which would have provided two years of start-up funding for a legal nonprofit. I was completely up-front about my position on fat liberation issues in the application. Finalists were flown to New York for a multi-day event that included live panel interviews. When I flew, I was worried about whether I would be turned away at the gate for being too fat for one airplane seat. When I was there, I worried I would be stranded in New York for the same reason. While I flew, I worried about a child who had been threatened with removal for their weight and how I could help fight that. As it happened, I knew another finalist—he was trying to start a transgender rights legal organization. My panel interview was so hostile to basic fat rights, I was shocked. Not shocked that people had those attitudes, but surprised that they would choose me as a finalist but install judges with those attitudes. My application was very straightforward about the civil rights issues fat people needed help with and my fat liberation politics. The panel was overwhelmingly concerned with fat children. "What about their health?!?" They wanted to know what doctors would be a part of my organization to weigh in on the issues. I calmly explained that my organization was a legal organization, and we would be arguing for fat children to receive medical care, but that we absolutely did not need the permission of doctors to advocate for the legal rights of fat people. They were so paternalistic! One judge even said they wanted to fund an organization "on this topic" so they were disappointed in my position (that fat people deserved civil rights regardless of medical approval). The most friendly member of the judging panel was actually a doctor who tried to explain to the panel that fat people were not fat just because they ate too much. It was inconceivable to the panel that a fat rights organization would not be advocating for fat children to lose weight and would not be run by doctors. I figured the panel was just very harsh and very concerned about the health of children.

Then I talked to my friend about his experience with that panel. It could not have been more different.

Despite the fact that he affirmatively discussed that his organization would be advocating for children to receive gender confirming hormones and procedures (decades ago when this was a novel concept with much less supporting research), he had not received even one single concern or question about that proposition, and not one single suggestion that he consult with a physician before doing that advocacy. To be clear, I don't think he should have been asked those things, but the right for self-determination regarding gender was easily embraced, whereas the right for fat children to have *any* of their rights protected was held hostage to medical approval. I was so confused and traumatized by this disparate treatment that I called Marilyn Wann that evening; she asked if I had seen the *New York Times* that morning. I had not. It had a huge fearmongering cover story about fat children and diabetes. And that explained everything.

I'm so proud of my friend, who deserved and did receive the fellowship: Transgender Law Center (TLC) has grown into the largest trans-specific, trans-led organization in the United States. Their advocacy and precedent-setting litigation victories protect and advance the rights of transgender and gender nonconforming people across the country. TLC assists, informs, and empowers thousands of individual community members a year and builds towards a long-term, national, trans-led movement for liberation. I completely support and am grateful for TLC; at the same time, I do use TLC's success as a yardstick for where fat justice could have been today with institutional support.

As an outsider-academic, I was as active as I could be in the field of fat law and justice. The field of fat studies had grown, and I felt like it was time the field itself had a book. While we were both visiting groundbreaking fat activist Judy Freespirit, I approached Esther Rothblum, PhD, who had conducted a study on weight discrimination in employment that I often used in legal arguments. In retrospect, she was a much better partner than I had anticipated; in addition to being brilliant and impeccably organized, as a highly successful professor with a lot of publishing experience she provided helpful perspective on the prejudice we faced in publication. We did publish *The Fat Studies Reader* in 2010, and it was honored with a few awards, meaning it was receiving recognition as a valid topic in academia. (Fun fact—there was such a lack of available fat-friendly imagery for the book cover, I had to enlist Max Airborne to collaborate with me—together in ki's living room, we created the cover art.) Adjunct professors don't receive academic salaries that anticipate covering time for writing and editing. Like all my other fat work, my fat studies academic work cost me money and time.

What other types of fat activism did you do, and what was your favorite project?

During my career I was honored to serve on a few advisory boards of folks doing visionary projects. Until around 2017 I volunteered on the NAAFA advisory board—this was one of my favorites because of the commitment and dedication of the people I met through NAAFA. For me, the only thing that makes this fight sustainable is working with amazing people who, even if we don't agree, bring respect and allyship to the fight. I was also an active board member of NOLOSE (National Organization for Lesbians of Size) for a few years, up until around 2013, and was instrumental in bringing the conference to California for the first time. I love the community NOLOSE created, the pockets of joy, and most important, the space NOLOSE carved out to center—or at least to learn about centering—BIPOC leadership and membership within fat community.

In the days before self-publishing was something you could do from your phone, I was involved with *FaTGiRL, FAT!SO?* and *SizeQueen* zines, which were all about creating space to be seen and to talk about things relevant to our communities.

I was part of the Bod Squad (a campy fat liberation cheerleading performance team) and Big Burlesque. I was the co-author of, and performer in, *The F Word/Fat Fuck,* which toured and sold out at festivals in San Francisco and New York, as well as performing at NOLOSE.

I have done a lot of talks and interviews at all sorts of venues—from the Dirtybird Music Festival to childhood "obesity" conferences.

I think my very favorite project, however, has been *Cupcakes and Muffintops,* which is a clothing and bake sale where "only the prices are small." This incredible event helps fat people clear out their closets, then sells those clothes at very low prices to raise funds for fat liberation causes. The sale was initially created in California with help from New York's Big Fat Flea to fund taking the cast of *Fat Fuck* to NOLOSE to perform the play there, which was the dream of Heather MacAllister, may her memory be a blessing. The sale then transformed through collaboration to become *Cupcakes and Muffintops* and involved the inspired, fantastic dance troupe Big Moves/emFATic DANCE. It is not perfect and is always working to improve physical and scent accessibility, but it is my favorite event because it helps fat community at every step of the way—from rehoming/recycling clothes, to getting affordable new wardrobes to fat folks, to supporting fat arts and activism—and because it creates and strengthens fat community. Volunteers are thanked with free clothes and baked goods. Unsold clothes are donated to local shelters or charities, improving the availability of large size clothes. The event opens first for disabled and superfat/infinifat shoppers. Everywhere there are fat liberation and body positive signs. And each time some shopper has the amazing experience of trying on clothing surrounded by supportive people. One person came out to applause—she was trying on a bathing suit for the first time in decades. Another person found a wedding dress after thinking they could neither find nor afford one. Another person got a whole new wardrobe for college.

Is there anything else you would like to share that we haven't talked about?

I am truly excited about what the FLARE Project will do with you as the legal director. It's been exciting to hand the project over to someone who was a law student of mine way back in the distant past. I am already so thrilled to see FLARE moving into more legislative work and pushing for equity in healthcare, including your Imaging Access Project! I am also very hopeful for the future of fat justice. When I was trying to put a fat justice organization together there was so much resistance and so little opportunity for funding. Today with the ability to crowd fund, I think the chance to create a sustainable, effective, intersectional, independent fat justice organization is within reach.

Thank you so much. It has truly been an honor to get to talk with you about all of these experiences. I love hearing the stories and learning from you.

FOOTNOTE

Apologies for anyone I am forgetting in this moment. I'd like to name and thank some of the people I personally encountered who participated or encouraged those important and unfunded fat legal battles— Carole Cullum, Mo Kalman, Julie Turner, Kyre Stucklin, Lilia Schwartz, Brandie Solovay, Beth Kenny, MC Linthicum, Elaine Lee, Jordan Ashe, and Marc Seawright. I'd also like to name and thank a few of the civil rights attorneys who were "early understanders" of the link between fat, disability, and intersectional legal issues and supported the field of fat justice—Elizabeth Kristen, Claudia Center, Shannon Minter, and Michael Adams. Finally, thanks to Brandie, Lilia, Ragen, Tigress, and Nancy for your incredible support on this piece.

WOMEN OF TREMENDOUS WEIGHT

A CONVERSATION WITH DEB BURGARD, PAT LYONS, CAROL SQUIRES, AND LISA TEALER
(*moderated by* TIGRESS OSBORN)

INTRODUCTION

I WAS A YOUNG ADULT when I moved to the San Francisco-Oakland Bay Area, and I had no idea when I landed in the Bay that it was an area of California where a deeply engaged multi-generational fat liberation community was part of the long and storied history of anti-oppression activism in the area. When I dipped my toe into fat activist waters in my early 20s, I didn't know yet that I would fully submerge in my mid-30s. That submersion would mean being surrounded by people whose names and faces and bodies I'd seen for years in books and articles about size acceptance and fat rights. Years later, I convened four of these respected activists to spend a winter afternoon as we so often do in the 2020s, on a Zoom call. We all dialed in from our homes (the four of them still live in the Bay) to discuss what their decades of work in body liberation has meant to them—its impact on their own lives, their impact on each other's lives, and the impact of their foundational work on the rest of us. I'd given them a few general questions to think about in advance, but we mostly let the conversation take us where it took us. Highlights are presented here in transcript form so that you, too, can experience the natural flow of that delightful and insightful winter afternoon dialogue.

THE INTERVIEW

Carol

I moved to the SF Bay Area in 1981 and I still live here. In 1986 I was first introduced to fat politics, and within a year I joined FAT LIP Readers Theatre, a group of fat women who wrote and performed about living in our fatphobic culture. I'm probably the most well-known for the 13 years I spent with FAT LIP. During this time I was also involved with *Radiance: The Magazine for*

Large Women as a photographer and an editor of the slush pile. In the early 2000s I was a performer and board member with Big Moves, a size-inclusive dance organization. Wow, I've been a public fat person for 37 years!

Deb

I'm Deb Burgard. I was dimly aware of the Fat Underground when I was in college in the late '70s and heard about the people in LA doing that, but I was really smack in the middle of second wave feminism on campus. After that, in 1983 I came to the West Coast, to the Bay Area, to do grad school in psychology. When I got here, I wanted to start teaching a class that would not be weight-loss oriented, but would be a space for larger people, larger women (we were using that language at the time), to just party, basically. I had that yearning and I had a lot of questions about whether I should be the person to do it, but I started doing it. I met Lisa and Carol in my class, and I met Pat when I was substituting for another person's class in San Francisco. The class ended up being this little laboratory or a little community that got formed, sometimes in Oakland, West Oakland, sometimes in Berkeley—there were a bunch of different locations where I was teaching. That just was amazing to me. People found each other and went on and did all this other stuff that was just incredible. And they had already been doing good stuff, too, of course, but it was a lovely little crossroads. Then Pat and I wrote the book *Great Shape* together.

Meanwhile, I was learning how to treat eating disorders, which wasn't even much of a thing in the '80s. The people who were in healthcare who didn't want to put people on diets were beginning to find each other. I had one foot in healthcare and eating disorders stuff, and psychologists were trying to teach me to put people on diets, and I was not going to do it. I had the other foot in the fitness world and dance world and I had the activism stuff that was beginning to become really important to me. I started the website Bodypositive.com in the mid-'90s, and some people found a lot of content there. I started the ShowMeTheData listserv for people who were doing research, which was an outgrowth of a section of the Think Tank Group Pat will talk about. The listserv began, I think, in 2001. The listserv was (and still is) a global list of people who were doing research and analyzing what's coming out in all the places where the weight cycling industry is reforming and coming back to push "obesity" as a disease.

Lisa

Lisa Tealer, pronouns she/her. You may remember *BBW* magazine. I think that was the first time I actually saw women that looked like me, and that opened up my head to the fact that there are women that were bigger, fatter.

And it opened up the world, just that possibility. I saw an ad for Deb's class and I met her and Carol. The way I entered it was the fashion show and then got into the fitness and health arena, and met Alice from *Radiance*. I was on the board of NAAFA (the National Association to Advance Fat Acceptance), and a charter member of Health at Every Size (HAES®) and got involved in the politics of it.

It was so funny, when I saw the questions for today, it was like flashbacks of us being on the corner of Van Nuys in San Francisco when 24 Fitness said, "When the aliens come they'll eat the fat ones first," and we were like, "Yeah, eat me!" We would just to try to create a safe space for all bodies. I had my toe dipping in a lot of different spaces.

Pat

I'm Pat Lyons, and my background was in nursing. I was a public health nurse on a tribal Indian health program in the Eastern Sierras when I first started hearing about the Fat Underground in the early '80s. I was running at the time, and I remember running out to the dump and throwing my scale into the dump! And that was my first experience of "Oh, I see, I could live without worrying about being fat," but still trying to run and get thinner if I could.

I left there and went to graduate school at Sonoma State in 1984. The first month I was there I saw FAT LIP Readers Theatre and it turned my head completely around. I said, "Oh, I see. I see. Here is a whole other wavelength!" I ended up doing my graduate thesis called "Fitness, Feminism, and the Health of Fat Women," where I was comparing situations that had been arranged specifically for bigger women. Deb and I wrote *Great Shape,* published in 1988. Laura Kiernan, who was the director of health education at Kaiser Permanente's regional health education office had been on the cover of *Radiance* magazine. I met her and took *Great Shape* to her, and she made it possible for us to do the Great Shape Program, and all the work that we did to develop the basic Health At Every Size paradigm.

I was at Kaiser until 1997. After that, I did some research on weight discrimination, health, and healthcare access at UC Berkeley. For that whole period of 10 and 12 years I spoke at a lot of conferences; I was probably the only person in the country that was being paid in my job to do fat liberation work.

I've not been involved in the last 10 or 15 years, kind of going to retirement. I guess one thing for me now is, I don't know most of the people that are doing the work, and it's fantastic. At one point in my life I owned everything that had ever been written positively about that stuff. And now it's so exploded all over the world, and it's so fantastic.

Tigress

I agree. It's so much harder to stay caught up! I often feel pressure to know everything about fat lib, to read every book, every article, and it's just not possible anymore. But that's part of what we're here to talk about—how fat community has moved from that place where you all could know each other because there were so few of you doing the work, to this place where the work is so expansive that we just can't keep up.

Carol

In 1984 I decided to start the-diet-to-end-all-diets. I was going to do it right this time. I just happened to see a flyer for Deb's We Dance class at a clothing store in Oakland. I thought, "okay, now I can really do it right, I'll do my 500 calories a day and I will exercise, I'll go to this class, and I'll get thin and it'll be wonderful. Life will be beautiful and perfect."

With some trepidation, I went to my first class. And I loved it. I never lost weight, but it was a pivotal point in my fat-body-loving journey. It was in this class that I saw a flyer for the fifth anniversary performance of FAT LIP Readers Theatre. You gotta remember, this is the days before everyone had computers. Everything was done by flyers, or phone trees, calling up people. Through Deb's class, I'd also gotten involved with *Radiance* magazine, because Alice Ansfeld, the editor, was there. I started taking some pictures for her of the class, and she also had *Radiance* Retreats. At the *Radiance* Retreat in '86 they had two people from FAT LIP come and do a writing exercise, and shortly after that I saw the ad for the performance.

This was the first time I'd ever gone to a performance by myself, which was a big deal, because you are always supposed to go with someone when you go out. And I took myself to Mama Bears, and I saw FAT LIP. The next thing I know they had a callout for new members and I applied! And then you had to use the word "fat" because it was right in the title of our name, FAT LIP Readers Theatre. I wasn't sure that I agreed with everything just yet, because I still had some diet hopes, but I faked it till I made it. From that day on "fat" has been my term, my choice. I will use it proudly. I will use it to shock people. Even today, you can shock people by saying "I'm fat" or using the word "fat" in any positive way.

Pat

This is one of my very favorite stories. We started having a Fat Swim for women at the beautiful pool up in Richmond. It was fat women in bathing suits, and everybody's so beautiful and it was just fantastic. I remember getting to the swim one day before anybody else was there. I was standing there, and one of the little 16-year-old lifeguards that they hired to save these 300-pound women if we were drowning came out and said, "Excuse me, excuse me, this is a private swim." I said "Yes, I know that." He said, "Well, are you a woman of tremendous weight?" I guess so! Oh, yeah. I think I told that story at every talk I ever gave after that, at conferences and speaking engagements. I would often tell that story about my way of accepting being fat.

The other thing I would often do is say, "I'm from California, sometimes I'll use the F word, so I'll just say it now so people won't be shocked or upset." And then I'd say "fat," and of course everybody else would think I was going to drop an F bomb. There could be this whole ability to put that out there in the way that people could laugh with me and say a word, it's just a word, and then talk about how it's been used against us.

When we were writing *Great Shape,* I remember Deb wrote a piece about language we were going to use, that we were not going to use "pleasingly plump" or other terms. "Large women" was the terminology we settled on. "Fat" was something we talked about as being in transition at that point, so I would change my language, sometimes, depending on the audience that I was dealing with, because I've worked with a lot of doctors and all sorts of folks. But I would always come into the thing about, it's a word that's been used to hurt people, we need to stop hurting people.

And "obesity." At the point where, at Kaiser, I was challenging the Everett Koop "war on obesity," I would always talk about how the war on obesity is a war on me, and a lot of the audience will stop and go, "Oh, that's not what we mean." Well, that may not be what you mean, but that's the effect. The whole issue about language and terminology and self-definition and all of those kinds of things are so critical and it continues.

Tigress

Do you remember what you actually said when that young man asked you if you are a woman of tremendous weight?

Pat

"Well, I guess I am!"

Tigress

I feel like "woman of tremendous weight" should be a hashtag on Twitter.

Lisa

Actually, if someone said that to me, I'd be like, "Oh, thank you!" Like a title.

I think for me, it was a gradual process, in the mid-to-late-'90s. Even getting comfortable saying the word, because, as we know, for so long "fat" has been used as the slur as opposed to just an adjective. Like Pat, I wouldn't use "fat" depending on the audience I was in. I'm in the world of diversity, equity and inclusion, so I started incorporating size diversity into my diversity work. Depending on the audience, I would introduce myself as a fat woman, and clarify it saying that it is a description, not a judgment. It was my own personal journey, as well as trying to weave it into my everyday professional life. Now it's just part of who I am as a person, but it was a gradual thing, and I watch people's response to it. They might say, "That's okay for you to describe yourself, but I couldn't go up to a client or a customer and say, 'there's that fat woman.'"

And I appreciate that, but that's part of the process of taking the power of that word in a different direction. I think I started also using it more when Dana and I opened up Women of Substance health spa in Redwood City back in the late '90s. We started using the language more in our materials, that this is a place for all women. We'd have conversations with customers, explaining to them that we're comfortable with using that word, because we're taking it back. That's a word that describes who we are, but it's not to be used as a negative.

I remember being at the grocery store and this little kid said to his mom, "Oh, hey, there's a fat lady." She, of course, was mortified and she came up to me, "Oh, I'm so sorry." I said, "Oh, I have no problem with that word, because it describes who I am. I'm a fat woman." She didn't know how to respond because she was so busy trying to apologize for it. When I disrupted that, then she didn't know how to have a conversation with me.

Tigress

Lisa, how did you settle on the name "Women of Substance" for the spa?

Lisa

I think because it was supposed to be sort of a double entendre. We are women of substance, women of tremendous weight, I just love that. It's so regal, right? I'm a woman of tremendous weight. It also described who we were striving to be. We wanted the place to speak to content and character, as well as to be a safe space for women of all sizes. Because that was the other thing, we wanted to have a place where your weight wasn't an issue. In fact, I believe our tagline was "the measure of a woman has nothing to do with the scale or measurements." We had women of all sizes. We had women that were very slender, and we had fat women. That wasn't an issue. We didn't have scales in our place, you just came and had fun, swam, exercised, whatever. In fact, we ended up having a training with our staff. Some of our instructors were on the thinner side of the spectrum, and we talked about how we're also supporting them at whatever size they happen to be, that if someone came to them and said, "Why are you teaching this class? You're not a fat woman," that was also not okay. That's what we wanted in the title, that this was a place for all women, regardless of size, age, whatever. Women of Substance was for women of all sizes, but also women who had substance and character.

Tigress

Something that I'm hearing from y'all is a very gendered approach to this work at the time of your origin stories. I wonder what thoughts you have about that. Why it was so important to focus on women, and what did that mean, both for men whom you encountered in your work, and for other gender minorities. We were using different language to talk about gender at the time than we are using now. Do you have thoughts on that?

Carol

In FAT LIP, when I joined there were two important rules. One, you couldn't be dieting for the purpose of losing weight. We recognized diet for health needs, but it couldn't be for the purpose of losing weight. The second one is you had to be, and these are the words they used, "a woman born woman." Now that phrase sets off TERF sounds in my head, but at the time it seemed reasonable.

Towards the end of FAT LIP, we had someone who transitioned to a trans man and left the group. That would have been maybe '96, '97. It was very tough on everyone. We didn't have all of the terminology for what was going on at the time. It was really hard because it split us. We had recently added new members, and they weren't yet fully integrated. It's a very personal thing to write and perform around your own story of being fat. In the early years they had women-only audience performances. Before I came in, they even had some fat-women-only audiences.

Even though we were fat and female, that was our primary focus, we did understand that we were not cardboard people, that we brought all of ourselves to the table. That included our sexuality, gender, race, economic status. In the last group that came in, there was a real divide about supporting this person staying in the group, although I don't really think that he wanted to stay. I was part of the third generation, I was not there when those rules were made, but I came in under them. It was a really hard time.

I think that even nowadays, women and trans women are much more scrutinized around our body size, we all know that. And while men get it, too, they often have more positive ideas about "big" and "strong" going together. "Big" and "sloppy" go together for women, "fat" and "sloppy" go together for women. Men, at a certain size, may get feminized. I think women are hit harder, for instance, with our clothes. For work, we couldn't just have a couple of good suits or a good pair of pants with a top. We had to have more outfits, and finding those kinds of things was really tied up with finding and keeping jobs. They used to say, "A thin woman in a T-shirt is just casual; a fat woman in a T-shirt is a slob."

Pat

I think in the early days, there was an issue of lesbians and straights because a lot of the Fat Underground stuff. I remember as a straight woman thinking, "are all rather brazen people lesbians?" And "is there a place for me as a straight woman?" There was that kind of tension sometimes at the *Radiance* Retreats initially. That was before the other gender issues came up. There was tension between straight women and lesbian women around who really was comfortable.

The other part of it was, "are you fat enough?" When Deb and I published *Great Shape,* we had a party at the Women's Building in San Francisco, and I was so excited about being there. This woman came up to me, I didn't know her, she was in the building but not really invited to the party, and basically she said to me that we weren't fat enough to write this book, what right did we have to do that, who do we think we are, and all that. I remember saying, "Well, I can't get health insurance," but it was a baffled tension. The language about mid-sized women or supersize women was much more focused on at that point, rather than conversations about men and women. When I did the research around the healthcare aspects, we did focus groups with Black women and white women and I did one with a very fat man. I think in the earlier days, the stereotype, historically, was of big men as bankers and fat cats and as a positive thing, like football players.

Tigress

It's really interesting to think about what you said, Pat, around feeling like all the fat feminists are lesbians and is there a place for me as a straight woman, because working with NAAFA, I hear that from the opposite direction, that this is a very heteronormative environment and is there space for a lesbian woman? Lisa, do you have any thoughts about that from your NAAFA years? And can you talk about the broader question of gender?

Lisa

I do remember when we opened up Women of Substance, we did have a trans woman join our gym. There was a conversation that we had up around that. I remember she wanted to join the gym because she felt like it was a safe space for her.

When I first got involved in NAAFA I went to a couple of conferences, and some of the social activities in the late '80s. I was in a much smaller body then and I remember someone saying, "Why are you here? You're not that big." So that was an interesting conversation. And I thought, "Well, isn't this this space for all sizes?" When I got involved, it was like, if you want the dating, social fashion show kind of stuff, that seemed to be very straight folks. And if you want to do the politics stuff, you had to be queer, lesbian. Those were the people doing the politics and protesting. And at least from my perspective, there weren't many people of color involved. It seemed like we should be working together.

Carol

When FAT LIP started in '81, it was nine women who identified as lesbians and one straight woman. When I came into the group there was an Asian woman in the group and a lot of the women were Jewish. It almost felt like that to be political, you needed to be a Jewish lesbian. Yes, that was where a lot of the politics came from, for the beginning members of FAT LIP. I came in with a group of four white women and three Black women. We were in our 20s to 40 so we had age diversity. I was bisexual, and I think three or four of the women were straight, and one or two were lesbians. We brought a lot of diversity to FAT LIP at that time. It was an interesting mix of people. Lesbian friends would say, when I would say I was going to go to a NAAFA event, that they're all about heterosexual people dating. And I said, "No, there's other stuff going on, too." And then, of course, when I was with NAAFA folks and I talked politics, they were like, "Yes, of course, we need to be in the streets." There was an overlap, but from the outside, it really looked very separate.

Deb

I came out during the lifespan of my class. I was aware of my sexuality in college, but I was in a pleasant relationship with a man. It was sweet. I really loved him. I had to personally get to the place where I could choose something that was really going to hurt somebody else. I was about to get married to him.

And I basically thought, "I'm going to vow to never act on these feelings." I thought, "what do I feel about this?" It sort of exploded everything.

I came out in 1987. I was teaching the classes from 1983 to 1989. I stopped teaching because I couldn't get enough traction to write my dissertation, doing too many things. It took me a while and I was exploring all those personal questions, not gender, but sexuality. And I was also really aware of the gay men's community, and I was aware of the body fascism in the gay men's community. Because AIDS was going on at the time, I want to bring that thread into this, too. I was an interviewer in a huge study that was going on with multiple waves that were trying to document when people were seroconverting, and what were their practices, and trying to correlate all this stuff. I was steeped in the practices of the second wave feminist movement, which was really a lot about consciousness raising by talking about stuff with other women. We weren't really thinking about gender with so much sophistication at all.

Being a therapist in the Bay Area over all these decades, I can tell you that after a while I had gone through this process so many times, where somebody was telling me something about a boundary that was in the culture, somebody was coming in who was assigned female at birth but saying, "I really feel like a gay man." I was listening and trying to learn about what people's own lived experience was of this. Every single time there was sort of one line being drawn, there was another group of people who were outside of that line saying, "This doesn't work for us, right? This is too, too hard. This is not really capturing what we're going through." It just got more and more and more nuanced. I just can't believe how vibrant and nuanced. I'm hoping we keep moving on this; it's certainly threatened at this moment very deeply.

I'm sitting here listening to you all, and I'm thinking about all these boundaries and groups. I was not sure if I should teach my dance class. In the beginning, I had a lot of back and forth in my head about this. I said, really concretely, "Please be over 200 pounds, if you're thinking about coming to this class." Not because I was going to be a bouncer or anything, but I was really trying to get the point across, because I had seen so many people my size and smaller who were complaining, "I'm so fat, I'm so fat" all the time, especially in gym spaces. I want to pace this class for people where the physics of what we are doing means we don't have to be doing "typical" exercise to get the benefits. You don't have to hang from the chandeliers to get your heart rate into the aerobic range. Knowing that opens up all kinds of movement that you can do, which is really fun and it's just as helpful to your goals about conditioning or whatever.

I didn't have the language then to say, "This is a space for people who experience being othered in the world in this way." Because we were still looking at bodies instead of the thing that's happening out here. This has been a huge thing in my mind. It's still there in academic studies; people will do academic studies and say, "I experienced discrimination because of my weight" or "I experienced discrimination because of my race." I keep thinking, "these are academics and they're still locating the problem in somebody's body." They're not saying, "I experienced discrimination because of this thing out here in the world that is bullshit." Even the language that's currently being used, you have to fight all the time against this body-blaming or focus on individual problems without looking at the structural problems.

So I was trying to figure out myself, "I'm not big enough for this class. Should I be teaching this class?" I settled it in my head by thinking, "There will be people who think I shouldn't be teaching this and that's a legitimate position. I can live with that. Actually I'm just fine with that, because I agree, there could be somebody who's better for this, but I don't see them yet. I'll try to put something together here, and if it's good enough, people will pick it up, and if it's not good enough, then they won't. And I'll try to keep learning as I'm doing this." That's how I settled it. I needed to recognize that I would not be harmed by people making that argument. I think that's important, you can hold all of that, and you can learn from it, and you can learn from people who've had these experiences. I wasn't really getting, in the beginning, that there had been principles that Black feminists have been talking about in the '70s, about centering the most marginalized people. If you do that, you cover a lot of the problem. I wasn't thinking in an intersectional way completely, then. I don't know if I have it even now. I'm still figuring this out. I had part of it, but not all of it.

I had someone who was fat come up to me later at a NOLOSE conference. She was one of the people who had felt critical of me, and she was so lovely. She was almost in tears, saying, "Deb, I heard you talking about how you weren't sure if you were going to start your dance classes because of this and I was one of those people. I really thought you shouldn't be doing this." And I said, "It's okay, it's really okay." We had this really lovely moment, and she said, "But I just think, what if you hadn't gotten involved in all this work? And what if you hadn't done all these things in the world?"

This is also something that I struggle with constantly. How do you help people wherever they are, as they're moving towards the movement work? Because we're not going to get it right, in some really important ways, as we're transitioning from where we are to where we're trying to get to. There's going to be harm done along the way, and how do we help each other with all of that in a way that isn't terrible and harmful on top of the harm? The accountability part is really important to me.

Pat and I had this come up with the cover of the book. The publisher was telling us, "You have to help us with the cover. Who do you want on the cover of the book?" Nell Carter, Oprah, these were the people who were in the public eye, but they flat out refused to put a Black person on the cover. I remember being like a deer in the headlights. Then they said, "We're going to put Deb on the cover, but not Pat." They had some arbitrary line between my size and Pat's size. We had worked so hard to get pictures of fat people into the text of the book so people could see themselves. I remember that was a really painful moment between Pat and me, when we protested that. And then they said, "Well, we're just going to find a model who's Deb's size if we don't use Deb." I could have said, "Well, fine, fuck you," and stood with Pat, and I didn't. I still didn't know how to navigate this shit. At least I could control what this picture looks like of me. But that really was painful. Then when Pat was looking for the softcover publisher, that was a big, important thing, that we would have control over that cover.

Pat

I want to say one more thing about the book. The letter that we got back from the editor said, "Couldn't you have found women who were younger and prettier than this?" And in the original hardcover version we had a picture of Carol Squires doing the splits and they would not publish that, because she had a gap in her teeth. A 300-pound woman is doing the splits, and you're going to see the gap in her teeth? It was ridiculous, but as Deb said, very painful, that idea of getting things published without having that control.

Tigress

I want to ask a little bit more from you, Pat, around what Deb said about what it felt like to be the smaller fat who got chosen. What was that negotiation like? How did it feel to be the larger fat who was told that you couldn't be on the cover of your own book?

Pat

I was pissed off! And at the same time, I certainly didn't want to turn it over to them to choose a model. That was the choice that we were left with. Deb worked really hard for everything. I wouldn't be caught dead in a leotard. It was amazing that we got the book published in the first place. It's the first book that said the words "fat and fit." Our determination was to have fat women with pictures without "before" underneath the picture. We were so committed to that. Giving up the cover? Okay, whatever, as long as we could get this published. That became the most important thing. Then we were able to turn it around with a soft cover. I had it from both directions. I wasn't fat enough for some people. I was too fat for other people, and I was like, "the hell with all these people. It's my story."

Tigress

What we're hearing in some of these stories that you all are sharing are aspects of power and privilege, where people in the movement were examining privilege, and where they weren't. One of the things that was really a struggle for me in the early 2000s was listening to white women talk about fat as "the last acceptable form of prejudice." Let's talk a little bit about the racial dynamics of the movement at the time that you all were involved. Lisa mentioned the lack of Black representation in NAAFA particularly, but what about in the other spaces where you all were, especially in your fitness and dance and performance spaces, because that's the thread here with this group. What was the racial representation like? And what were the dynamics around understanding privilege or lack of understanding of privilege related to race?

Lisa

When I started getting more involved in the movement, I didn't see a lot of folks who looked like me. I was kind of used to it anyway, because I went to a school that didn't have a lot of people of color in it. You get immune to it. Then there are times where people remind you that you're the only. Sometimes I wasn't even aware that I was the only one, or one of very few, because I was so used to being in that space. It just came with the territory. I just accepted it, although it would have been nice to see more people of color involved in the movement. I can't remember what conference it was, there were breakout groups. There was a group of women of color, or African-American women. We talked about all that, that there's very few of us, and how to create a safe space for ourselves and for others who might want to participate in the movement, but don't see people that look like them in the movement.

Even when we had Women of Substance health spa, it was in Redwood City and the membership was very white, somewhat upscale, because it was in a somewhat affluent area. There were clashes at times where those comments were made, that this is the last form of discrimination. A lot of times I felt like that was an additional burden for me. I'm a woman, a Black woman, and I'm a fat Black woman. Three strikes, you're out. We had conversations about it, sometimes it was heated, but it was constructive. I'm seeing more people of color involved in the movement. It's really nice to see that. In those early days, people of color in general were not part of that. They weren't active or in leadership roles in the movement. It was just something you deal with as a person of color, a Black person. You get used to not having that support or seeing people like yourself, you just deal with it. It's just part of everyday life.

Deb

There was somebody teaching back then who I tried to get in contact with on Facebook for this interview—her name is Rosezella Canty-Letsome. She and I used to swap people back and forth all the time between our classes because she had a more exercise calisthenic-y vibe to her class and I had more of a dance vibe to my class, and so people would wander into one or the other. That was a sweet connection. My classes were through Oakland Parks and Rec, places where it would be accessible to people. And I think it was a little bit better than a lot of things that we were doing at the time. One of the more diverse places in my life was my dance classes, but it wasn't good enough.

When we talk about who were the people in the movement, that is a thing to be critical about, right? There were people doing this work in a different way who should be thought of as ancestors to the work. We're still defining the people who are part of the movement as the mostly white, mostly straight women who were fat. That is the branch of this work that has gotten the legitimacy. But if you really think about it, the things that bring us to this work are the ways that we don't have our white privilege. Things like, we're not getting our medical care. Well, a lot of people don't get their medical care. Most people don't get it. But we're white women who are middle class, we're supposed to get our medical care. We're enraged about that. That becomes a thing, but the fact that we aren't also trying to solve all these other oppressions means that we create a movement that is about solving this one thing in the abstract, which is not abstract. Weight stigma is an unstable element. It's something that is deeply, deeply connected to these other forms of oppression that we weren't experiencing.

Now, we are beginning to make some progress, because people who have a lived experience of how these things are all connected are in more leadership roles and they are saying that the analysis has to come at a much deeper level. Because there's been a critique of our earlier work, a critique that I think has legitimacy, that is basically "you were just trying to get your privilege back," which makes a lot of sense. I was going into this from my own experience, but I wasn't really putting myself in any space of critical thinking. I hadn't gone far enough.

Carol

FAT LIP was a feminist political group, and we took those words really seriously. Of course, at that time, we're really talking white feminism. That is only clear in retrospect. I will say, for FAT LIP, I came in with the most diverse group in '87. In '88, I think, we had an Unlearning Racism workshop with a Black woman and a white woman, and what I took away from that is that racism can only come from a position of power. That's why there can be no such thing as "reverse racism." I have fought people over that for 30 years. That's what came out of that for me, and for whatever people I've managed to beat into submission around not saying "reverse racism." That was a powerful change in me, and in our group as we went forward. We already had made connections with gender, sexuality, social and economic class, and race, and size, because we did also recognize the privilege of people on the smaller size of the spectrum of what we described with the word "fat." In fact, we had a parody song, "What do you do with a mid-size woman?" sung to the tune of the traditional sea shanty "What shall we do with a drunken sailor?"

Tigress

Two of you have now made references to being in your 60s. How do you relate to being labeled as an elder in the movement? What does that mean to you? What learnings do you hope younger activists will get from you and others? What stories and lessons do you wish to see carried down? What is the long view, and what do you think it does (or should) mean to folks coming up after you?

Pat

I'm 77 and I'm the elder here today. I heard a podcast about six months ago with younger women who are very active now. They were talking about all the same stuff that we had developed, and I was like, "God, we were talking about that 30, 35 years ago, and it's still meaningful," and that felt really good. It was recognition of some of the work that we did that has lasted and helped people through the years, and that people have built on.

For me, working with Indians and being on a reservation where there's lots of fat Indians, and at that time I had long black hair, and I could be with the Indians and be treated like an Indian, so I learned about racism in that way. But there was also this whole concept of tribal sovereignty, and the idea that the federal government doesn't get to tell Indians what to do, and I took that to heart. I remember later on doing a whole spiel about body sovereignty, and that whole sense of self definition, and the issue that the pressure is out there.

Sovereignty from whatever the source is, whether it's race or gender or age or size, is integrated. That whole sense of self-determination and sovereignty is so critical.

I don't mind at all being thought of as an elder. I had a very close brush with not being here about six months ago. I was very ill. So I'm just glad to be here. There's that sense of survival, and what's really important. Age is so relative. For people, whatever generation they're in, this is our work, and we are on the shoulders of all the people who came before us. There's much more work to be done on all these issues, and I'm always just so thrilled to see how work is progressing.

Deb

That's so moving. I don't even know how to think about the privilege of look-ing back on my life and feeling like what I decided to do is something that's mattering. It's gotten me through the shitstorm over the last few years, in par-ticular, to think about a connection that I feel with people whose work made it possible for me to do the things that I did. I have this feeling of, "okay, you're up at bat right now, do your thing, because the next people who are coming up at bat are going to be able to have certain advantages or skills or tools, or not, based on what your choices are right now. Try to keep the beat, try to keep the rhythm." These other people who came before me, they're never far from my mind. Growing up as a little kid during the civil rights movement, and all the other movements of the '60s and '70s, was an incredibly huge part of my awareness. So for me to now see younger people so invested, it is like that weird feeling of, "oh, my gosh, there's people who want to take over the family business." I don't have children, so this is an incredibly important part of my generativity in the world, feeling like I gave the right gift.

I guess what I wish I would have known before is how relentless the ma-chinery is, that it will take what you do to resist the bullshit, and spin it into the next thing that you're supposed to do. Everything that we were doing to resist becomes the new demand. The new demand is to never feel bad about your body. Now you're supposed to be filled with a confident attitude. Those marketing things, they are just going to take what you're doing and spit it out in the same old shapes.

Carol

It's the appropriation of so much of what we did in fat liberation, talking about our bodies in a positive way. They use it. Like Deb said, they chew it up. I guess what I want the younger folks to know is this: I don't know if there's a way to stop that. I know we tried things like, for instance, with the term Health at Every Size, which was trademarked to try to prevent having Health at Every Size become the next weight-loss diet.

I'm happy to be an elder and I'm happy to be a resource whenever I can. As we were talking about before, there was a time when we knew everybody doing the work, pretty much. Even with people on the East Coast, there was enough communication, since there was stuff happening there, too. Now, I can't keep up with it. I still try to go to as many things and be available when possible for the community.

I guess I hope that the young folks out there coming up don't reinvent the wheel. Improve the wheel! It's like we were Calistoga wagons with the hard wheels and then they came with the tires and the inflated wheels. Don't reinvent it, but improve on it. Don't lose the basic structure because the basic structure is strong. What we were saying about body autonomy is strong. Be aware of what the culture has tried to put on all of our bodies as fat folks. Be careful, because they're out there and they will take the work that you do, and they will try to find a way to monetize it for themselves. So, I don't know, should we monetize it for ourselves first? No, that wouldn't work.

Deb

I want them to know, too, that when we come together, and we do things together, and we build these spaces where people have a little bit more room to move, room to breathe, a little bit more protection, that is everything.

It's inside of all of us to heal. We don't have to think of ourselves as machines that need to be fixed; we just need to get the shit out of the way. And then people know what to do, our bodies know. Our impulses towards each other, that are about connecting and loving each other, that really works! It really works. And it's the thing that you have to work with, it really is about getting stuff out of the way. That would have helped me. I think it's always been clear to me as a therapist, that that's true. There's not something I'm doing in therapy, it's really about the relationship that we have with ourselves, and really understanding getting some shit out of the way. And then people can do what they need to do.

Lisa

I feel blessed to be an elder. In fact, yesterday, I was at a meeting with some younger folks. I mentioned the word "old" and they all went, "No, don't use that word! Use 'seasoned!'" And I was like, "I'm good. I'm good, with both, actually."

Tigress

Women of tremendous age.

Lisa

Yes, a woman of tremendous age. I love that.

Carol

My seasons are old.

Lisa

I don't really have a problem with the word "old" even though it has all this negative stuff associated. I feel it as a blessing to be my age. I had to explain that to the younger folks, but I appreciate that they were being sensitive. They're like, "Oh, we don't see you as old. We see you as seasoned." I was like, "Yeah, I'm all that and a slice of bread! I'm fine with that."

I love how I see young people galvanized and don't take any shit from anybody. I really appreciate that. And then there's the tremendous pressure that young people are under from social media. If I see one more thing come across my feed about the Kardashians, I just want to throw my phone across the room. We weren't dealing with all that, with Twitter and Instagram and Tik Tok, blah, blah, blah. It was phone, or the written word. And TV commercials, then emails. Now, it's in your face 24/7. I try to be sensitive to that.

I hope that young people take a minute to learn the history, to know what was created, or what the efforts were in those early days, and do the research and dig deep as they move on their journey to improve, enhance, whatever is the next step with the movement. And, at the same time, listen to those folks who came before them. I am even more appreciative of that now, as I listen to my elders. As an older person, seasoned, whatever you call it, you don't always remember everything, and then sometimes something comes up and, "oh, that's related to this." It's not just that one-time conversation, it's constantly having that dialogue and conversation, so that as things come up you can talk about it, and you can appreciate what elders have gone through and experienced, and that can even give you ideas and suggestions, even though you're going to create your own and make it your own.

But to listen for that minute of talking to the Pats and the Debs and the Carols and all the folks that came and set the path and built that road map that folks can follow, and if you deviate, you know why. You want to try something different, but at least spend that time to know the history. That's with anything, not just the topic we're talking about now. We're in a world where we don't really listen to each other. We don't appreciate people's differences. We can have a difference of opinion and not get violent. It concerns me that when people have differences about things, we automatically cut them off. "I don't want to talk to you, you're the enemy, you're the other."

I'm hoping that the young folks are really just attuned to the fact that we don't always have to agree on everything, that we can still work together, and have a common goal, and be respectful of our different ways of doing things.

Tigress

Do you have some lessons for younger activists about how we manage disagreement in our community? Can you share experiences with reconciliation processes or stories about times when someone was wrong, but they were still able to be part of the community because the community worked through that?

Deb

I think that's more recent history for me, for example, the Association for Size Diversity and Health (ASDAH) started with one group of people, and then went through this period where it got into a kind of "HAES® Lite" version—intuitive eating, and pleasurable movement, and that's what it is—without considering the social and structural determinants of health. When we brought more people to the work, the people who were not white and thin got hurt a lot, and that education was really important to me. I was just not understanding how damaging these tables were that we were inviting people to, tables that weren't built for everybody.

What happened with ASDAH was a combination of things. They sort of did an artificial graft of diversifying the input by having an advisory board that was made up of a whole bunch of people who were not in the dominant group of the membership. The advisory board tried to do their thing and ran into a leadership that was clueless and harmful. There were some efforts at that point to bring in an organizational consultant whose work was about this kind of transformation and getting people into those leadership positions who are going to have a lived experience. That transition was very painful for some people. But if I look at ASDAH now and I look at the leadership now, they have completely shifted the bylaws of ASDAH in order to pay the people who are doing the leadership, to not make it a situation where there's a bunch of white professional healthcare people in the membership who decide who the leadership is. Also, they opened up membership, because of the accessibility and the financial part of that, to everybody who wants to join, so there's thousands of people in ASDAH now! Oh, my God, it's just so great. All these workshops, and all the things that are being generated, are centering the most marginalized people over and over and over, period. And you see this incredible, incredible change, but that needed to happen with a bunch of structural support, that isn't something that an organization is just going to do with good intentions, right? That process was really interesting to me, and somebody ought to document that someday.

My experience with some of these other pieces would lead me to say [in HAES® and eating disorders spaces], you've got to have breakout rooms that are BIPOC only, you've got to have places where people can go process the damage that we're doing. If they're coming to conferences to find each other, that's a really important thing. The eating disorders organizations are in a crisis, because they are so terrible. The academic elite, dominant groups are holding all of that hostage. People are moving on, there's a whole bunch of grassroots stuff that's happening with eating disorders that is pulling the field in an important direction. After all this time of people with lived experience calling bullshit on the idea of prescribing one body as the norm, this horrible idea of "Everybody should pursue weight loss; everybody's body's got to be normal. And if we just make everybody's body normal, everything will be fine." There's a lot more pushback on that.

I want Pat to reminisce about the beginnings of the Think Tank because it is still going, young people who are interested in this work are coming. It's just beautiful, people are talking about important things, about their lived experience, and they want the connection.

Pat

It really grew out of AHELP. In 1989 Joe McVoy in Virginia put a conference together with Susan Wooley, Janet Polivy, and the original people who published the research. We went to Virginia, and that became this horribly codependent Association for the Health Enrichment of Large People, which I always hated. It was a national group of all the thinkers and authors and activists and people in that sector. Setting up a group at Kaiser was an outgrowth of that. Because Laura Kiernan had such a commitment to community organizing, and community development and the idea of how you make change in the community, this was an outgrowth of that. I think for people who originally came to those kinds of meetings with some of this AHELP codependent help kind of thinking. Every time new people would come, we would have to go back to the beginning, explain it all, do the basics. I got tired of telling the story.

I think for me, it was an attempt to have the ability to use Kaiser effectively.

To be able to do letters on Kaiser stationery, it legitimized that this was important work that needed to happen. The Think Tank was the idea of coming together with these ideas, and then how do we support and move it and change?

Carol

I was there for the very first meeting at Oakland Kaiser. One of the connections that was made there for me was Marilyn Wann. I don't know if she came to the first or second or third one, but she came in with her very first issue of *FAT!SO?* zine. And several of us bought the issue and/or subscribed. That was the next generation, the overlap generation with Marilyn and her activism, and all the ways that touched people.

Deb

Marilyn organized the 24Hour Fitness protest.

Pat

At the AHELP conference in Chicago, the non-dieting people were talking about this "mouth hunger" versus "stomach hunger" and I remember Marilyn standing up, "This reminds me of 'is it vaginal orgasm, is it clitoral orgasm.'" She always brought humor and brilliance, right on the money.

Deb

She was right on the money because she picked up on the prescriptive quality of what was going on with Hirschman and Munter, which was exactly this thing that we've been talking about where the thing that you're trying to do as a point of resistance morphs into the next oppressive structure. And she was right there. It was fantastic.

Pat

Joanne Ikeda was another person who did a lot of work with dieticians and with the idea that health professionals were doing harm, and that "do no harm" is for everybody. I remember Marilyn said to me, "I always felt more protected when either you or Joanne were in the room," because we had credentials. I was an RN and Joanne was an RD and that legitimized all the things that we were saying. How much privilege is given to that?

I remember when I saw the cover of *Great Shape* and they have "Pat Lyons, RN" on it, that was the first time I knew they were going to use RN after my name. I thought, "Don't say that, people will think I'm one of the bad guys!"

Carol

We often spoke about needing allies with initials after their names, because when we fat people talked about it to non-fat people, we were just talking to our own self-interest, because we didn't have the willpower, we didn't have enough whatever to diet successfully. Therefore, anything we had to say was just talking in our own self-interest. We didn't want to do the work to lose weight; we were too lazy.

I just wanted to say that 32 years ago (1991) was the Oakland Hills fire. That day, FAT LIP performed on the Capitol steps in Sacramento, doing our anti-bariatric surgery script. I don't remember what group put this together, but they brought a cardboard coffin as a statement about the deaths from weight-loss surgery. We were doing it at this spot because across the street at a big hotel, bariatric surgeons were having a conference. We did our performance to a small but enthusiastic audience. This was pre-social-media so we couldn't put out a post telling folks to come see us and expect to reach a large number of people. After our performance, they carried this coffin to the hotel and disrupted the bariatric surgeons' conference. Driving back from Sacramento, we saw the smoke in the Oakland Hills that would become the tragic conflagration that burned for two days.

I was also there 11 or 12 years ago when Marilyn did a thing where we disrupted an information meeting of bariatric surgeons at a hotel in San Francisco. We danced into the conference room singing an anti-weight-loss-surgery song. The WLS doctor at the podium was having a breakdown, screaming, "You guys get out of here!" They had people come in and escort us out. It was so jazzed to just be there and be so disruptive. I remember there was this one fat woman in the room and as we walked down, I connected eyes with her, and she kind of smiled. So it's like, "well, there's at least one fat person in that room that was happy to see us." Everybody else was like, "Keep them out of here! We gotta get back to talking about how we can cut up the fat people and make them skinny!"

Pat

Lynn McAfee and the Fat Underground did that at a medical conference in LA, in what would be late '70s, I think, where they had people who basically locked the door and they went up on the stage and they interrupted this whole medical conference until they were dragged off.

Deb

That was the same era as the people in the American Psychiatric Association, the gay men in the APA, disrupting the APA conference and saying that homosexuality is not a disease. Everybody was using that tactic to disrupt. I've used that tactic within the Academy for Eating Disorders. I'm always trying to get to the mic at the Q&A. I'm always thinking, "What have people not heard from the speakers that is important not to leave out? Who is not getting a voice?" I have almost gotten thrown out of there, even though I'm a fellow. They're reluctant to do something that's going to have that big of a visibility, but they can't stand it. They're always talking about civility, and rules, and basically how we should be polite when they are talking about how our bodies shouldn't exist. They're fucking scared when we don't cooperate. And it's one of my favorite things to do.

Pat

I raised my hand at this conference. And the speaker goes, "Oh…" He kind of grabbed the podium and said, "Okay…what do you want to say?"

Carol

Isn't it good when we have these reputations of being a disrupter!

Deb

I would usually get applause. People in the audience want to hear this conversation. And it's the people who are at the podium who are reinscribing all the same bullshit, and the people in the audience know that.

Pat

I remember at a conference we did at American College of Sports Medicine, with Glenn Gaesser, Wayne Miller, Steve Blair, talking about the fat and fit stuff, and for three- or four-hundred people, and somebody stood up in the audience, "Well, somebody has to speak for the other side." And I said, "How about the other 200 sessions that are going on at this meeting? That's the other side. This is the only one talking about this!"

Carol

There's this whole idea from the disability community: "Nothing about us without us." If the people in the audience really wanted to hear what you have to say, but the power dynamics on the stage that control the organization wanted to go some other way, then this group out here in the audience are the folks that should be at the table!

LOOKING FORWARD

TIGRESS OSBORN

IN THE FALL OF 2021 I posted a note on Facebook telling folks that I was hoping to collect stories from people of color who had a long history in the fat liberation movement. I soon found a note from Nancy Ellis-Ordway in my inbox. "I'm working on a history project, too," she wrote. "Can we talk?"

I'd met Nancy virtually the previous summer, when she led an online workshop for NAAFA's webinar program. I was the director of community outreach for the organization at the time. I loved her presentation, and we became Facebook friends, but we didn't know each other well. We set up our first video call. As of this writing, we've had a few dozen of those.

In that first call Nancy explained that she wanted to gather stories from people who had been working in Health at Every Size (HAES)®, eating disorders treatment and prevention, or fat acceptance for at least 25 years. She'd put together an ambitious list of folks she wanted to reach out to, some of whom I knew quite well, some of whom I had admired from afar, and some whose reputation and work I would get to know over the course of this project. I know quite a bit more than the average American, or even perhaps the average fat activist, about the history of Health at Every Size. But HAES and ED spaces are far less familiar to me than size acceptance or fat activism. And although I have many years of experience as an advocate for fat people, and way more years of lived experience as a fat Black woman, I am 10 years shy of the vintage Nancy was aiming for in collecting the untold tales of these movements. Nancy assured me this was precisely why we would make a good team—we have the same commitment to making the world a better place for fat people, but we approached that commitment with different lenses based on our lived experiences and professional expertise in different areas.

At the time of Nancy's invitation I had been spending several hours a week tracking down or talking to people with a deep investment and/or very strong critical opinions of NAAFA. Until very recently, I was not a paid employee of NAAFA—no one had been in over two decades—but I was the board chair, working intensely to strengthen infrastructure there and to create a much more intersectional approach to the organization's work. The history project I'd had in mind was specifically focused on identifying people of color from fat liberation's first and second waves, especially those who had been directly involved in NAAFA at some point. Many of them are unnamed and under-remembered, and most never racked up 25 consecutive years of participation in these spaces, in large part because these spaces were often not as warm and welcoming to us. They weren't on Nancy's draft list, and I couldn't even add very many to the list because I hadn't found very many yet. I wasn't sure I wanted to take time away from working on my Black and Brown project to work on one that was likely to involve few POC voices.

Still, I'm quite a bit of a geek when it comes to fat history, and I thought I could learn a lot from Nancy and from the many contributors to this collection. I was right about that. I also thought I could continue to give a lot of time to seeking out more about the POC past of body liberation work. I will always be collecting bits and pieces of that past and trying to figure out how to weave those stories into our present and into our future.

I am also someone who likes to see those who have been around this movement for a long time take responsibility for harms they caused—whether intentional or not—and help lead the way to others doing better. There were a few people on the list of contributors to this book whom I knew could and would do that. As we worked on this project, I was pleasantly surprised that several more owned up to the white privilege and heteronormativity they had upheld in their own work. I am thankful for this accountability. And I am especially thankful to the people of color and queer folks in this collection who were forthcoming and vulnerable in sharing their realities in these movements, even though doing so in the past has often cost them dearly.

It's been just under two years since Nancy extended the invite to work on this project, and it'll likely be closer to three years by the time you are holding this in your hands or scrolling through it on your screen. This book that I'd thought of as just a "25-year history book" is now one I think of in hundreds—over a hundred video calls with Nancy and others, hundreds of emails with contributors (mostly helmed by Nancy, with tremendous gratitude from me!), hundreds of minutes interviewing, and thousands of minutes reading and editing. Some folks who know about the project seem to think it has taken us forever; others seem amazed that we made it to the finish line this quickly.

During the course of our work on this book, HAES, ED, and fat liberation worlds faced many individual and collective challenges. Many of us involved lost loved ones to the pandemic, to other crises, or simply to time. We lost our own friends and family, and we lost folks from these communities that mean so much to us. Our dedication list grew faster than we could have imagined. It is an honor to honor these folks, but we wish they were here to hold this book in their hands, to have put words into this volume as others did.

During the time we've worked on this project, our communities have also grappled with major disagreements and disappointments involving prominent people and organizations from these histories, including some referenced in this book. There's been stress and distress, hopelessness and anger, misunderstanding and mistrust. Many relationships—between individuals, between organizations, between communities—were damaged in what still appear to be irreparable ways.

But there has been repair, too, if not to the specific current crises, at least to some oversights and exclusions of the past. In many HAES, ED, and fat liberation spaces we've developed a deeper understanding of and commitment to intersectionality. We've made more room, literally and figuratively, for fat people from all identities. We've earned to better partner with other social justice movements, including the movement for Black Lives, disability justice, and LGBTQIA+ rights. New connections and friendships have been forged, new voices and perspectives have emerged, and new research has added nuance to our knowledge. There's so much more to do; we have to move past creating spaces that only pay lip service to diversity and inclusivity, and instead cocreate spaces that truly integrate all members of our communities. But I hope we're on the right track.

I hope that the history and perspectives collected in this book invite those who were there to take another look through different lenses. I hope, too, that those who weren't there will find answers to questions they may not even have known they had. I hope readers, regardless of generation, saw themselves somewhere in these pages.

Most of all, Nancy and I hope you found not only information but inspiration here. Look how far we've come! But we still have a long, long way to go.

May we find the way together.

ADDITIONAL READING

Additional reading about the history of pushing back against weight stigma, including body liberation, fat activism, eating disorders treatment, fat studies, weight neutrality, etc.

PRINT RESOURCES

Bock, L. (2017). *Red Diaper Baby: Three Generations of Rebels and Revolutionaries.* Second Wave Press.

Boero, N. (2013). *Killer Fat: Media, Medicine, and Morals in the American "Obesity Epidemic."* Rutgers University Press.

Bruno, B. (2018). *History of the Health at Every Size Movement.* https://naafa.org/other-resources

Burgard, D., Dykewomon, E., Rothblum, E. & Thomas, P. (2009). Are We Ready to Throw Our Weight Around? Fat Studies and Political Activism. In E. Rothblum, S. Solovay, & M. Wann, (Eds.), *The Fat Studies Reader.* (pp. 334-340). New York University Press.

Cooper, C. (2016). *Fat Activism: A Radical Social Movement.* HammerOn Press.

Cooper, C. (2009). Maybe It Should Be Called Fat American Studies. In E. Rothblum, S. Solovay, & M. Wann, (Eds.), *The Fat Studies Reader.* (pp. 327-333). New York University Press.

Cranberry, J. (2015). Civil Rights and Size Acceptance: A Personal History. In R. Chastain (Ed.), *The Politics of Size: Perspectives from the Fat Acceptance Movement* (pp. 19-30). Praeger.

Daufin, E. (2015). Black Women in Fat Activism. In R. Chastain (Ed.), *The Politics of Size: Perspectives from the Fat Acceptance Movement* (pp. 163-186). Praeger.

Ellison, J. (2009). Not Jane Fonda: Aerobics for Fat Women Only. In E. Rothblum, S. Solovay, & M. Wann, (Eds.), *The Fat Studies Reader.* (pp. 312-319). New York University Press.

Ellison, J. (2019). *Being Fat: Women, Weight, and Feminist Activism in Canada.* University of Toronto *Press.*

Flegal, K., (2021). The Obesity Wars and the Education of a Researcher: A Personal Account. *Progress in Cardiovascular Diseases*, 67, p 75-79.

Gordon, A., (2023). Body Positivity is About Feeling Better About Yourself, As Long As You're Happy and Healthy. In A. Gordon, *You Just Need to Lose Weight and 19 Other Myths About Fat People.* (pp. 88-97). Beacon Press.

McAllister. H. (2009). Embodying Fat Liberation. In E. Rothblum, S. Solovay, & M. Wann, (Eds.), *The Fat Studies Reader.* (pp. 305-311). New York University Press.

McCalphin, I., & Tango, J. (2015). Women of Color in Size Acceptance Activism. In R. Chastain (Ed.), *The Politics of Size: Perspectives from the Fat Acceptance Movement* (pp. 139-150). Praeger.

Pausé, C. J., Wykes, J., & Murray, S (Eds). (2014). *Queering Fat Embodiment.* Ashgate.

Schuster, D. & Tealer, L. (2009). Exorcising the Exercise Myth: Creating Women of Substance. In E. Rothblum, S. Solovay, & M. Wann, (Eds.), *The Fat Studies Reader.* (pp. 320-324). New York University Press.

Smith, E. (2015). The Pragmatic Attitude in Fat Activism: Race and Rhetoric in the Fat Acceptance Movement. In R. Chastain (Ed.), *The Politics of Size: Perspectives from the Fat Acceptance Movement* (pp. 151-162). Praeger.

Snider, S. (2009). Fat Girls and Size Queens: Alternative Publications and Visualizing of Fat and Queer Eroto-Politics in Contemporary American Culture. In E. Rothblum, S. Solovay, & M. Wann, (Eds.), *The Fat Studies Reader.* (pp. 223-230). New York University Press.

Solovay, S. & Rothblum, E. (2009). Introduction. In E. Rothblum, S. Solovay, & M. Wann, (Eds.), *The Fat Studies Reader.* (pp. 1-7). New York University Press.

Wann, M. (2009). Foreword: Fat Studies: An invitation to revolution. In E. Rothblum, S. Solovay, & M. Wann, (Eds.), *The Fat Studies Reader.* (pp. xi-xxvi). New York University Press.

Wann, M. (2015). Anatomy of an Activism Campaign: A 2003 Action Against Weight Loss Surgery Marketing. In R. Chastain (Ed.), *The Politics of Size: Perspectives from the Fat Acceptance Movement* (pp. 43-54). Praeger.

ONLINE RESOURCES AND ARCHIVES

https://asdah.org/blog/
The official Health at Every Size® Blog of the Association for Size Diversity and Health (ASDAH).

https://biblio.uottawa.ca/atom/index.php/canadian-womens-movement-archives

Canadian Women's Movement Archives in Ottawa, Canada.

http://cswd.org/
Council on Size & Weight Discrimination.

https://www.glbthistory.org/
GLBT historical society in San Francisco.

https://rmc.library.cornell.edu/EAD/htmldocs/RMM08748.html
Health at Every Size records, 1980-2012, Collection Number: 8748. Division of Rare and Manuscript Collections, Cornell University Library.

https://naafa.org/community-voices/category/Health+At+Every+Size
NAAFA Community Voices Blog.

http://revolutionsresources.blogspot.com/
New Year's ReVolutions Resources: website of Fat Resources developed by fat activists in 2012–13, including links to fiction, non-fiction, blogs, vodcasts, and activist campaigns of the time.

https://cherrymax.medium.com/community-origins-of-the-term-superfat-9e98e1b0f201
Community origins of the term "superfat."

INDEX

J

Johnson, Craig, 120, 127, 138, 140, 178

K

Kaiser Permanente, 14, 19, 23, 59, 229, 231, 246, 247
Kinsey, Dalia, 18, 146–152

L

Lemire, Deb, 63, 64
Levine, Michael, 10, 18, 170–181
Louderback, Lew, 7, 77, 78, 80
Luna, Caleb, 5, 9, 18, 27–28
Lyons, Pat, 11, 14, 19, 25, 48, 56, 59, 60, 69, 73, 74, 112, 227–249

M

Maine, Margo, 10, 19, 20, 170–181
Matz, Judith,10, 20, 162–169
Maudsley, 9, 102, 104, 105
McAfee, Lynn, 8, 49, 67, 68, 248
Minnesota Starvation Study, 27, 55
Munter, Carol, 110, 162–166, 168, 247

N

National Anorexic Aid Society/NAAS, 109, 111, 137–139, 141, 172–174, 178, 180
National Association to Advance Fat Acceptance/NAAFA, 9, 13, 15, 17, 18, 21, 23, 25, 28, 29, 43, 48, 52, 63, 64, 68–70, 76, 78–92, 98, 163, 190, 193, 200, 203–212, 215, 219, 225, 229, 234, 235, 239, 250, 251, 253, 255
National Eating Disorders Association/NEDA, 10, 16, 19, 28, 139, 141, 142, 170, 174, 176, 178, 180, 181
National Institute of Mental Health, 137, 140
No-Diet Day, 82
NOLOSE, 187, 225, 237

O

O'Hara, Allegra, 9, 20, 36–45
O'Hara, Lily, 9, 21, 36-45, 113
Omichinski, Linda, 56, 69
Optifast, 9, 71, 72, 162, 163

V

W

Y

ABOUT PEARLSONG PRESS

PEARLSONG PRESS is an independent publishing company dedicated to providing books and resources that entertain while expanding perspectives on the self and the world. The company was founded by psychologist Peggy Elam, Ph.D.

FICTION

If We Were Snowflakes—YA novel by Barbara D'Souza

Heretics: A Love Story & *The Singing of Swans*
novels about the divine feminine by Mary Saracino

Judith & *Under the Pomegranate Tree*
historical novels by Leslie Moïse

Fatropolis—paranormal adventure by Tracey L. Thompson

*The Falstaff Vampire Files, Bride of the Living Dead, Larger Than Death,
Large Target, At Large* & *A Ton of Trouble*
paranormal adventure, romantic comedy & Josephine Fuller mysteries
by Lynne Murray

The Season of Lost Children—a novel by Karen Blomain

Fallen Embers & *Blowing Embers*—Books 1 & 2 of The Embers Series,
paranormal romance by Lauri J Owen

The Program & *The Fat Lady Sings*—suspense & YA novels
by Charlie Lovett

Syd Arthur—a novel by Ellen Frankel

Measure By Measure—a romantic romp with the fabulously fat
by Rebecca Fox & William Sherman

FatLand & *FatLand: The Early Days*—Books 1 & 2 of The FatLand Trilogy
by Frannie Zellman

ROMANCE NOVELS & SHORT STORIES FEATURING
BIG BEAUTIFUL HEROINES
by Pat Ballard, the Queen of Rubenesque Romances:
Once Upon Another Time | *Adam & Evelyn* | *ASAP Nanny* | *Dangerous Love*
The Best Man | *Abigail's Revenge* | *Dangerous Curves Ahead: Short Stories*
Wanted: One Groom | *Nobody's Perfect* | *His Brother's Child* | *A Worthy Heir*

by Rebecca Brock—*The Giving Season*
& by Judy Bagshaw—*Kiss Me, Nate!* & *At Long Last, Love*

NONFICTION

Flying On Invisible Wings, Poems of Reckoning and Hope,
& *Fire Island and Their Sister*—poetry by Félix Garmendía

Fat Poets Speak: Voices of the Fat Poets' Society,
Fat Poets Speak 2: Living and Loving Fatly,
& *Fat Poets Speak 3: FatDance Flying*
Frannie Zellman, Ed.

Other Nations: An Animal Journal—poetry by Maria Famà

Soul Mothers' Wisdom: Seven Insights for the Single Mother by Bette J. Freedson

Acceptable Prejudice? Fat, Rhetoric & Social Justice
& *Talking Fat: Health vs. Persuasion in the War on Our Bodies*
by Lonie McMichael, Ph.D.

Hiking the Pack Line: Moving from Grief to a Joyful Life by Bonnie Shapbell

A Life Interrupted: Living with Brain Injury—poetry by Louise Mathewson

ExtraOrdinary: An End of Life Story Without End
memoir by Michele Tamaren & Michael Wittner

Love is the Thread: A Knitting Friendship by Leslie Moïse, Ph.D.

10 Steps to Loving Your Body (No Matter What Size You Are) by Pat Ballard

Something to Think About: Reflections on Life, Family, Body Image & Other
Weighty Matters by the Queen of Rubenesque Romances by Pat Ballard

Beyond Measure: A Memoir About Short Stature & Inner Growth
by Ellen Frankel

Taking Up Space: How Eating Well & Exercising Regularly Changed My Life
by Pattie Thomas, Ph.D. with Carl Wilkerson, M.B.A.

Off Kilter: A Woman's Journey to Peace with Scoliosis, Her Mother
& Her Polish Heritage—a memoir by Linda C. Wisniewski

Unconventional Means: The Dream Down Under
spiritual travelogue by Anne Richardson Williams

Splendid Seniors: Great Lives, Great Deeds
inspirational biographies by Jack Adler

www.ingramcontent.com/pod-product-compliance
Lightning Source LLC
Chambersburg PA
CBHW080644270326
41928CB00017B/3182